A Unified Theory of Collective Action and Social Change

Analytical Perspectives on Politics

ADVISORY EDITORS:

John Aldrich, Duke University
Bruce Bueno de Mesquita, Hoover Institution and New York University
Robert Jackman, University of California, Davis
David Rohde, Duke University

Political Science is developing rapidly and changing markedly. Keeping in touch with new ideas across the discipline is a challenge for political scientists and for their students.

To help meet this challenge, the series Analytical Perspectives on Politics presents creative and sophisticated syntheses of major areas of research in the field of political science. In each book, a high-caliber author provides a clear and discriminating description of the current state of the art and a strong-minded prescription and structure for future work in the field.

These distinctive books provide a compact review for political scientists, a helpful introduction for graduate students, and central reading for advanced undergraduate courses.

Robert W. Jackman, *Power without Force: The Political Capacity of Nation-States*

Linda L. Fowler, *Candidates, Congress, and the American Democracy*

Scott Gates and Brian D. Humes, *Games, Information, and Politics: Applying Game Theoretic Models to Political Science*

Lawrence Baum, *The Puzzle of Judicial Behavior*

Barbara Geddes, *Paradigms and Sand Castles: Theory Building and Research Design in Comparative Politics*

Rose McDermott, *Political Psychology in International Relations*

Ole R. Holsti, *Public Opinion and American Foreign Policy, Revised Edition*

Luis Fernando Medina, *A Unified Theory of Collective Action and Social Change*

A Unified Theory of Collective Action and Social Change

Luis Fernando Medina

The University of Michigan Press
Ann Arbor

A CIP catalog record for this book is available from the British Library.

Library of Congress Cataloging-in-Publication Data

Medina Sierra, Luis Fernando, 1968–
    A unified theory of collective action and social change / Luis
Fernando Medina.
        p.   cm. — (Analytical perspectives on politics)
    Includes bibliographical references and index.
    ISBN-13: 978-0-472-09995-5 (cloth : alk. paper)
    ISBN-10: 0-472-09995-7 (cloth : alk. paper)
    ISBN-13: 978-0-472-06995-8 (pbk. : alk. paper)
    ISBN-10: 0-472-06995-0 (pbk. : alk paper)
    1. Patronage, Political. 2. Patron and client. 3. Social action.
4. Social change. I. Title.

JF2111.M43   2007
303.48′4—dc22   2006050007

77011438

Contents

Preface

The following pages constitute a book with an unusual structure, a structure that may be hard to negotiate without an initial summary. Part of the difficulty is due to the book's unusual genesis: although this is ostensibly a volume on the theory of collective action, my original purpose was not to write on this topic. In fact, I did not set out to write a book at all. My goal was rather to write a short paper on political clientelism in developing countries, a paper that ultimately became Chapter 5 in this book.[1] As I progressed in this project, I began to realize that it was built on shaky ground and that I could only salvage its initial insights, which I still found valuable, by going back to its theoretical foundations. This book is my response to this original impasse and much about it can be clarified by retracing the steps I had to follow.

I began working on the problem of clientelism hoping to develop a model that would extend to the study of patronage regimes the rigor of standard electoral models. Since my preparation consisted solely of some familiarity with modeling and some personal acquaintance with clientelism, I was fortunate to collaborate in the early stages with Susan Stokes, a scholar with ample research experience with this problem. From the outset I was convinced that whatever model I developed should capture two basic properties of clientelism: the fact that, at least as a first approximation, clientelism tends to be weakened by economic development and the fact that, judging from the narrative of clients in a political machine, politi-

---

[1]Some of its main ideas also form part of another joint piece: Medina and Stokes (2007).

cians in a clientelistic regime wield with respect to their voters a power unmatched by anything in a fully mature democracy. While patrons can lavish their voters with all kinds of favors, they can also punish disloyal behavior with the loss of jobs, goods or services.

Since the literature in industrial organization is full of game-theoretic models of such power asymmetries, at first I thought I would adapt any of the models on offer to the specifics of the problem at hand. But soon I realized that there was a significant difference between the threats issued by a patron and the threats with which, say, a firm can discipline its workers, or an investor can discipline a manager: in an electoral context, the power of the patron depends crucially on having the voters confirm his position via the ballot box. Bosses exist independently of the wishes of their workers just as investors exist independently of the wishes of managers. But patrons of a political machine owe their position as such patrons to the very people they try to control: the voters.

This meant that, instead of the usual models of industrial organization, I would need to rely on the theory of collective action. After all, voters in this situation are trapped in a coordination problem: while they can get rid of an undesirable patron if enough of them vote against him, dire consequences await those who try if they end up going it alone.

There were, then, two paths open at this juncture. I could conceptualize this collective action problem as an Olsonian Prisoners' Dilemma or I could, instead, adopt the framework of tipping games proposed by Thomas Schelling, where coordination problems have multiple equilibria. I quickly ruled out the first option for reasons that will become apparent in Chapter 2. The Olsonian model is very fragile and even tiny changes in its specification are enough to destroy its main result, viz. universal free-riding. But, for my purposes, models with multiple equilibria were not much better because it is not clear how they respond to exogenous shocks. Within that framework I would not be able to study the connection between exogenous variables, especially economic ones, and the survival or demise of clientelism; I would have had to give up my original goal.

So I probed a different approach. Once we go beyond the mere reporting of equilibria in a game and inquire about their robustness, or lack thereof, we realize that the multiple solutions of a game are not entirely capricious and instead, their relative likelihood depends in intuitive and illuminating ways on the exogenous parameters that govern the payoffs. This means that, going back to the problem of clientelism, in a precise and formal sense, the probability that the voters coordinate against the patron depends on economic variables such as levels of development. Such approach would allow us to formulate rigorously the connections between economic transformations and the putative demise of clientelistic machines. Having produced a fully working "toy example" of an economy with two voters and one patron, I was soon convinced that, even at the price of departing from the canon, it was worth putting together these ideas in a more systematic framework.

The method of stability sets is just such framework. It may not be the only possible one, or even the best one. It has its limitations, which will be discussed later on. But it has several advantages that convinced me to put it into print. First, it is not entirely original. Although we all place a premium on scientific innovation, there is something to be said for gradualism and cumulative progress as opposed to sweeping changes in outlook. The method of stability sets builds on ideas already developed in game theory, especially by John Harsanyi and Reinhardt Selten in their joint work *A General Theory of Equilibrium Selection*. In developing the method of stability sets I have borrowed liberally from their classic work but I disagree with its ultimate goal. The method of stability sets is, deliberately, *not* a method of equilibrium selection. Another advantage is its comparative simplicity, which makes it a good tool for obtaining results when we do not have much information or when we are simply in the initial stages of model building. Although the method of stability sets requires mathematical tools that may not form part of the average political scientist's toolkit, it is relatively simple. Nowhere is this more apparent than in the study of large-scale coordination games.

As I will show in Chapter 4, with the method of stability sets we can compute the relative likelihood of equilibria in games involving large numbers of players. Using this result, it is possible to extend the intuition of the two-voter clientelistic election to a true electoral model involving an arbitrary number of voters and two candidates. In fact, thanks to the method of stability sets it is straightforward that some types of economic growth can alleviate the coordination problem of voters in a clientelistic polity and, thus, erode the advantages enjoyed by their patron. The intuition is simple: changes in the economic environment that make the voters less dependent on the patron's resources reduce the weight of his threats and, therefore, make it more likely that the voters will coordinate against him if a better alternative comes around. But it should be noted that this intuition cannot be represented formally with the tools of standard game theory because, with their exclusive focus on the equilibria themselves rather than on their stability conditions, these tools cannot establish a link between the predictions of the game and its exogenous parameters.

The results pertaining to the method of stability sets and its extension to large coordination games, presented in Chapters 3 and 4, form the backbone of the present book. Chapter 3 introduces the method and Chapter 4 shows the results of applying it to the standard models of collective action already discussed in Chapter 2. These parts are the most mathematically demanding of all the book and many readers will prefer not to spend much time on them. Aware of this, I have written these chapters trying to keep separate the purely formal foundations, of interest only for readers familiar with game theory, and the substantive results that will be necessary later on in the book.

For readers uninterested in following all the technical arguments, down to the tiniest detail, there are several ways of navigating this part of the project. The easiest is to look at the central result of the method of stability sets applied to collective action games (pg. 136) and then move on to the chapters where that formula is used. For some purposes this might be an efficient way to use this book but, of course, readers who follow this path will have to accept as a given central conclusions of this book that are at odds with some received wisdom on the matter. A second option is to read the verbal discussions of the method. I suspect this is what most readers will do and, undoubtedly, for many it will be the wisest choice. But I think that some readers in that group may benefit from a third course of action: looking occasionally at the numerical examples of 2×2 games. I am convinced that the key elements of the method of stability sets are accessible to people without a state-of-the-art technical training. In fact, these examples are written at a level of mathematics not too different from the one that students often attain in their first course on game theory. Furthermore, attentive readers will realize that some topics that are a constant source of confusion in elementary game theory, especially the concept of mixed strategy Nash equilibria, come under a new, simpler and more intuitive light once connected to the notions of stability. In sum, although there is no guarantee that these examples will work for readers already familiar with basic game theory, there is no harm in trying them. They can clarify much of the method's fundamental principles and even some notions of game theory in general.

Beyond the interest that the method may have for game theory, however, I concluded that it had several substantive ramifications, sufficient to support a research program on collective action. If the method of stability sets could bring the precision of formal analysis to the idea that economic development lowers the barriers to collective action among clients of a political machine, this suggested that similar progress could be made in other areas. Collective action is a potent mechanism of social change but it always occurs within a particular set of structural conditions. As social scientists, we should try to make sense of how changes in said structure lead to changes in the possibilities of collective action that individuals face. This would be a crucial step toward a rigorous theory of social transformations. I am convinced that the method developed in this book offers promise in such an endeavor and have tried to defend this view at length throughout the text. To that end, I offer two lines of argument, each one somewhat independent of the other: one, comprising Chapters 1 and 2, that pertains to the general structure of the theory of collective action and another, developed in Chapters 5 and 6 where I present examples, admittedly crude, of the research program I envision.

The first such line of argument pertains to the general structure of the theory of collective action. Its main arguments are contained in Chapters 1 and 2. For all their accomplishments, the existing approaches to collective action from the perspective of rational-choice theory are unable to answer some fundamental questions. If we want to develop a systematic treatment of collective action we cannot just look at the mechanisms that individuals use to coordinate. We also need to investigate how the circumstances in which they operate help or hinder their efforts. Such is, precisely, the central objective of the method of stability sets.

Thanks to its ability to handle this problem the method is a useful tool in areas where other methods more elaborate and with a more solid foundation have not worked thus far. I give special importance to one such area: collective action as a counterfactual. Although real episodes of large-scale coordination are rare in societies, latent coordination is a potent undercurrent running through most social affairs. An example from the game of chess is entirely appropriate here, given the extensive use of game theory in this book.

Checkmate is the ultimate goal in chess; whoever checkmates the opponent wins. In professional chess, however, only a handful of games end with checkmate. In the vast majority of tournament matches one player resigns when the situation seems hopeless, even if the prospect of a checkmate is still several moves away. In fact, there is something of a convention: a player who waits until the bitter end of a checkmate is regarded as either too incompetent to realize that a checkmate was in the making or too arrogant to believe that the opponent would be able to pull it off. While observationally, checkmates seem negligible, it would be absurd to conclude that they are.

It is not possible to understand chess, to make any sense of the moves of the players at any juncture of the game, without knowing what a checkmate is and how to produce it.

Collective action is the checkmate of social sciences. The members of a society can destroy all its existing institutions, no matter how old and revered, through collective action and yet such action surfaces only in exceptional times. Beneath the surface, its possibility guides the choices of political actors at any given moment, no matter how quiet things seem.

This poses a technical problem for any game-theoretic enterprise. If the multiplicity of equilibria is one of the defining features of collective action, how can we study threats of collective action as opposed to actual instances? What threat assessment can we attribute to the players involved if we do not even know which outcome is the right one? A moment's reflection shows that this question, although entirely pertinent, should not be blown out of proportion. In real life we are constantly making decisions that we regard as good because they avoid other sequences of events. But those sequences themselves may be contingent and we can nevertheless see that we are better off avoiding them. Many drunk drivers, perhaps even a majority, make it safely to their destination. But, although it is not a sure thing that taking a ride from an ostensibly drunken friend will result in disaster, we often think it is wise not to: the risks entailed can be too high, and are higher the more inebriated he seems or the more difficult the road. When we make our decisions, we rely on risk assessments of events that do not occur and, in making such assessments, we draw from our knowledge of how those events could come to happen.

With its emphasis on relative likelihood rather than point-predictions, the method of stability sets can help us develop assessments of the likelihood of coordination in a collective action game even if we never observe it. Those assessments capture in an intuitive and rigorous way our knowledge about the objective circumstances where said collective action could eventually occur. I doubt that something similar can be formulated with the existing methods.

Chapter 1 makes these reflections explicit and spells out the goals of my research program. After clarifying the program the way I envision it, in Chapter 2 I lay down its foundations. In its current state, the rational-choice theory of collective action is not entirely unified and there are some loose ends in some of its formulations. In fact, although having several schools of thought can be healthy, the coexistence of the Olsonian and the Schellingean paradigms is on occasions unfortunate. Quite often one scholar considers some phenomenon an instance of a Prisoners' Dilemma and another scholar sees it instead as a tipping game and it is hard to see the underlying reasons for each choice. The difference is far from trivial: Olsonian models have one equilibrium, Schellingean models, many. In this chapter, then, I offer a unified framework for the study of collective action problems, a framework that covers both the Olsonian and the Schellingean cases. Although models of iterated games are not strictly speaking a particular case of the framework I propose here, I show that they are connected to the other models in ways that can be studied with the method of stability sets. This chapter may be of interest independent of the rest of the book since its results do not require the method of stability sets. Expressing both models as cases of the same mathematical structure allows us to bring out their implicit assumptions so that, when we analyze a collective action problem with the help of game theory, we can know which model is better suited for our purposes.

The analysis developed in that chapter is not kind to the Olsonian model of collective action. As it turns out, the central prediction of the public goods model, that individuals will always free-ride unless they are offered selective incentives, is an artifact of some parameter choices that are hard to justify. Once we relax the restrictions imposed by this model, we realize that collective action problems rather resemble games with multiple equilibria, in the spirit of Schelling's tipping games. This is not to say that the public goods model is useless, but simply that its scope is much more limited than what is often asserted.

The method of stability sets is not simply an alternative to the Olsonian model. It is a method that can be applied to any game, Olsonian, Schellingean or otherwise, even games that do not involve collective action. To prove that point, in Chapter 4 I apply it to the models of collective action already discussed, showing the results it allows us to obtain. Since the method of stability sets is designed to deal with multiple equilibria, when applied to a model with a unique equilibrium, such as Olson's, it gives results that are true but trivial. Its true relevance becomes apparent only when studying games with multiple equilibria, such as the Schellingean models or the models of repeated interactions.

This concludes the first part of this book, the part where I develop the technical foundations for my research program. In the second part I exemplify the work that such a program can generate. Since this part ventures into substantive issues, it is likely to be more controversial than the first one. To mature, a research program must leave behind its speculative stage and produce results that can be compared with already existing knowledge. Beyond a certain point, it becomes futile to argue in the abstract about the connection between collective action and the socioeconomic structures in which it occurs.

As already mentioned, Chapter 5 presents my discussion of clientelism in light of the preceding study on collective action and its game-theoretic underpinnings. Confirming the intuition with which I began this project, the model shows that, under very general circumstances and holding constant other elements, economic growth undermines the grip of a clientelistic machine. But the real test for models is not whether they ratify our previous intuitions but whether they allow us to develop other new intuitions that would have been harder to articulate without a precise language. Thus, I use the same model to study the connection between clientelism and policies of universalistic redistribution, a connection that has not been explored as extensively as the link between clientelism and development. For all the model's limitations, I think these results constitute a first success for the method of stability sets: thanks to it we can formulate new hypotheses about the relationship between clientelism and its wider politico-economic environment.

The path that led me to Chapter 5 also convinced me that with the method of stability sets we can expand the range of applicability of our ideas about collective action. Whereas with the standard tools we can only deal with explicit manifestations of collective action, with this method we can also study its more hidden instances and their far-reaching politico-economic effects. I would not have wanted to put into print a book where all the methodological weight lifting comes down to developing one model of one particular characteristic of some electoral regimes. If, as I believe, the work in this book can serve to launch a research program, it should be possible to show more than one instance of it. In Chapter 6 I do so. Its starting point is simple enough: modern democracies are more than just electoral systems; democratic rights include not just the right to vote, but also the right, subject to varying constraints, of engaging in collective action with other fellow citizens.

Whereas an outstanding literature in political economy has studied the consequences of expanding the right to vote, much less is known about the consequences of expanding the right to associate in collective action. This is a regrettable omission because a society's fundamental institutions owe their stability to the acceptance, or at least acquiescence, they command from the citizens. If that acceptance or that acquiescence disappears, the said institutions go with it as the floodgates to collective action open up. This book is not the right place to elaborate this principle in full detail so I decided instead to illustrate it with an example.

A vast literature in economics has studied how different institutional settings to regulate labor markets can lead to different patterns of economic performance. As some of that literature has already recognized, these regulations emerge from a process of confrontation between capital and labor where collective action is the ultimate source of power, especially for the latter.

The labor market illustrates the role of collective action as a threat and, hence, the need for a method to understand it. Strikes, lockouts and other forms of industrial conflict are, even at worst, a rarity. In most countries, most of the time, the factories and the labor market run smoothly without being disrupted by class struggle. But this normalcy represents a consensus between all the parties involved about many aspects, e.g., wages, paid leaves, pensions. Ultimately, the specifics of this consensus are determined by collective action, understood not as an overt explosion but as a constant threat that both parties wield to make sure that the terms agreed upon are honored.

In their current form, techniques such as those of tipping games and focal points are at a loss in studying games where collective action is only a possibility, so to speak, off the equilibrium path. Instead, with the method of stability sets it is possible to analyze this problem and establish what structural conditions inhibit the possibility of labor's collective action. Such latent collective action plays a decisive role in determining an economy's performance and distribution and, hence, the political coalitions that such economy will engender. Since the method of stability sets shows the connections between the potential for collective action and the economic structure that supports it, the result is a model that explains how the asset distribution and the technology of an economy shape the prospects for different types of interclass political coalitions.

In what I regard as a very fortunate development, the recent literature has already produced deductive arguments of this type, the best of them being real exemplars of rigor and relevance in political economy. Chapter 6 can be read as an attempt to supplement some of that literature. While most of the models in this tradition consider elections as the link through which economic structures affect political outcomes, the model I present here, while recognizing the centrality of elections, goes on to show that more nuanced patterns of coalition building emerge once we make clear the importance of extra-electoral collective action.

By now it must be clear that my original project became something entirely different. Such transformation came at a price. I did not obtain all the results I wanted about political clientelism. For example, I wanted to study the effects of trade on these political systems, in particular, whether it is possible to discern differences in those effects depending on the sector where trade occurs. In principle, one would expect that whatever effect trade has on the stability of a clientelistic regime must depend on its relative factor intensity, on the volatility of the income it generates, on the exchange rate regime that harnesses it, on the infrastructure it needs and so on. But I have no regrets for not having gotten there. Such studies are still possible and, moreover, I think that the method of stability sets is the most appropriate tool to conduct them. I did not arrive at the port I intended but I believe that, in the process of trying, I learned how to build a sturdier vessel that will take me there next time. The vessel can use several improvements and there are many more places to explore with it. This led me to a second conclusion: the next journeys will be much more interesting if accompanied. That is why I have decided to publish this book.

Acknowledgments

It began as a quickly scribbled graph. It was not a new or unusual graph, let alone a pretty one. I had seen it hundreds of times before, only this time it looked different. But it could not yet become a book. I needed first to understand what was special about it, determine whether it merited a book, write it and then publish it. In retrospect, I am happy I did not appreciate at that time how hard each of these steps would be and how long they would take. Such knowledge would have overwhelmed entirely the brief elation of that moment, a moment that has already receded four years into the past. That original instant was followed by others, thus becoming a sizeable segment of my life; its brief loneliness gave way to the presence of many people that helped me as that sheet from a notepad was joined by more pages and, ultimately, by two covers.

Before anything else, I needed to make sure that those marks populating my notepad were not utter nonsense. Daniel Diermeier, Sven Feldmann and Roger Myerson offered the necessary reassurance at a moment when the wrong doses of curtness could have proven fatal. Given how sketchy my reasoning was at that point, it is remarkable that they could overlook its ostensible flaws long enough to see something worthy in it. Roger Myerson even brought the tracing procedure to my attention, a piece of advice whose value grew tremendously over time. Already believing that my views on the problem of multiple equilibria could find support in game theory, I wondered if political scientists would agree with the implications I wanted to draw from them. Carles Boix, John Brehm, Daniel Gingerich, Jeff Grynaviski, Stephen Haber, Gretchen Helmke,

Jim Johnson, Stathis Kalyvas, Jack Knight, Scott Mainwaring, Joan Serra, Susan Stokes, Mariela Szwarcberg and Alex Wendt were subjected to my first, not wholly persuasive, attempts. In fact, I first imagined this book while driving alone, somewhere in Rhode Island, after a conference with some of them. In my search for a solid mathematical foundation, I tested Ethan Anderes's patience until he finally disabused me of the hopes I had placed on an earlier attempt at formalization. Although he expressed it just as an afterthought, Michael Stein made what turned out to be an incredibly prescient mathematical remark.

Then came the false starts. Steven Brams and Peter Stone made very thoughtful comments on a first attempt at a paper-length exposition of my ideas. Robert Bates and Randall Calvert read what proved to be the first in a very long chain of iterations of manuscripts and offered great insight and support. Several audiences witnessed my grappling with some of the issues involved in this book, with varying degrees of success and, fortunately, kept their promise of giving me a hard time. I should thank seminar participants at CIDE (Mexico), Duke University, Harvard University, ITAM (Mexico), Northwestern University, Notre Dame University, Rochester University, Stanford University, Tulane University, Universidad Carlos III de Madrid (Spain), Universidad Externado de Colombia, University of Chicago, the IV Conference on Collective Intentionality in Siena (Italy) and the Inaugural Jorge Eliécer Gaitán Lecture in the Universidad Nacional de Colombia. The journal *Rationality and Society*, in whose pages I embarked upon the search for this book's voice, was also a very valuable part of this stage.

In spite of their changing physical form, books remain the tool with which our ideas defy oblivion, hopefully for long enough to reappear in other people's notepads. In my case, this is where Bruce Bueno de Mesquita and James Reische came in. They believed in this manuscript and led the great editorial crew of the University of Michigan Press to turn it into a published outcome.

The Department of Politics at the University of Virginia has been more than a wonderful institutional home to finish this project; it has also been the place where I have met engaging colleagues and friends, purveyors of both intellectual light and personal warmth. From his chairmanship, Sid Milkis went out of his way to make sure that I had the right environment to focus on this book. Dale Copeland, George Klosko, John Maclaren, Carol Mershon, Len Schoppa and Herman Schwartz have led me to think and rethink my ideas, making me a happier author, albeit a more hesitant one. In the lonely crowd of academia, you can consider yourself lucky if you find someone who is half as encouraging, half as probing and half as congenial as David Waldner has been to me. Melissa Ptacek helped to clean up the manuscript by going through it with all sorts of brushes and with amazing attention to detail. This book is guilty of having distracted from more worthy tasks the minds of two bright young scholars that gave it serious scrutiny: Cristian Ponce de León and Ernesto Cárdenas. Among many other things, the latter found the needle of a misplaced subscript in a haystack of equations. To technical readers, this should say it all. Non-technical readers should understand that the metaphor falls short: you can find a needle if it pricks you by chance.

Through a brilliant twist of fate, I began typing these acknowledgments in a beautiful office with one of the best possible views of Bogotá, the city where I grew up. I can hardly think of a more appropriate way to wrap up an itinerary that began precisely in these same streets, many years ago. With its generosity, the Universidad Externado de Colombia, through the gentle but determined leadership of Mauricio Pérez, keeps reminding me of all the wonderful people, ideas and things that populate that part of my life governed by the accident of birth. While a strong believer in rational choice, I acknowledge the wisdom of chance: there is something profoundly good about a milieu that offers you friends, mentors and peers such as Marcelo Bucheli, Jorge Iván González, Gabriel Misas and Manuel Ramírez. Probably the single most decisive juncture of the itinerary that led to this book was made possible by the Banco de la República de Colombia when it overwhelmed me with a generous scholarship. Whatever the merits of this book, a country that, in the middle of trying times, through one of its foremost institutions, privileges to such an extent an ordinary citizen solely because it trusts his intellectual abilities deserves a future brighter than its present.

Authors make books, but books also make authors. The most vivid discoveries of this book are nowhere to be found in its pages. I kept them to myself in the form of lasting memories. In an apt symbol of this process my family's three generations were, literally, standing next to me during the darkest hour, right after hanging up from a fateful phone call. It is now time for me to part company from this book, to let it stand for itself. Some readers might put it down, some critics might destroy it. It may lead a tough life and come to know some of the hardship it caused me for four years. Anyway, to me it will always be the same unruly mix of hopes, exhilaration, frustrations, absent-minded breakfasts and, especially, the gift of having shared it all with Claudia, my wife, and Alejandra, my daughter.

Part I

Theory

Chapter 1

Why Another Book on Collective Action?

1.1 The Book's Basic Claims

For decades, country X has suffered under the iron-fisted dictatorship of General A. Even in his advanced age, the General has continued his kleptocratic policies, impoverishing the populace while he and his entourage live in astonishing luxury. Daily, government minders send more and more reports about the growth of discontent, especially after last year's economic crisis, triggered by a monumental decline in the price of exports. Amid this situation, the Finance Minister brought a proposal to the cabinet in a recent meeting: a five-fold increase in water fees. General A, a man with no formal training whatsoever in social sciences, a man who has spent his life in the barracks, immediately fulminated: "You are crazy! You want to get us all overthrown!"

"Your Excellency," interjected one of his most trusted political advisors, Advisor 1, "I think the Finance Minister has a point. I have studied the contemporary theories of collective action as a public goods problem and they concur in one conclusion: the level of water fees has nothing to do with the regime's survival. You see, our opponents are trapped in what theorists call a Prisoners' Dilemma (PD). They would want to get rid of you but they are all better off if somebody else does

3

it for them. So, they will all try to free-ride on each other. If there's any clear teaching in the theory of collective action is that, as Mancur Olson (1965, pg. 2) would put it: 'rational, self-interested individuals will not act to achieve their common or group interests.' There is always the risk that some kind of political entrepreneur could provide them with selective incentives to rebel. But thus far that doesn't seem to be happening and, in any event, selective incentives should be enough to compensate the cost of cooperating in a rebellion, a cost that has everything to do with our secret police and nothing with water fees. If there's any political entrepreneur out there trying to provide selective incentives, we're not making his job any harder or easier by changing water fees. I think we can just go ahead with the Minister's proposal."

The general then turned to Advisor 2, who had been expressing discomfort with some of Advisor 1's views. "Well, Excellency, I don't think that Mr. 1 is using the right tools to analyze the problem, but, although I would state them differently, his conclusions seem right overall. It bothers me that he sees this problem as a PD. He is, to use Hardin's concise formulation (Hardin, 1995), confusing exchange power with coordination power. PDs happen when people rely on the exchange of resources to induce each other to act, and then only under some specific circumstances. Coordination is different. A group can create power through coordination. If the would-be rebels coordinate in enough numbers, we are all in real trouble. Apart from that caveat, I must confess that Mr. 1's basic point is hard to refute. Instead of using the language of PDs, I would frame this situation in the language of games with multiple equilibria, as Thomas Schelling (1978) taught us, some years after Olson . The opposition is facing two possible equilibria: one in which no one cooperates because they are afraid of going it alone, and one in which they do coordinate and they succeed in taking over the government. Which one they will play depends on whether each individual expects others to join. That is the famous 'focal point effect.' If cooperation becomes focal, then everyone will realize that they have nothing to lose by joining, and they will join. Otherwise, they will all stay home. Still, for all my differences with Mr. 1, I concur that water fees do not play any particular role here. Focality does not depend on water fees; it depends on what you think others will do. To be honest, it remains something of a mystery what makes some equilibria focal and not others, but I cannot see what water fees have to do with this. As Mr. 1 said, maybe you will be overthrown, that's just, dare I say, an occupational hazard. But water fees do not change that fact; they do not make it more or less likely."

During Advisor 2's speech, Advisor 3 had been scribbling in his notepad. Upon being subjected to the General's stern stare, he began with some hesitation. "I think Mr. 2 has done us a service by forcing us to think in terms of games with multiple equilibria. But I also think he is simplifying things too much. Schelling shows clearly that focality is not the only possible mechanism. In fact, he is rightly credited with developing the analysis of tipping games, games where, before making a decision, agents consider how many people they expect to join some common effort. See, I've drawn here what I believe is the right representation of our case. (Shows his notepad with Figure 1.1.) This is a typical Schelling diagram. In the horizontal axis I've put the percentage of people expected to join a revolt and in the vertical axis, the percentage of people who will actually join. As you see, this situation has three possible equilibria, points where the S-shaped curve intersects the 45° diagonal. For the time being, look only at the solid curve. As Mr. 2 says, in one case everyone joins the revolt (point R), in the other no one does (point Q). The case in the middle (point U) is unstable so we should not worry about it. If people are on a point to the left of U, then the logic of the tipping model says that they would all rather remain quiescent: the equilibrium is Q. If they are to the right of U, then their expectations for revolt will be self-fulfilling and they will 'tip' toward equilibrium R. Alas, tipping games do not tell us what determines the levels of critical mass but it is safe to say that the populace right now is to the left of U even though we cannot know where they will be once you raise the water fees. At any rate, notice that levels of critical mass

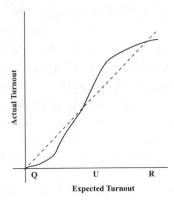

Figure 1.1: Advisor 3's Schelling Diagram

depend on how many people you need to see joining a revolution before you decide to join. The tipping point depends on amounts of people in the revolution, not on what people want from the revolution; it depends on the size of militant groups, not on water fees. So, with these qualifications, I agree with my colleagues: water fees do not matter for the immediate likelihood of a revolt."

The General looked icily at the Finance Minister but then made the already legendary silent nod that for years had meant approval of a proposal. At that point, General B, the feared chief of the secret police and his long-time friend, banged the table: "This is ridiculous! How can you entrust your political future to these armchair advisors, after all these years in the business? Look, unlike these guys, I've been out there. I know this country. I've been doing my job for over 20 years and this much I can tell: four years ago we had a crop failure. We received aid from international donors but we in this room all know what happened to that aid. Let me tell you. Things got really tough then. My men had to work extra hard making sure nobody would stir up trouble. Even the toughest guys were showing unease with so many arrests and ... intensive inquiries, if you know what I mean. We got lucky back then but I don't think this time we'll be that lucky. A five-fold increase in water fees? This is crazy! 20 or 30% and I think I can keep the lid on things. But 500%? Look, you raise water fees 500%, I'm out of here and, let me warn you, soon you will be too."

In this meeting we have encountered four different theories of collective action, three of them deeply rooted in the rational-choice paradigm, with the fourth one a simple layperson's theory without any analytical justification. The chief of the secret police has in mind what we may call a layperson's theory of collective action (henceforth LPT). Although hard to formulate precisely, we can, provisionally, summarize it with the following statement: *When individuals can achieve some beneficial result by coordinating in a group, they are likely to coordinate. As the potential benefits of coordination increase (or the costs decrease), these individuals are more likely to coordinate and, conversely, as the potential benefits decrease (or the costs increase), they are less likely to do so.* In the previous example, the LPT says that an increase in water fees increases the likelihood of a rebellion, that 20-30% increases in water fees lead to modest increases in such likelihood but that 500% increases have a much more sizeable effect. This theory's conclusions differ substantively from those of the first three, suggesting that we need to decide which theory to adopt. One way of choosing would be with the following sequence of claims:

Claim 1 Logical consistency is the primary value of a theory. If a logically consistent theory contradicts the impressions of the layperson, the latter ought to give way. In these instances, the theory leads to counterintuitive results that should be embraced as genuine contributions to our knowledge of a problem.

Claim 2 Unlike LPT, the rational-choice accounts are logically consistent. In particular, they have microfoundations, which is to say, they can be derived from a theory of individually rational behavior.

Claim 3 Because of these microfoundations, rational-choice theories are more useful than LPT. They can be formalized and tested in ways the other cannot.

Although not stated explicitly, this reasoning seems to animate much of the rational-choice scholarship in collective action. In a dissenting mode, I want to propose the following sequence:

Claim 1′ It is debatable that logical consistency should overrule common sense in the social sciences. Social scientists do not have a privileged access to human behavior, beyond the layperson's reach. Counterintuitive results may be artifacts of a poorly contrived theory. They should only be accepted after the theory itself has been subjected to serious scrutiny. In fact, a good criterion for choosing a theory is the degree to which it can make sense of our everyday intuition. It may teach us something we would not know from mere intuition, but we should be cautious if the theory does serious violence to it.

Claim 2′ Even if the previous claim is rejected, the layperson's theory of collective action is also logically consistent by the same standards of rational-choice theory. It can be expressed and formalized with the same tools that we use to express and formalize the extant rational-choice paradigms. If anything, the rational-choice explanations of collective action are special cases of the general theory underlying the layperson's approach. The layperson's theory covers a wider set of cases of that general theory and is true in more of its instantiations. The rival views cover only very restrictive, and even uninteresting, cases.

Claim 3′ Once we acknowledge that the layperson's theory is also compatible with microfoundations, it is clear that it can also be formalized and tested. Moreover, there are many relevant social-scientific questions that cannot be an-

swered with the standard rational-choice theories and that can, instead, be addressed in
a systematic way with the formalized layperson's theory.

This book is a defense of Claims $2'$ and $3'$. Elsewhere I
have defended a position close to that of $1'$ but the case for
it cannot be as conclusive as the one for $2'$ and $3'$. Defending
$1'$ requires a set of philosophical assumptions that some readers may find controversial.[1] Instead, Claims $2'$ and $3'$ can be
proven without appeal to any argument that rational-choice
scholars might reject. In other words, Claims $2'$ and $3'$ are theorems, as it were, of the axiomatic body of rational-choice theory. As the reader will notice, in this book there is nothing but
rational-choice theory in a very orthodox version. This is not
because I reject other types of approaches. To the contrary, I
believe that the gap between approaches is much smaller than
we usually think, and that genuine exchange is possible, a subject on which I will make some remarks toward the end. But to
engage in serious dialogue between approaches, it is important
that each approach stretches itself to the maximum, trying to
give as much as it can. A dialogue is much more productive
if the interlocutors are fully articulate and lucid rather than
mumbling and distracted.

1.2 A Plea for Comparative Statics

Even if Claim $2'$ is proven, a skeptic may argue, it would be a
simple intellectual curiosity. If LPT can be formalized using
game theory, it will join the already large variety of theories of
collective action but there would be no reason to believe that it
stands out in this crowded field. I disagree. Formalizing LPT
is essential because it, alone among the rational-choice theories, offers something indispensable for the scientific understanding of collective action phenomena: comparative statics
on the environmental parameters.

---

[1] My defense of this view is expressed in Medina (2004).

In the example above, LPT offers a comparative statics of collective action as a function of changes in the environment: an exogenous shock (increase in water fees) has a discernible, systematic effect over the endogenous variable (revolt), at least in probabilistic terms. Foes of LPT may say that this is a specious progress because LPT has still to explain why collective action is possible in the first place. But here I am asking this hypothetical foe to suspend disbelief momentarily and entertain the possibility that LPT is successfully formalized. Then, many interesting questions, questions that thus far cannot even be posed, could be addressed rigorously. In what follows I will give some examples. To answer them rigorously, we need what LPT has: a comparative statics of collective action, focused not on explaining *why* collective action occurs, but *how likely* it is.

By itself, the question "why collective action happens?" is not a useful one. There are many answers we can give to this question and, absent any further details, we have no grounds to accept one over the rest. Any set of statements that concludes that collective action happens would do. A theory that simply explains why collective action occurs, while remaining silent about how likely it is and how this likelihood changes with observable changes in the environment, is ultimately an untestable theory. There are many possible ways of explaining why collective action occurs; some may rely on the actors' rationality, some on their irrationality, some may even invoke divine intervention or the specific location of celestial bodies. The only way to accept or reject theories is by looking at their further implications, their comparative statics. Collective action happens, but it also happens with some specific patterns. People vote, but they vote in ways that are connected to objective features such as their ethnicity, socioeconomic status, geographic location or occupational choice. Groups engage in protests, but they do so in response to specific circumstances: if a country has an economy that grows at 10% per annum, with inflation rates of 2%, with record-high prices for its exports, and a spotless-clean administration, observers would be stunned to see its government collapse under the pressure of a massive citizens' revolt. Asking "Why does collective action happen?" places the scientific bar too low. A harder question, one whose answers are testable, is: "Why does collective action happen when it happens?" This is the central question of formalized LPT.

It may seem grossly unfair to say that the current rational-choice theories of collective action do not have comparative statics. Olson's classic *The Logic of Collective Action* has been credited for generating predictions of comparative statics previously unavailable.[2] Results on the effect of group size over the probability of collective action are the quintessential example of such comparative statics.

Granted, there already are results of comparative statics such as this one. But these are not enough. Results like this pertain only to the devices agents can use to overcome collective action problems. But a fully testable theory must also look at the problem from the point of view of its exogenous parameters, those beyond the control of the agents.

Economic Determinants of Organized Political Action. Suppose, for instance, that LPT is right so that we can ascertain the likelihood of collective action as the objective parameters of its environment change. In the case of the imaginary country described at the opening of this chapter, it would now be possible to ask questions such as: If the five-fold increase in water fees is politically infeasible, what about other options, such as a higher tariff, an increase in the VAT, possibly altering its base? What is the political impact of these options, compared to that of the water fees increase? Is country X more likely to meet the IMF's stabilization goals than country Y, a neighboring and embattled democracy? What about country Z, which has managed to establish solid democratic institutions but has hit hard times because of the regional economic crisis? If, instead, the three countries have roughly similar political systems, but in one of them the exports are much more labor intensive than in the remaining two, which is more likely to suffer political unrest following a decline in

---

[2]See, for instance, Fiorina (1996) and Sandler (1992).

the price of exports? To put it in terms familiar to political scientists, the current theories of collective action do not allow us to study questions where collective action phenomena appear as the dependent variable and economic processes as independent variables.

Collective Action off the Equilibrium Path. One of the greatest strengths of game theory is its treatment of counterfactuals in explaining social phenomena. Without the kind of comparative statics that LPT can offer, we cannot make the most of that strength in the study of collective action. In every polity, collective action is the dog that did not bark. Most waking hours of heads of state are spent forestalling the kind of collective action that could topple them. Massive, outright rejection of a government is an off-the-equilibrium-path behavior that explains a good deal of the decisions governments take. Governments often shelve plans for trade liberalization, privatization, tax increases, abolition of political rights and so on because of fears that they may set off organized resistance. Potential collective action acts as a brake on governments' behavior. But if we do not have comparative statics of collective action as a function of its environment, we cannot have an idea of how big a threat it is, and hence how strong a brake it is, in specific circumstances.

Counterfactuals and Forecasting. One of the major limitations of the standard theories of collective action is their focus on sufficient conditions for its success. This focus does not yield interesting comparative statics as a function of the environment and forces collective action theory to study processes only after the fact. We can only know that a set of sufficient conditions has been met after we observe their outcome, in this case, collective action. When we explain the success of the American Civil Rights Movement as the result of focal point effects (Chong, 1991), or of the revolutions in Eastern Europe as the result of informational cascades (Kuran, 1991; Lohmann, 1994), just to take examples of some of the best studies available, we are focusing on the sufficient conditions that can only be ascertained once we know that these movements were successful.

Doubtless, studies like these make valuable additions to our knowledge. But they are not equipped to answer many other important questions. For every successful social movement, there are many others, often even in the same country and with the same agenda, that fail. By concentrating only on successes, we risk selecting on the dependent variable (King, Keohane and Verba, 1994). A good theory of collective action must also know how to make sense of failures. These failures have much to do with the organization of those movements but also with their timing, with the objective circumstances they faced. The opposition to the SED regime in East Germany succeeded in setting off an informational cascade in the midst of dismal economic and political performance on the part of the regime. Would it have been equally successful if, through some exogenous mechanism, the GDR ended up posting amazing growth rates of 10% per annum from 1980 on and during the same period West Germany's output contracted at an annual rate of 3%, with unemployment reaching levels over 35%? Suharto's regime in Indonesia lasted for more than 30 years through which time its opponents tried all kinds of means to overthrow him. Arguably we can read the collapse of this regime in 1997 as the result of some kind of focal point. But then, what if the rupiah did not enter a free fall at that point? What if it depreciated only by half of what it did? One fourth? What if, instead of currency meltdown, the Indonesian economy suffers from a spike in interest rates? (In fact, in the East Asian crisis of 1997 this is what governments were willing to put up with, if only creditors would lend them money at those interest rates.) Of course, we will never know the answers to these questions. But we need a disciplined way to formulate them. After all, right now, many groups throughout the world are trying to set off some informational cascade, or to generate a focal point around some specific agenda. If I want to make probabilistic assessments of their chances of success, and understand how their presence impacts the political decisions of other actors, I need to know what is the context in which they are operating and I need systematic propositions about how that context affects the likelihood of organized collective action ... and I need these propositions now, not in 5 or 10 years when these movements have already been successful, and then I can attribute their victory to some tipping mechanism.

1.3   LPT's Privileged Status

In this book I will make no attempt to prove Claim 1′. But here I will make some remarks about it to dispel a very persistent objection: that there is no need to formalize LPT's comparative statics because the current theories of collective action already have one and it has been treated kindly by the data.

True. In a way the prevailing theories of collective action have a comparative statics of collective action with respect to its environment. Let's call it a "null comparative statics," echoed by the advisors in the previous example, where the environment plays no role whatsoever in explaining organized collective action. As empirical studies keep accumulating political scientists are gaining confidence in this result.[3] So, it might be that the rational-choice literature on collective action is already chalking up a major victory in showing that revolts, insurgencies and other types of organized collective action are, after all, not related to their economic context. If that is true, one major argument in favor of formalizing LPT collapses. One of the best scholars in this area cautioned me in a private conversation that: "you are interested in a collective action story driven by the payoffs. But that story may be wrong and the true story may have to do with culture, institutions and history." I do not deny that culture, institutions and history may play a crucial role in shaping collective action outcomes and the formalism I propose makes this clear. But I

---

[3]This seems to be the attitude among scholars in civil conflict as they probe into the conventional "grievance" model. See, for instance, Collier (2000) and Fearon and Laitin (2003). An earlier, more benevolent yet still skeptical appraisal is that of Lichbach (1989).

do not think that they are the "true" story. The "true" story includes the payoffs as well.

Rational-choice theorists claim, rightly, that if this null comparative statics is correct, it will overturn the time-honored beliefs of many social scientists. This is an understatement. If true, the null comparative statics would overturn the time-honored beliefs of everybody, especially, political actors, always mindful of objective circumstances when making their decisions, the better to ride the waves of organized collective action. When crops fail, savvy rulers see the writing in the wall and react; they put together aid packages, or lower taxes, or convene representative bodies, or step up repression, or even perform a combination of all these measures and many others. When a time-saving technology is developed in a research lab, industrialists and labor organizers brace themselves for a new battle over labor legislation. When the majoritarian ethnic group of a country goes through an unprecedented economic boom, absorbing labor from peripheral minorities, autonomist intellectuals start pondering the advantages of assimilation versus confrontation and autonomist leaders call for intense meetings to discuss membership, strategies and demands. In all these instances, the actors may come to different conclusions and some of their choices may prove to be unfortunate. But, whatever decision they make, it is informed by the understanding that structural changes will affect the prospects of different types of collective action.

So, it would indeed be very remarkable if this null comparative statics were a truth of logic, not just of empirics. It would mean that a good deal of recorded political history has been the result of a huge mistake. It would mean that, after all, Louis XVI did not need to shuffle his economic cabinet and convene the Estates General during the 1788-89 crisis because it had no impact over the endurance of his reign. Or that Czar Nicholas II did not need to be bothered by the dismal news coming from the front in World War I, and take the risky move of assuming direct command of the troops, because the imminent bread shortages would have no meaningful political effect. Or that all the meetings of the Communist Parties in

Eastern Europe that for decades called for increased production of consumption goods in the next five-year plan were a waste of time because the shortages of these goods and their poor quality did not constitute a serious political issue for the regime's survival.

But if this is correct, this would be a Pyrrhic victory for rational-choice theory, a self-refutation of sorts. If political actors can deceive themselves so much when they make some of the most crucial decisions they can make in their lives, then a theory based on rationality may not be relevant at all to study political processes.

The null comparative statics, however, may be validated by empirical studies. This seems to pose a serious dilemma. But such dilemma arises from confusing empirical truths with logical propositions. When building a theory, there is a danger in allowing its internal logic to follow too closely the facts it intends to explain. Let me give an example taken from individual decision theory. Here is a theory about lottery purchases: there are individuals in society who dislike money so much that they give it away to the state by purchasing lottery tickets. From an empirical point of view, this theory is highly successful. It predicts that people who play the lottery will end up losing money and, in fact, the overwhelming majority of lottery players lose money. Sure, there are a handful of cases in which lottery buyers end up winning money but the theory is consistent with upwards of 95% of the observations. Not many theories in the social sciences correctly predict 95% of their sampling universe so it may seem inappropriate to object simply because of a few, pesky anomalies. Human beings are not perfect; they make mistakes. It should come as no surprise that among the group of money-haters that buy lottery tickets there is a tiny fraction of them who are woefully incompetent in achieving their goal and, instead, end up making more money than what they had at the beginning.

Obviously, this theory is silly. Regardless of its empirical success, it should be rejected on logical grounds. In fact, its empirical success is partly the source of the problem. The theory's logical construction already includes its empirical conclusion. The seemingly impressive 95% success ratio is an artifact of the theory that should carry no weight whatsoever because the remaining 5% of cases, the failures, reveal how much the theory distorts its subject, neglecting that people play lotteries because there are low chances of winning large sums and high chances of losing small sums.

Going back to the case of collective action, it is true that there are countries where the situation deteriorates for decades and yet they never see a revolt against the regime. For instance, in the literature on civil strife, the "grievance" theories are becoming somewhat old-fashioned as cross-sectional analyses fail to find connections between objective economic circumstances and popular uprisings. But this empirical result should not be built into the theory's logical structure. Such structure should contain only statements about what collective action is and only then, try to explain empirical observations.

1.4 A Short Methodological Note

Sitting at the crossroads of many different lines of inquiry, political science hosts permanent methodological disputes. With its extreme rationalist stance, this book is likely to attract various methodological criticisms. A full defense of my views on the matter would require something of a companion volume so I will not even attempt to defend rational-choice theory and the particularly orthodox version I use here. Ultimately, the taste is in the pudding. Whether the tools I present contribute to a better study of collective action is something that can only be decided after using them judiciously.

But some may doubt that there is a pudding to taste, to begin with. While I defend my techniques for their potential empirical applications, in this book I illustrate this potential offering purely deductive models. But there is no contradiction in this; not, at least, for those who share the views of mainstream economics on what makes a theory "empirically useful."

Modern economic analysis arrived at its current methodological stance after several disputes in the 1940s. This was a time where economists had already gathered massive amounts of data in the hope of explaining phenomena as relevant as the business cycle. In 1946, Arthur Burns and Wesley Mitchell, from the already prestigious National Bureau of Economic Research, published a volume, *Measuring Business Cycles*, that culminated their efforts at data gathering on economic performance. It was a herculean task going through huge amounts of time series with a fine-toothed comb and computing statistical correlations between them all. But it was met with a scathing, if mild-mannered, review from Tjalling Koopmans (1947), who summarized in a three-word title the attitude of economists ever since toward this kind of work: "Measurement without Theory." Koopmans decried how, in their fixation with the data and in their reluctance to come forward with theoretical conjectures, the authors of the study had missed the opportunity to really explain business cycles, as opposed to just reporting them. This is what he had to say about their choice of variables to measure:

> The choices made may have been the best possible ones. But "good" choices mean relevant choices. What is relevant can only be determined with the help of some notions as to the generation of economic fluctuations, and as to their impact on society. (Koopmans, 1947, pg. 164)

Koopmans's critique explains the otherwise odd habit of economists of developing simplified models, with heroic assumptions, to explain phenomena that any ignoramus would recognize as bewilderingly complex. True understanding, as opposed to plain reporting, results from measurement *and* theory. Without theory, without arguments that guide our thinking as we glance at the data, we cannot discern the relevant from the superfluous, the fleeting from the permanent, the general from the particular. Deductive models, then, never substitute for empirical inquiry, but neither can such inquiry progress without them.

What, then, makes simple models empirically useful? Their comparative statics. With their abstractions, simple, deductive models aim at identifying the underlying forces of a process, telling us what to expect from the data and where the important findings may be. To guide us in this process, such models must explain how some part of the data can react to changes in another; they must partition the data into exogenous and endogenous and show the connections between the former and the latter. This is the essence of comparative statics.

Chapter 2

Rational-choice Models of Collective Action: A Generalization and Critical Assessment

2.1 Introduction

A systematic study of collective action informed by game theory must deal with the problem of multiple equilibria. Equilibrium is the polar star of game theory: the whole purpose of a game-theoretic model is to arrive at an equilibrium that can serve as its testable prediction. Yet, when a game has multiple equilibria, many possible outcomes are compatible with individual strategic rationality and the theory does not lead to a unique prediction.

Multiple equilibria are ubiquitous in collective action theory. This may seem an exaggeration given that a large and prominent share of models of collective action, those based on the public goods approach introduced by Olson (1965), have indeed only one equilibrium and, hence, a unique and deterministic prediction. Although models involving multiple equilibria have been a lasting and influential presence since the development of focal point arguments and tipping games by

Schelling (1960, 1978), it would seem that they cannot claim any privileged status within the theory of collective action.

The subdiscipline seems split on this matter, with different scholars often using different models to capture the same situation. Tullock (1971) considers that the public goods argument, typical of the Olsonian approach, captures the essence of all known revolutions, and Muller and Opp (1986) follow some of these insights in their analysis of Peru's guerrilla movement. But Wood (2002) uses a Schellingean model to analyze the Salvadoran insurgency. Kuran (1991) argues that the collapse of the Eastern European regimes obeyed the logic of multiple equilibria, in keeping with Schelling's original insight, but Finkel, Muller and Opp (1989) analyze German protest movements using an Olsonian theoretical template. To take a closely related example, the standard formulation of the "Paradox of Voting" is couched in terms of the analysis of public goods, but other treatments (e.g., that of Schuessler (2000)) adopt the perspective of tipping games. This abundance of collective action models in the literature is eloquent testimony of the creativity of contemporary political scientists but is in some ways an unhealthy development. Without a unifying framework, we do not have a firm basis for deciding which model is correct.

This chapter will develop such a unifying model, allowing us to appreciate the extent to which collective action phenomena are indeed interactions with multiple equilibria. The single-equilibrium simplicity of the public goods models is the result of too many restrictive assumptions. Although logically consistent, these models are critically fragile: tiny changes in the assumptions destroy their fundamental conclusion.

To prove this, in this chapter I will specify a model of collective action that subsumes both the single-equilibrium (Olsonian) approaches and the multiple-equilibria (Schellingean) ones. Instead of arguing about the relative merits of, say, the Prisoners' Dilemma versus tipping games in a vacuum where each has an air of plausibility, this model shows what assumptions are critical in each case so that we can make better modeling choices. Later, once the book's basic technique is in place, we will be in possession of a fully general and fully systematic framework of collective action: deriving implications about its comparative statics will be largely a matter of choosing in each case the relevant specific model.

2.2   A General Model of the Collective Action Problem

Whatever else we want it to represent, a model of collective action should capture the essence of situations that (*a*) involve more than one, preferrably many, agents who (*b*) have to decide whether to take a costly action that, in turn, (*c*) increases the likelihood of a goal that is (*d*) desirable by all the agents. Remove any of these, and the situation at hand stops being a collective action problem.

At a minimum, a game-theoretic model must describe the agents, what they can do (i.e., their strategies) and what happens to them when they do what they do (i.e., their payoffs). From these three ingredients we obtain the basic decision problems that go into describing an equilibrium. Therefore, a model of collective action must include:

a. Several agents. In this case, I will use i (occasionally j) to denote an arbitrary agent, where $i - 1, \ldots, N$. N is a natural number subject only to the restriction that $N > 2$.

b. A strategy space for each agent, representing her two possible actions (Cooperate or Defect). I will use the notation $A_i = \{C_i, D_i\}$ where C_i stands for "Player i cooperates" and D_i for "Player i defects."

c. A construct to represent the likelihood of success and the fact that it increases as the number of agents who cooperate increase.

d. A representation of the agents' preferences.

Representing the Likelihood of Success. Denote the share of agents who decide to cooperate by $0 < \gamma < 1$, success of collective action by *Succ* and failure by *Fail*. The generic probability of an event E will be denoted as $\Pr(E)$ and the probability of event E conditional on event H as $\Pr(E|H)$. The function F will represent the probability of success, for every value of γ: $\Pr(Succ) = F(\gamma)$. I will assume that, all else being equal, higher levels of participation increase the likelihood of success so that F is increasing in γ. It also makes sense to assume that $F(0) = 0$, that is, that collective action cannot succeed without at least some agent cooperating. Often, the calculations will be easier, without any conceptual loss, if we assume that collective action is assured success if every agent participates, something that we can represent with $F(1) = 1$. Later I will consider what happens as we introduce further assumptions.

Representing the Agents' Preferences. Following the standard procedure of collective action models, I will assume that each individual agent cares only about the final outcome and whether she cooperated. To get an idea of the possibilities that these assumptions exclude, notice that in this model agents do not care about how the outcome is obtained, the exact identity of other cooperators or the payoffs of other players. There might be good reasons to introduce all these other factors in a more general treatment, but I shall not do so here, mostly for two reasons. First, I want my discussion to stick to the standards of most models of collective action. Second, I believe that much can be accomplished within that standard framework: the main ideas I want to get across need not depart from it.

The agents' payoffs will depend, then, only on the strategy they choose and the final outcome. Since there are two possible strategies and two possible outcomes, this gives us four possible payoffs which may differ across agents:

- If a player cooperates and collective action succeeds, her payoff is $u(C_i, Succ) = w_{1i}$.

- If a player defects and collective action succeeds, her payoff is $u(D_i, Succ) = w_{2i}$.

- If a player cooperates and collective action fails, her payoff is $u(C_i, Fail) = w_{3i}$.

- If a player defects and collective action fails, her payoff is $u(D_i, Fail) = w_{4i}$.

By assumption, participating in collective action is costly but, when successful, results in an outcome that is desirable for all the agents involved. So, the payoffs must satisfy the condition that, for every agent i: $w_{2i} > w_{4i} > w_{3i}$ and $w_{1i} > w_{4i} > w_{3i}$.

From now on, this general structure, the agents, their strategies, their payoff functions and the likelihood of success will be called **Model 0**. All the models that follow are special cases of this general setting.

The central question of rational-choice models of collective action is under what conditions an individual will find it in her best self-interest to cooperate. In the language of game theory, this amounts to asking when the expected payoff from choosing C_i is larger than the expected payoff from choosing D_i.

The function $v_i(\sigma_i, \sigma_{-i})$ denotes the payoff for individual i from choosing an arbitrary strategy σ_i provided that the rest of the players are choosing σ_{-i}. Since a player's payoffs depend only on her strategy and the outcome, all that matters about σ_{-i} is the aggregate level of turnout associated with it, $\gamma(\sigma_{-i})$. So, unless it leads to confusion, I will drop the term σ_{-i} and the player's subindex, and denote the expected payoffs with the shorthand notation $v(\sigma_i, \gamma)$ (especially in the nontechnical sections).

With this notation, the decision problem of any given agent becomes:

$$
\begin{aligned}
v(C_i, \gamma) &= w_{1i}\Pr(Succ|C_i, \gamma) + w_{3i}\Pr(Fail|C_i, \gamma) & (2.1) \\
&= w_{1i}\Pr(Succ|C_i, \gamma) + w_{3i}(1 - \Pr(Succ|C_i, \gamma)) \\
&= (w_{1i} - w_{3i})\Pr(Succ|C_i, \gamma) + w_{3i} \\
&= (w_{1i} - w_{3i})F(\gamma + 1/N) + w_{3i}. & (2.2)
\end{aligned}
$$

$$
\begin{aligned}
v(D_i, \gamma) &= w_{2i}\Pr(Succ|D_i, \gamma) + w_{4i}\Pr(Fail|D_i, \gamma) \qquad (2.3) \\
&= w_{2i}\Pr(Succ|D_i, \gamma) + w_{4i}(1 - \Pr(Succ|D_i, \gamma)) \\
&= (w_{2i} - w_{4i})\Pr(Succ|D_i, \gamma) + w_{4i} \\
&= (w_{2i} - w_{4i})F(\gamma) + w_{4i}. \qquad (2.4)
\end{aligned}
$$

Then, the agent will cooperate if:

$$
\begin{aligned}
v(C_i, \gamma) &\geq v(D_i, \gamma), \\
(w_{1i} - w_{3i})F(\gamma + 1/N) - (w_{2i} - w_{4i})F(\gamma) &\geq w_{4i} - w_{3i}. \qquad (2.5)
\end{aligned}
$$

Equations 2.1 - 2.4 characterize the decision problem and Inequality 2.5 shows us the conditions under which its solution will be to cooperate. Inequality 2.5 is the foundation of all the subsequent analysis: it will appear under several guises over and over again.

2.3 A Formalization of Model 0[*]

Readers interested in the mathematical details of this book's arguments will benefit from seeing the basic concepts and notation introduced in one place with all the rigor that is necessary for the later computations.

2.3.1 Definitions

2.3.1.1 Strategies, Payoffs and Outcomes

A **threshold game** (Γ) is a triple $\langle N, (A_i), (u_i) \rangle$ with the following elements:

- N is the set of players.

- A_i is the set of pure strategies of each player. In particular, $A_i = \{C_i, D_i\}$ where C_i stands for "Player i cooperates" and D_i for "Player i defects." For every player, the parameter $\alpha_i \in [0, 1]$ describes the set of mixed strategies, $\Delta(A_i)$: mixed strategy α_i means that

---

[*]Technical section.

Player i chooses a lottery that assigns probability α_i to strategy C_i and $1 - \alpha_i$ to strategy D_i.

- A set of two possible **outcomes**: $\mathcal{O} = \{F, S\}$, where F stands for "Failure" and S for "Success."

- A set of two possible **probabilistic states**: $\Omega = \{0, 1\}$. The probability (π) of each of these states will depend on the strategy vector so I will denote the conditional probabilities, that is, the probability of state ω conditional on strategy vector a, as $\pi(\omega \mid a)$.

- An **outcome function** $g : A \times \Omega \to \mathcal{O}$. By convention, this function will be such that: $g(a, 0) = F, g(a, 1) = S$.

- u_i is a Bernoulli utility function defined over the vectors of strategies.[1] Formally, we say that $A = \times_{i=1}^{N} A_i$ and that $u_i : A \times \Omega \to \Re$.

The probabilistic states introduce some uncertainty over the outcomes because, in general, success or failure of collective action is not just a function of the players' strategies but depends on other exogenous factors as well. This uncertainty differs from the one typical of Bayesian games because here the (uncertain) payoffs are common knowledge. This is in keeping with the spirit of leaving private information out of the picture.

From now on I will assume that players only care about their individual strategy and the outcome, something I represent with *separable* Bernoulli utility functions. Formally, $u_i(a, \omega) = u_i(a_i, g(a, \omega))$. This results in the following payoff function:

- $u(C_i, S) = w_{1i}$;
- $u(D_i, S) = w_{2i}$;

---

[1] In using the term "Bernoulli utility function," I follow the convention recommended by Mas-Colell, Whinston and Green (1995) to distinguish utility functions over states from utility functions over lotteries (the von Neumann-Morgenstern utility functions). Although the confusion they intend to avoid does not occur very often among experienced game theorists, when it does, it may have disastrous consequences.

- $u(C_i, F) = w_{3i}$;

- $u(D_i, F) = w_{4i}$.

For the most part, I will study models where all players have an identical payoff function; this will simplify the analysis while retaining the fundamental properties. When that is the case, I will assume that, for instance, for two arbitrary players i, j, $w_{1i} = w_{1j} = w_1$.

As already discussed, these payoffs can only be an adequate representation of collective action problems if $w_{1i} \geq w_{4i} \geq w_{3i}$ and $w_{2i} \geq w_{4i} \geq w_{3i}$. Later we will see the implications of further assumptions on this ordering.

Let $\mu : A \rightarrow [0,1]$ be a probability distribution over all the possible strategy vectors a so that μ is subject to the constraints: $\mu(a) \geq 0, \forall a$ and $\sum_{a \in A} \mu(a) = 1$. For each player the von Neumann-Morgenstern utility function is $U_i : \times_{i=1}^{N} \Delta(A_i) \times \Omega \rightarrow \Re$ such that:

$$
\begin{aligned}
U_i(\mu, \omega) &= \sum_{a \in A} u_i(a, \omega)\mu(a) \\
&= \sum_{a \in A} u(a_i, g(a, \omega))\mu(a), \\
U_i(\mu) &= \sum_{\omega \in \{0,1\}} \sum_{a \in A} u(a_i, g(a, \omega))\pi(\omega \mid a)\mu(a)
\end{aligned}
$$

The following function expresses how the probability of collective action depends on the share of people who participate in it. Let $F : [0,1] \rightarrow [0,1]$ such that F is continuous, monotonically increasing and subject to the condition $F(0) = 0$. For every profile a, a scalar $\gamma(a) = \frac{1}{N}\#\{i : a_i = C_i\}$ represents the share of cooperators in strategy profile a. So, the probability of success of a is: $\pi(1 \mid a) = F(\gamma(a))$. Continuity of F implies that no individual decision of cooperating has a sizeable impact over the chances of success. With monotonicity, more cooperators mean a more likely success. Because $F(0) = 0$, there is no chance of success if no individual cooperates. As already stated, sometimes I will also assume $F(1) = 1$.

2.4   Single-equilibrium Models of Collective Action

2.4.1   The Olsonian Model of Collective Action

Olson's model of collective action is a special case of Model 0. According to the public goods model, the logic of a collective action problem is dictated by the fact that: (*a*) there is a positive cost $c > 0$ of cooperating and (*b*) no agent's specific decision to cooperate will have a significant effect on the probability of succeeding.

The assumption that individual agents have a negligible effect over the likelihood of success can be captured by making the function F continuous in γ: a single player's decision to cooperate will result in an infinitesimal increase in the turnout rate γ and, since F is continuous, in an infinitesimal increase in the probability of success. In the standard Olsonian model, the benefit an agent obtains from successful collective action (what Olsonians call the public good) can be denoted by $B > 0$. In the notation introduced above, Olson assumes that, for every agent i:

$$
\begin{aligned}
w_{1i} &= B - c, \\
w_{2i} &= B, \\
w_{3i} &= -c, \\
w_{4i} &= 0.
\end{aligned}
$$

We now ask under what conditions an agent will decide to cooperate. We can answer that question by substituting for the corresponding terms in Inequality 2.5:

$$
\begin{aligned}
v(C_i, \gamma) &> v(D_i, \gamma), \\
B(F(\gamma + 1/N) - F(\gamma)) &> c.
\end{aligned}
\tag{2.6}
$$

Inequality 2.6 is the key to the public goods model of collective action. The left-hand side represents the benefit that agent i receives from cooperating while the right-hand side represents the cost of doing so. If F is continuous, for large values of N, i.e., for collective action problems in large groups, the difference $F(\gamma + 1/N) - F(\gamma)$ is negligible so that this inequality reduces to $0 > c$. But this contradicts the assumption that cooperation entails a positive cost. In other words, under the assumptions we have introduced thus far, individuals do not find it rational to cooperate.

2.4.2   Selective Incentives

In a very influential move, Olson argued that the only way to overcome the collective action problem is to have an organization that would reward those agents who cooperate in the production of the public good with an excludable resource, a prize that only the cooperators can enjoy. Formally, Olson's argument boils down to assuming that, thanks to this external agent that provides selective incentives s_i to those who cooperate, the payoffs players face now become:

$$
\begin{aligned}
w_{1i} &= B - c + s_i, \\
w_{2i} &= B, \\
w_{3i} &= s_i - c, \\
w_{4i} &= 0.
\end{aligned}
$$

If we plug these new values into Inequality 2.5, we obtain the result that the new condition for cooperation is:

$$
\begin{aligned}
v(C_i) &> v(D_i), \\
B(F(\gamma + 1/N) - F(\gamma)) &> c - s_i.
\end{aligned}
$$

Once we let $F(\gamma + 1/N)$ converge to $F(\gamma)$, this new inequality reduces to

$$
s_i > c. \tag{2.7}
$$

In other words, collective action occurs when the players receive selective incentives that compensate them for the cost of cooperation.

2.4.3   Implications of the Model

Was Advisor 1 in the book's opening scene truly an Olsonian? Thanks to the inequalities above we can answer yes to this question. According to the Olsonian model, in deciding whether to cooperate, individuals only consider the value of the selective incentive and the cost of cooperation. For the hapless citizens of Country X, the water fee scheme will increase B by a substantial amount: overthrowing the regime now could spare them this added hardship. But, as the advisor puts it, B is irrelevant. Only the selective incentives can account for collective action. An organization that wants to secure some outcome must compensate its members until they find it advantageous to participate.

This doctrine has disturbing implications that should count as grounds for caution. Let's look at some of them.

This null comparative statics denies any connection, empirical or logical, between objective conditions in a polity (e.g., water fees) and organized collective action (e.g., protests). It says that, as discussed in the introduction, the government of Country X can simply raise the water fees without taking any extra precaution. For what is worth, I do not know any person who would, in fact, take seriously the advice of the hypothetical Advisor 1.

Not only does the public goods model arrive at implausible conclusions about the role of external payoffs, it also has difficulties offering a rationale for selective incentives. According to the theory, when the member of an organization decides to cooperate, he increases the probability of attaining the collective good in a magnitude $\Pr(Succ|C_i, \gamma) - \Pr(Succ|D_i, \gamma) = F(\gamma + 1/N) - F(\gamma)$. From the leadership's point of view, then, $B(F(\gamma + 1/N) - F(\gamma))$ represents the benefit resulting from offering a selective incentive to an individual. This same selective incentive has a cost to the leadership which, for argument's sake, we may fix at s_i. A rational leadership will only provide selective incentives to individual i if, from its standpoint, the benefits exceed the costs:

$$s_i \leq B(F(\gamma + 1/N) - F(\gamma)).$$

But s_i, the selective incentive, is a nonvanishing term, a discrete amount of resources, while, according to the theory, $F(\gamma + 1/N) - F(\gamma) \approx 0$. This inequality can only hold if the leadership can provide resources s_i at virtually no cost or if it values B at levels that approach infinity. In this case, the leadership is willing to give away a discrete unit of payoffs (a t-shirt, a pin button, a bottle of rum) just to extract an infinitesimal increase in the probability of attaining B.[2] Plausible or not, this assumption is implicit in every use of Olson's theory of collective action. Olsonian analyses should either state it clearly and defend it or say that the leadership is acting irrationally. But if our theory assumes that leaders have the kind of preferences I just described, we could also assume the same preferences for the populace which, then, would not need to be induced to cooperate with selective incentives.

The calculations above do not require that B is a collective "good." They would obtain all the same if we assume that B is a "collective bad" ($B < 0$). From Inequality 2.6, expressed only in terms of the selective incentive and the individual cost, we conclude that a political entrepreneur could use selective incentives to get individuals to cooperate in attaining goals they dislike.

In the tongue-in-cheek formulation of Green and Shapiro (1994, pg. 79):

> A Christian fundamentalist walking through a park
> in which two demonstrations are going on simulta-
> neously – a pro-choice rally to her left and a pro-life

---

[2]With a finite number of actors this is not literally true and, hence, we could expect to observe some positive level of selective incentives. But then we should observe that the size of the selective incentives declines with the size of the group and, moreover, that that decline should be extremely fast, especially if we want to stay true to the assumption that marginal contributions become insignificant. Sven Feldmann rightly pointed out to me that this argument may not work if we assume some fixed cost in the production of the public good because then the leadership will not necessarily equate the selective incentive to the marginal contribution of the members. But, if there are fixed costs in the production of the public good, then free-riding is not the only equilibrium. (See 2.6.1.)

rally to her right – might easily join the former if the refreshments provided were sufficiently enticing ...

What should we make out of these disturbing implications? Arguably, nothing. If a theory is built rigorously, we cannot reject it simply because it reaches conclusions we do not like; all we should do is to test it.

But this line of defense misrepresents the objections. To say that these are implications that may not seem likeable belittles the issue to a matter of taste. These implications do not point to an aesthetic criticism; they point to a view of the world that Olsonians must accept if they wish to remain consistent. If we believe the public goods model is right, we must: be ready to offer examples of governments that take decisions most analysts would call suicidal while being entirely oblivious to their political consequences; be able to show leaders with preferences that are either lexicographic or irrational; be able to point to groups that mobilize for causes that will unmistakably hurt them, that is, be ready to find black members of the KKK or Jewish members of the Nazi Party. In short, these implications are already, as it were, tests of the theory, tests the theory is unlikely to pass with flying colors.

While personally I find these problems grounds enough to reject the theory, I cannot leave the matter at that, given the procedure I wish to follow in this chapter. Instead, I will show the set of assumptions that precipitate these implications. That way, both critics and defenders of the model will be able to decide what they want to do with it.

2.4.4 Outcome-independent Preferences in the Public Goods Model

Beginning with Riker and Ordeshook (1968), a variant of rational-choice theory has tried to generalize the concept of preferences to include interests that are not purely self-regarding. This view has influenced the theory of collective action because it holds a promise of explaining cooperation by means other than material selective incentives. In principle, we could explain collective action if we think that, in making their decisions, individuals value not just the results, but the actions that create them.

There is a kernel of truth in this notion and, as we will see later, some versions of it may form part of a general model of collective action. But some of the proposals, the ones I will discuss here, are beholden to the Olsonian framework and, hence, inherit its weaknesses. Later I will have more to say about alternative specifications.

These models specify individual preferences that include, next to the objective state of the world (viz. the success or failure of achieving the collective goal), mental states that depend only on the decisions made by the individual. Riker and Ordeshook (1968) offered "civic duty" as a possible explanation for voting and, presumably, for participation in other collective action problems. Tullock (1971) proposed that the search for entertainment could lead some individuals to participate and Brennan and Buchanan (1984) argued that voting could be motivated by the expressive rewards that citizens obtain when they go to the polls. Moe (1981) revised Olson's original model by assuming that individuals can misperceive the efficacy of their actions and derive utility from "doing their share." Moral considerations also drive the analysis of Muller and Opp (1986); Finkel, Muller and Opp (1989). All these candidates for an explanation are outcome-independent: they claim that some rewards accrue to the individuals for performing one action (viz. cooperating) regardless of the consequences. So, supporters of the losing candidate derive as much expressive pleasure, or satisfaction for performing their civic duty, as supporters of the victor. Protestors experience the same entertainment even if the demonstration ends up being a fiasco, and so on. I find this hard to justify. Even if we can pin down what psychic benefits are, they seem to depend on the outcome. Failing at a collective endeavor imposes a cost on its participants so, if we want this argument to succeed, we have to explain why we assume that these psychic benefits would outweigh the cost of failure. As I will show later, if we assume otherwise, the resulting model is no longer a single-equilibrium one.

The question remains, however, whether this generalization may lead to a different kind of comparative statics. To study this question, let's introduce a "duty" term d_i in the payoff for individuals who decide to cooperate and experience a (material) cost c_i. In this case the model's preferences become:

$$
\begin{aligned}
w_{1i} &= B - c + d_i, \\
w_{2i} &= B, \\
w_{3i} &= d_i - c, \\
w_{4i} &= 0.
\end{aligned}
$$

We have already encountered this model. These preferences are identical to those of the Olsonian model with selective incentives except that here instead of a selective incentive s_i we have a duty term d_i. Just as in the Olsonian model the condition for cooperation was given by Inequality 2.7: $s_i - c > 0$, here the condition will be $d_i - c > 0$, implying that, once again, the decision to cooperate is not related at all to the size of the benefits. In essence, this type of psychic benefits does not change the logic or the results of the Olsonian model.

2.5 Strategic Dominance and Equilibrium Uniqueness

For the time being, this finishes our study of single-equilibrium models of collective action. But before we turn to the study of models with multiple equilibria, let's make explicit the game-theoretic principle that precipitates equilibrium uniqueness in the models studied thus far: strategic dominance.

public goods models, like Prisoners' Dilemmas, their two-player counterparts, are games where noncooperation is a *dominant strategy*, a strategy that is better for a player regardless of whatever choices the other players make.[3] Inequality 2.6

---

[3]Strictly speaking, we should differentiate between strictly dominant strategies (those that are always better than others) and weakly domi-

shows the role of strategic dominance in the Olsonian model. As far as F is continuous, this inequality is false, that is, defection is better for Player i, regardless of the value of γ.

The Prisoners' Dilemma offers a useful two-player interface to bring out this point. Consider the following game matrix (Figure 2.1):

$$
\begin{array}{ccc}
 & & 2 \\
 & C \qquad\quad D \\
1 \begin{array}{c} C \\ D \end{array} &
\begin{array}{|c|c|}
\hline
1,1 & -1,2 \\
\hline
2,-1 & 0,0 \\
\hline
\end{array}
\end{array}
$$

Figure 2.1: Prisoners' Dilemma

If we use this payoff matrix to represent a collective action problem, we are implicitly assuming strategic dominance. Notice, for example, that for Player 1, the payoff from cooperating is 1 when Player 2 cooperates and -1 when Player 2 defects. But her payoff from defecting is 2 when Player 2 cooperates and 0 when Player 2 defects. No matter what choice Player 2 makes, it is always best for Player 1 to choose D. Defenders of the Olsonian model claim that this game captures the essence of collective action. After all, in this game cooperation entails an individual cost but if both players cooperate, they obtain a better outcome than if they defect.

But not every model of collective action assumes strategic dominance. Assurance games, for instance, are a longstanding alternative that has given rise to some important criticisms of the Olsonian model. At least since Taylor (1987), this case has been formulated forcefully and it has created room for doubt about the Olsonian model, as Hardin (1995) exemplifies.

In an assurance game no strategy is unconditionally the best. The optimal choice depends on the choices of the remaining players. To illustrate this, consider Figure 2.2, which represents the 2×2 version of the assurance game:

---

nant ones (those that are never worse than others). Such distinction is irrelevant in this context but is the source of important debates in game theory.

2

	C	D
C	1,1	$-1,0$
D	$0,-1$	0,0

1

Figure 2.2: Assurance Game

This game does not display strategic dominance. For any player, choosing D is better than choosing C *if* the other player also chooses D, but not otherwise.

Despite their seeming similarities, these two games could hardly be any more different. The PD is a game with a unique Nash equilibrium (D, D), whereas the assurance game has three Nash equilibria, two of them in pure strategies $(C, C$ and $D, D)$ and a third equilibrium in mixed strategies that will be later discussed at length.

The models that will be discussed next differ on several counts but they all share one specific property with the assurance game: none of them has one dominant strategy. This lack of strategic dominance is a necessary, though not sufficient, condition for the existence of multiple equilibria.

2.6 Multiple-equilibria Models

2.6.1 Threshold Games

Thus far I have exemplified assurance games in a 2×2 setting to illustrate their differences with respect to the PD approach. But one of the central goals of this book is to develop a useful analysis of large collective action games with multiple equilibria. In other words, we need to develop versions of Model 0 that do not have dominant strategies. Here I will discuss one such possibility, threshold games, more for the sake of completeness than because of its intrinsic merits.

One argument in favor of assurance games as the right framework, as opposed to the PD, is that collective action may be subject to "fixed costs." Instead of assuming that the probability of success increases gradually as the number of co-operators increases, the argument goes, we should rather assume that, once some critical level of participation is reached, the probability of success increases dramatically.

We can use Model 0 to represent introducing a discontinuity in the F function at some critical value γ^*. Since F is monotonically nondecreasing, this may result in additional equilibria. To see why, let's go back to the basic inequality $v(C_i, \gamma) > v(D_i, \gamma)$ evaluated at that critical level:

$$v(C_i, \gamma^*) > v(D_i, \gamma^*),$$
$$(w_{1i} - w_{3i})F(\gamma^* + 1/N) - (w_{2i} - w_{4i})F(\gamma^*) > w_{4i} - w_{3i}. \quad (2.8)$$

If F is nondecreasing and discontinuous at γ^*, experiencing an upward jump at $F(\gamma^*)$, it is no longer true that $F(\gamma^* + 1/N)$ converges to $F(\gamma^*)$. Then, Inequality 2.8 may well be true, depending on the values of the payoffs. If it is true for every player i, the game has an equilibrium where a share $\gamma^* + 1/N$ of agents cooperate. Indeed, for levels below that value, every player faces an inequality with the opposite sign, just like in the Olsonian case and the same is true for levels above that value. But at $\gamma^* + 1/N$ all the players that are already cooperating face an inequality $v(C_i, \gamma^*) > v(D_i, \gamma^*)$, which means that they have no incentive to defect. At the same time, those players who are not cooperating have no incentive to cooperate because doing so would raise the level of cooperation to a new value of γ where the function has no discontinuity. In sum, this critical level of cooperation is a Nash equilibrium: no player can benefit from a unilateral deviation.

We could create more equilibria in the model if we simply introduce more discontinuities at different values of γ, as long as those discontinuities also satisfy Inequality 2.8. While fixed costs exist in collective action problems and, to that extent, a model with a discontinuous F function may capture important properties of coordination, there are problems with this approach. As modelers we rarely have a criterion to determine the location of those points of discontinuity; the amount of guesswork needed to get the model right makes it unreliable.

2.6.2 An Olsonian Model with Differential Costs

According to the public goods approach, in a collective action problem, absent selective incentives, the players' dominant strategy is to defect, whereas if they receive the right inducements, their dominant strategy will now be to cooperate. Much of the theory's success depends on the status of this finding. But, as it turns out, it is not robust. Even tiny changes in the model are enough to destroy strategic dominance and precipitate the existence of multiple equilibria. In this section and the following I will show two such changes.

The Olsonian model assumes implicitly that the cost of cooperation will not depend on the outcome. If we go back to the payoff structure in 2.4.1 , we will see that, for any player, the cost of participating in a successful collective endeavor $(w_2 - w_1)$ is equal to the cost of engaging in failed coordination $(w_4 - w_3)$, viz. c. This is too restrictive and, other than algebraic convenience, no other justification has been offered for such an assumption. For the participants, the costs of collective action depend on the actual outcome. If we join a successful protest movement and, in a sunny, exhilarating afternoon manage to topple a government we hate by marching to the public square, our cost is likely to be simply the wear and tear on our shoes. But if the protest fails and the government can react by sending in tanks, shooting at the crowd, arresting and making disappear those it captures as they try to escape the carnage, the costs are significantly higher.

If we combine this assumption with selective incentives, the result is decidedly non-Olsonian. To see why, consider the following payoffs:

$$
\begin{aligned}
w_{1i} &= B - c_0 + s_i, \\
w_{2i} &= B, \\
w_{3i} &= s_i - c_1, \\
w_{4i} &= 0,
\end{aligned}
$$

where the costs of cooperation are such that $c_1 > c_0$, i.e., the cost of cooperating in a failed instance of collective action is higher than the cost of cooperating in a successful one. The term s_i represents, as before, the selective incentive an individual receives if she decides to cooperate.

Then, letting, as usual, N go to infinity, the standard inequality that determines cooperation becomes:

$$v(C_i, \gamma) > v(D_i, \gamma),$$
$$s_i > c_1(1 - F(\gamma)) + c_0 F(\gamma). \qquad (2.9)$$

This last inequality implies that the selective incentive needed to induce an individual to cooperate is a weighted average between the two costs of cooperation and that the weights depend on the level of aggregate turnout. In other words, even with selective incentives, there is no dominant strategy. For example, consider a selective incentive $s_i = c_0 + \epsilon$, with ϵ being a very small quantity and assume, for the sake of argument that if everybody cooperates, success is guaranteed, so that $F(1) = 1$. Would this be enough to induce cooperation? We cannot know a priori because the game has multiple equilibria. If nobody cooperates, then $\gamma = 0$ and $F(\gamma) = 0$. Inequality 2.9 would become $s_i > c_1$, which is false: nobody would find it beneficial to cooperate, validating the equilibrium $\gamma = 0$. But if everybody cooperates, $\gamma = 1$ and the inequality becomes $s_i > c_0$, which is true: every player would prefer to cooperate and $\gamma = 1$ would, in fact, be an equilibrium.

This has serious implications for the general validity of the Olsonian model. If strategic dominance cannot survive a seemingly innocuous change such as differential costs of cooperation, then the theory's range of applicability becomes intolerably narrow.

2.6.3   The "Stock-option" Model

Selective incentives are a mechanism to induce cooperation among agents in a collective action problem. But it is wrong to claim, as Olson himself did, and Tullock after him, that these are the only kind of incentives that can do that. Other incentive systems, leading to drastically different results, are possible.

The Olsonian theory claims that the only way to induce players to cooperate is with rewards that compensate their cost of cooperation regardless of the outcome. It is not gratuitous that the examples Olson adduces to support this notion are transfers of resources entirely unrelated to the group's purported goal. Subscription magazines for members of a lobby, car insurance discount rates for members of a union and things of this like are transfers that cooperators receive independently of the results their organization obtains. To that extent, there is no difference between a labor militant and the janitor of the union's building: they both receive compensation, no matter what.

But there is a difference between the two: the militant has a stake in the organization's success, whereas the employee does not. In his attempt to extend the Olsonian analysis to the study of revolutions, Tullock (1971) is at the same time aware of and confused on this point. Tullock argues that all revolutions result from the search for private benefits, by which presumably he means the spoils of victory. (He does not state this in so many words.) But the Olsonian model, which Tullock uses, makes no distinction between the spoils of victory and the "spoils of defeat." For Olson, selective incentives are rewards that an organization can hand out regardless of its success.

In collective action, organizations can, and do, resort to the same mechanism that start-up firms use in the market: issuing "stock" with a value conditional on the end result. We see this all the time in the stock market and we should not be surprised at all to see it in politics. Start-up firms often do not have the cash flow that would allow them to take a loan large enough for their intended growth. To solve this problem they issue stocks which are little else than a promissory note to the buyers. The buyers of stock know full well that if the firm goes under they will lose their investment, but hope to gain handsomely if, instead, the firm is a success. A similar mechanism can be put to work in political organizations: victorious organizations tend to reward their members according to the effort they put in before victory.

Let's see what happens to the Olsonian model once we introduce success-contingent rewards. To that end, consider the following slightly modified version of the payoffs:

$$
\begin{aligned}
w_{1i} &= B - c + s, \\
w_{2i} &= B, \\
w_{3i} &= -c, \\
w_{4i} &= 0.
\end{aligned}
$$

These payoffs are almost identical to the ones of the Olsonian model with selective incentives except for a small difference: the reward s is something that the would-be cooperator only receives if the collective goal is, in fact, attained. Just as we have done with all the previous specifications, let's study the inequality $v(C_i, \gamma) > v(D_i, \gamma)$ to see under what conditions a player will cooperate.

$$
\begin{aligned}
v(C_i, \gamma) &> v(D_i, \gamma), \\
(B + s)F(\gamma + 1/N) - c &> BF(\gamma). \quad (2.10)
\end{aligned}
$$

If we let N grow arbitrarily large, then Inequality 2.10 converges to:

$$
F(\gamma) > \frac{c}{s}.
$$

If $0 = F(0) < c/s < F(1) \leq 1$, the contingent reward is larger than the current cost and defection is no longer a dominant strategy for any player. The game has now three equilibria, two of them in pure strategies ($\gamma = 0$ and $\gamma = 1$) and one in mixed strategies ($F(\gamma) = c/s$).

Readers unfamiliar with the notion of Nash equilibrium may benefit from studying this result at more length. If $\gamma = 0$, $F(\gamma) < c/s$ and, as a result, no player finds it beneficial to cooperate. In other words, $\gamma = 0$ is a Nash equilibrium because, provided that no player is cooperating, no individual player has incentives to change her strategy from D_i to C_i. Likewise, if $\gamma = 1$, $F(\gamma) > c/s$ and, then, for every player it is optimal to cooperate. Given what all other players are doing, no player benefits from changing her strategy, which is the exact definition of a Nash equilibrium. Finally, if $F(\gamma) = c/s$, then every player is indifferent between cooperating and defecting and will then choose a mixed strategy. Mixed strategy Nash equilibria play a crucial role in the analytical technique I will introduce in Chapter 4 and I will have much to say about them.

Through this simple change in the payoffs we have gone from a dominance-solvable model to one with multiple equilibria, a move that has several implications. First, the model no longer makes a deterministic prediction. The public goods model says that without selective incentives participants will never cooperate and that with such incentives they always will. This multiple-equilibria version does not make a unique prediction. Detractors may say that, in fact, it makes no prediction at all. But, as I will argue later, if we use the method of stability sets this is no longer true.

Second, this model, in contrast to the Olsonian one, can explain the difference between militants and employees of an organization. The former have a stake in the organization's success in ways that the latter do not.

Third, this model allows us to make more sense of the "psychic benefits" arguments. Whenever psychic benefits are introduced in an Olsonian model (see above 2.4.4), the modeler is burdened with explaining why the psychic benefit of doing one's share is not outweighed by the grief of defeat in case of failure. I regard the lack of a straightforward argument to that effect as a fatal flaw. Instead, scholars who work within the multiple-equilibria setting are on firmer ground here. When, for instance, Wood (2002) weaves the notion of "pleasure in agency" into a tipping game to explain peasant insurgencies, or when Schuessler (2000) invokes "expressive benefits" to explain voting also as a tipping game, their arguments are not vulnerable to that objection because those benefits are clearly contingent on the outcome, as nonmaterial counterparts to the stock-options that investors receive in a start-up firm. Models of this type do not need to assume anything about psychic benefits of failure; they might as well be nonexistent. In Section 2.6.5 I will show that, in fact, the framework I have just presented leads us directly into the kind of tipping models that some scholars have used in the study of collective action. Before doing that, let's consider a prominent case of the multiple-equilibria paradigm: focal points.

2.6.4   Focal Points

The focal point argument (from the pioneering work by Thomas Schelling (1960)) correctly notices that in a game with multiple equilibria, the end result depends on what players believe about each other. In the collective action game of Figure 2.2, if there were some external mechanism through which each player came to believe that the other one will choose C, then both players would choose C. Likewise, if each one believed that the other one will play D, then the result of the game would be (D, D). If we know how that external mechanism works, we can refine the predictions of the model and derive comparative statics.

The "focal point effect" is an attempt to provide such a mechanism. In his already famous example, of two people choosing in isolation where to meet in Manhattan, Schelling noticed that there are some equilibria, such as "At noon in the Grand Central," that are more likely to be common belief among the players (as opposed to, say, "At 2:41 in the intersection of 67th and Madison"). To that extent, we can say that those equilibria are *focal points* of the game. As this example illustrates, focality does not depend on the payoffs of each equilibrium; it results from one equilibrium having some property that, although irrelevant from the standpoint of payoffs, serves players to coordinate their beliefs once all of them notice it.

In principle, focal point effects may help us narrow the set of predictions from a game to just one, fully restoring the theory's predictive power. But game theory cannot determine where a game's focal point is because the answer depends on properties that do not affect payoffs. Knowing which equilibrium is focal in a game requires knowing something about the process of collective belief-formation that takes place outside of the game: it is a task for social psychology or sociology, not for game theory. Each time we invoke focal points to solve a game with multiple equilibria, we must then furnish evidence from those disciplines or some other relevant body of knowledge to support our choice of focal point. Otherwise, our prediction should be demoted to the status of a guess.

2.6.4.1 Alternative Specifications of the Focal Point Effect

Let's see how this insight can be used to generate comparative statics. To that end, consider the following generalized version of the previous collective action game (Figure 2.3):

$$2$$

		C	D
	C	w, w	$-1, 0$
1	D	$0, -1$	$0, 0$

Figure 2.3: Collective Action with Generalized Payoff

For simplicity, I have kept intact all the payoffs except those of the strategy profile (C, C), which are now allowed to vary. This game can only be a true collective action problem if $w > 0$, so that D is not a strictly dominant strategy. We can think of w varying as a way to represent changes in the environment of the collective action problem. If, as in the introduction's example, the government decides on an astronomic raise of water fees, then the benefits of revolt (w) increase.[4] But, to fix ideas, we can imagine that a successful revolt requires the concerted effort of both players. Otherwise, the government will be able to capture and punish horribly whoever dares to challenge it alone. As long as $w > 0$, this game will have three equilibria: (C, C), (D, D) and a mixed

---

[4]Alternatively, I could have introduced this effect as reducing the benefits of the status quo. This would not change anything substantive in the current analysis and would complicate the resulting algebraic expressions.

strategy equilibrium, an equilibrium where players, instead of choosing one strategy, choose a lottery among them.

We can compute the mixed strategy equilibrium of this game as follows. Let α_1 denote the probability of Player 1 choosing C, α_2 the probability of Player 2 choosing C, and $v_i(S)$ Player i's expected payoff from choosing strategy S, then, following classical game theory, we obtain that:

$$
\begin{aligned}
v_1(C) &= w\alpha_2 - 1(1 - \alpha_2), \\
v_1(D) &= 0, \\
v_2(C) &= w\alpha_1 - 1(1 - \alpha_1), \\
v_2(D) &= 0.
\end{aligned}
$$

The mixed strategy equilibrium is the pair α_1^*, α_2^* that solves:

$$
\begin{aligned}
v_1(C) &= v_1(D), \\
v_2(C) &= v_2(D).
\end{aligned}
$$

In this case, the solution is:

$$
(\alpha_1^*, \alpha_2^*) = \left(\frac{1}{w+1}, \frac{1}{w+1} \right).
$$

This completes the list of equilibria of this game. Let's now consider some alternative focal point mechanisms:

Mechanism 1 (Fear):   "The two players in this game live in constant fear. The reports they have heard about horrible tortures in the government's prisons are deeply impressed in their minds. These images ensure that the equilibrium (D, D) is the game's focal point."

The comparative statics predicted by this mechanism is very simple: regardless of the values of w, collective action will not take place. In some sense, this is an Olsonian model that assumes a payoff structure with no strict dominance but specifies the focal point mechanism in a way that it reintroduces the deterministic prediction of free-riding.

Mechanism 2 (Agnosticism): "Collective action is inherently uncertain. We can never know when some equilibrium will become focal because focalness depends on salience and salience, in turn, can be the result of psychological frames that individuals come to adopt. But these psychological frames are not accessible to the game theorist.[5] Maybe the 'fear factor' of the previous mechanism has been operating for a long time but this may change for reasons pertaining to the psychology and sociology of the problem. These players could overcome fear through some change in their attitudinal makeup, they could build confidence in each other after lengthy interactions in social networks, they could arrive at a common mental model of the problem that enables them to coordinate and so on. But these reasons have nothing to do with the payoff structure of the game and hence, absent any knowledge about the culture, institutions, history and traditions of these players, the prudent forecast is that cooperation is as likely as non-cooperation."

This is the mechanism that Advisor 2 of this book's introduction had in mind. Although rarely expressed in these exact terms, I think this reflects Schelling's original views on the matter and, if I read him right, Sugden's view in his formalization of focal points.[6] Since focality *may not* be related to the payoffs, then the safest thing is to assume that it *is not*

---

[5]Recently, Richards (2001) has incorporated issues of cognitive representations of games in the analysis of collective action. Her novel approach, however, confirms that mental models are not results of strategic choice.

[6]Sugden (1995) has this to say in this regard:

> Schelling explicitly rejects the idea that focal points might be fully assimilated into conventional game theory. For example, he claims that "the propositions of a *normative* theory [of rational play] cannot be derived by purely analytical means from *a priori* considerations" (pg. 163, italics in original). If Schelling is right, no theory of focal points, of the kind presented in this paper, can ever be complete: some mechanisms by which human beings coordinate will always defy deductive analysis. ... I suspect that Schelling is right. (Sugden, 1995, pg. 549)

related to them. According to this mechanism the benefits of collective action do not determine its likelihood.

Mechanism 3 (Salience): "Although focality may not depend on the payoffs, this does not mean we must assume it is not. Here the payoffs from coordination (w, w) are larger than the payoffs of non-coordination. Players ought to take this into account. These payoffs give salience to the cooperative equilibrium."

This mechanism is often invoked in the analysis of collective action problems. For instance, Sandler and Sargent (1995) recommend it when players know each other's intentions. This raises the question of what intentions are and what it means to know them, a fascinating question in its own right but one that the current formalism seems ill-equipped to answer.[7]

The comparative statics implied by this mechanism is the opposite of the first mechanism. In a mirror image of the Olsonian model, this mechanism predicts that, whenever players face a situation where they can accomplish a Pareto-improvement through coordination, they will decide to cooperate. Pareto-optimality is often considered a good criterion for selecting equilibria in games of this kind. Taylor (1987), for example, invokes it in his analysis of this same assurance game. But such suggestion is at odds with the ample literature, both empirical and theoretical, in topics ranging from economic growth (Murphy, Shleifer and Vishny, 1989) to technical change (David, 1985), which suggests that players may end up in a sub-optimal equilibrium.

Mechanism 4 (Ad hoc LPT): "It seems odd to suggest that the likelihood of coordination does not depend on the payoffs. Everyday experience tells us that, quite to the contrary, people are more likely to cooperate when they stand more to gain from it. The previous mechanisms have not de-

---

[7]For a glimpse into the philosophical intricacies of defining intentions, especially in situations of interdependent decisions, see, e.g., Bratman (1993), Bratman (2000), Tuomela (1991).

fined precisely what focality *is* and instead trade on what it *is not*, making much of the fact that it is not related to the payoffs in any a priori, theoretical sense. But then we can fill in the blank of focality with whatever mechanism we deem more plausible. We are free to conclude that the probability of coordination increases with w. For instance, we can say that it is equal to $w^2/(w+1)^2$ so that when $w = 0$ the probability is 0 and this same probability converges to 1 as w approaches infinity. There may be no game-theoretic reason for this conjecture but game theory remains silent on this issue; from that point of view, any guess is as good as another. This one has the added advantage of looking good when compared with what common sense tells us about coordination."

To my knowledge no rational-choice theorist has proposed a mechanism like this. However, when applied to this particular example, the theory developed in the next chapter will give a result similar to this, although with a different justification.

Mechanism 5 (Mixed strategy Equilibrium or Anti-LPT): "Without a good reason, the previous mechanisms have excluded the mixed strategy Nash equilibrium. With his purification theorem, Harsanyi (1973) has shown that the mixed strategy equilibrium approximates well situations where players are uncertain about each other's payoffs. In the real world uncertainty is ubiquitous so, if anything, we should base our predictions on this equilibrium."

Palfrey and Rosenthal (1983, 1985) implicitly adopt this mechanism in their analysis of the voting paradox, although their defense is motivated by symmetry rather than by Harsanyi's purification result. Another attempt at using this motivation is that of Sandler and Sargent (1995).

Unlike the previous mechanisms (except ad hoc LPT), this one expresses the probability of cooperation as a function of w. Its results, however, are exactly opposite to those of LPT. Since in the mixed strategy equilibrium each player chooses C with probability $1/(w+1)$, the probability of the coordinated outcome is then the probability of both players choosing C, which is $1/(w+1)^2$. *Increases* in the payoff of cooperation *decrease* its likelihood. In analyzing the water fees problem, an advisor equipped with this mechanism would have recommended the measure as a way to enhance the regime's stability.

2.6.4.2   Evaluating the Different Mechanisms

Except for Mechanism 5, no other is justified by the game's structure. The first three invoke processes through which individuals come to believe things about each other, processes that are not themselves part of the game. The ad hoc LPT mechanism simply states the analyst's intuitions without any theory to justify them. In contrast, Mechanism 5 invokes the existence of uncertainty, an explicit property of the game. On these grounds, Mechanism 5 deserves special consideration.

But its theoretical rationale is wrong. Harsanyi's purification theorem demonstrates that the mixed strategy equilibrium of a perfect information game provides a good description of (i.e., mathematically, is located in an arbitrarily small neighborhood of) *an* equilibrium of a version of the same game where players are uncertain about each other's payoffs. But the indefinite article is essential. Harsanyi demonstrated (Theorem 2) that if the perfect-information game has multiple equilibria in pure strategies, these same equilibria will also be equilibria of the imperfect-information version. In other words, the purification theorem does not privilege the mixed strategy equilibrium over the rest. Harsanyi himself did not intend the purification theorem to do so. In fact, long after publishing this result he still considered open the problem of which equilibrium to choose, open enough to publish jointly with Reinhardt Selten *A General Theory of Equilibrium Selection*, fifteen years after proving the purification theorem.

Once Mechanism 5 is deprived of this advantage, it becomes clear that none of them is justified on game-theoretic grounds. They can be justified by an appeal to psychology, sociology, anthropology, history, culture or even to the fact that they feel right, which is what Mechanism 4 does. But none of these results of comparative statics is deduced from the model: they are all assumed by invoking some other criterion, unrelated to game theory.

This is unsatisfactory. The comparative statics of any model is one of its most crucial properties. It should not be left up for grabs so that different scholars can obtain contradictory results without a theory to determine which should be believed. It is not surprising, then, that focal point arguments are rarely invoked with any systematic predictive purpose and are, instead, used to rationalize outcomes that we already know.

2.6.5 Tipping Games

Introduced by Schelling (1960), tipping games are one of the best-known analytical devices in the study of collective action. Just as focal points do, tipping games bring out explicitly the interaction between beliefs and strategies in games with multiple equilibria, although with more generality. The method of stability sets I introduce in Chapter 4 owes some of its fundamental principles to tipping games. I would even go as far as to say that the method of stability sets formalizes the reasoning behind tipping games. Readers uninterested in the mathematical intricacies of stability sets might want to study with care this specific model since it offers a conceptual template for what comes next.

2.6.5.1 Basic Elements

The tipping model proposed by Schelling (1978) generalizes the focal points model by assuming that the players may hold beliefs that are not already equilibrium strategy profiles. In the words of Schelling:

> [S]uppose that for some activity ... there are some people who will attend regularly no matter what the attendance is and some who will never attend, but most people will attend if, but only if, enough others do. Everybody has his own definition of how

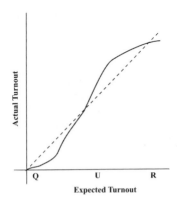

Figure 2.4: Advisor 3's Schelling Diagram

> many is "enough." ... For everyone whose atten-
> dance depends on the attendance he anticipates,
> we have a number: the minimum attendance that
> will just induce this person to attend. (Schelling,
> 1978, pg. 102)

This is the model that Advisor 3 had in mind when he
drew the diagram which is reproduced here again for convenience (Figure 2.4.). Potential participants of a popular uprising face a tipping game because their willingness to join the
revolt depends on how many players are already participating.[8] Plausibly, the model assumes that in a revolt there is
safety in numbers so that low levels of expected turnout actually deter participants while high expected levels encourage
them.

Unlike the focal points model, this tipping model considers the possibility that players have beliefs about each other
that are not in equilibrium. Disequilibrium beliefs are not
self-fulfilled and, instead, are revised until the game arrives
to an equilibrium. Beliefs to the left of the unstable equilibrium are mapped into the low-turnout equilibrium and beliefs
to its right lead to the high-turnout equilibrium. Instead of

---

[8]Some examples studying protests as tipping games involving a critical mass are: Oliver (1981), Kuran (1991), Lohmann (1994), Karklins
and Petersen (1993), Yin (1998).

assuming a specific set of collective beliefs, the tipping model analyzes the game's outcome under different possibilities.

2.6.5.2   Key Assumptions

Tipping games generalize the games with multiple equilibria already discussed but are in turn a special case of Model 0. Although the structure of tipping games is often taken for granted in many applications, it turns out that to derive it from first principles we need a lengthy but, fortunately, plausible set of assumptions. Furthermore, although it is not hard to find sets of sufficient conditions to ensure that the model does indeed behave as a standard tipping game, it is not possible to obtain critical sufficient conditions (Milgrom and Roberts, 1994), that is, sufficient conditions that cannot be weakened without the result at hand failing in at least some cases. In other words, we can easily verify if a model is a tipping game, but we cannot rule out other specifications that will also make it a tipping game.

These difficulties notwithstanding, if we remain committed to the notion of a continuous function F, the following assumptions are certainly necessary for a tipping game:

Assumption 1 *For every player i: $w_{2i} > w_{4i} > w_{3i}$ and $w_{1i} > w_{4i} > w_{3i}$.*

This assumption ensures that success is, indeed, better than failure and that to cooperate in a failure is worse than to defect in a failure. Notice that all the models we have covered thus far, both Olsonian and Schellingean, satisfy these conditions.

Assumption 2 *For at least some Players i: $w_{1i} > w_{2i}$.*

This assumption turns out to be of the utmost importance. It is the one that precipitates the existence of multiple equilibria. As I will show later, if it is violated, the game becomes dominance-solvable. In other words, any collective action model that relies on tipping games is, wittingly or unwittingly, endorsing this assumption.

To understand why this assumption is so crucial, let's consider the decision problem of an arbitrary agent i. This agent will cooperate, if $v(C_i, \gamma) > v(D_i, \gamma)$. This is once again Inequality 2.5 and, if we allow N to converge to ∞ and rearrange terms, it becomes:

$$F(\gamma) > \frac{w_{4i} - w_{3i}}{(w_{4i} - w_{3i}) + (w_{1i} - w_{2i})} \equiv t_i. \qquad (2.11)$$

This expression tells us the aggregate turnout γ that is enough to persuade Player i to participate. If $w_{1i} < w_{2i}$, the value t_i is greater than 1, which means that the player will not participate even if everybody else is already choosing C_i: this is the Olsonian case. If, instead, $w_{1i} \geq w_{2i}$, then t_i is less than 1 and there will be some level of participation γ such that it is optimal for Player i to choose C_i: this is the essence of the Schellingean case.

For convenience, let's refer to t_i as the *individual threshold value* of Player i since it represents the participation threshold above which Player i will cooperate. Because of Assumption 1, it is a non-negative value and, because of Assumption 2, it is less than 1 for at least some subset of players. Given these assumptions, $t_i = 0$ for players for whom $w_{1i} = \infty$. Those players are what some tipping models call "first movers," players who will participate even if no one else does. These are players that derive infinite benefits from successful collective action. Since these benefits can be material or psychological, this may well be a possibility. But, whereas it is legitimate to postulate the existence of such first movers, users of tipping games that rely on such agents would do well to make explicit this assumption so that the model is easier to assess.

A minor point of clarification: although necessary, this assumption is not sufficient for a tipping game with multiple equilibria. For example, if the condition $w_{1i} > w_{2i}$ is true only for a handful of players, their number may be so small that it is not enough to reach the critical mass. In that case, the tipping game will resemble Curve A below (pg. 59). In light of the upcoming analysis of sufficient conditions, this will not be a problem here.

Let the function G represent the statistical distribution of values t_i across players so that, as usual, $G(t)$ is the proportion of players for which $t_i < t$. So, if we start with an arbitrary value γ, the proportion of players that, given that value, will find it optimal to cooperate is $1 - G(F(\gamma))$. Therefore, the expectations of turnout will be self-validating, i.e., the game will reach an equilibrium at those values of γ that satisfy the equation:

$$\gamma = 1 - G(F(\gamma)). \qquad (2.12)$$

This model can display many types of behavior, many patterns of equilibria. It would take us very far from the current purposes to show that there is at least one equilibrium.[9] But beyond that, we cannot tell without further assumptions.

Figure 2.5 illustrates an ambiguity typical of this type of model: unless we make some further assumptions, a tipping game may have more than three equilibria. In the collective action problem it represents, the participants' group may linger at some intermediate size that is neither big enough for its ultimate success nor small enough to lead to its dissolution. If we observe a sudden increase in the movement's size, we have reasons to believe that it has surpassed a tipping point. But, which one? Is it the inferior one and the movement will get stuck somewhere in the middle? Is it the superior one marking the beginning of the end? We cannot know without knowing the location and number of those equilibria and both depend on the shape of the distributions F and G. A deficiency in the literature on tipping games is that it seldom makes explicit its assumptions about these distributions and, instead, assumes arbitrarily that there will be three equilibria.

Throughout this analysis I will assume the customary pattern of three equilibria. But I will soon show that, although that pattern can be the result of a set of plausible assumptions, it is not trivial. It would be salutary if users of tipping

---

[9]The interested reader should notice that the functions in this equation satisfy the assumptions of Brouwer's fixed-point theorem and so an existence proof for an equilibrium can invoke fairly standard arguments.

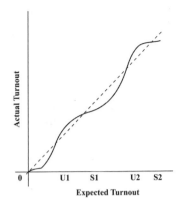

Figure 2.5: A Tipping Game with Two Tipping Points

models stated clearly their assumptions about the underlying distributions and probed the consequences thereof.

2.6.5.3   Deriving the S-shaped Curve of a Tipping Game[*]

Although it is not crucial for the remaining parts of this study, here I will stick to the standard practice of studying a tipping game that has only three equilibria: two stable ones (one of which is $\gamma = 0$) and an unstable one that occurs at an intermediate level $\hat{\gamma}$. As an illustration of how laborious it is to establish the S-shaped pattern that most tipping games assume, it may be useful to see how it can be proven in one particular case. So, I shall make the following two assumptions:

Assumption 3 *The function F is concave*

Assumption 4 *The threshold value t_i follows a truncated normal distribution $\Phi(\mu, \sigma)$ where $\mu > 0$.*

With these assumptions we can prove the following result:

---

[*]Technical section.

Theorem 1 *In a collective action model that satisfies Assumptions 1 - 4, the equation*

$$\gamma^* = 1 - G(b^*(\gamma))$$

has either a unique solution $\gamma^* = 0$ or three solutions $(0, \hat{\gamma}, \tilde{\gamma})$ where 0 and $\tilde{\gamma}$ are stable equilibria and $\hat{\gamma}$ is an unstable equilibrium.[10]

Proof: See Appendix 2.A.

These two assumptions are not implausible ones. In fact, to say that F is concave means that, although higher turnout increases the likelihood of success, there are diminishing returns in this process. In turn, the assumption about a normal distribution of the individual threshold values is hard to attack. To say that this distribution has a positive mean implies that at least half the players have a positive individual threshold value and, hence, are willing to cooperate, at least for some value γ. The fact that these assumptions are so mild suggests that, although not deriving the usual S-shaped curve from first principles may be an analytical offense, it may well be a minor one.

Still, it should be noted that these two assumptions are sufficient for an S-shaped pattern of the tipping curve, but not critically so. One could develop a model with weaker assumptions (for instance, allowing for tiny "wrinkles" in the distribution of t_i) and still have the same pattern. Apparently, it is not possible to find critically sufficient conditions that do not merely restate the conclusion. A model of collective action that relies on tipping phenomena should not just take the standard S-shaped function for granted.

---

[10]Strictly speaking, we should say that, under these assumptions, almost every pair of functions G, F generates a model with either one equilibrium or three equilibria. The reason for this qualification is that it is possible for the model to have two equilibria but that happens only for razor-edge conditions on F, G. Any tiny perturbation of such conditions and either the second equilibrium will disappear or a third one will appear. I will not pursue this topic further since it is not directly relevant for our purposes and would require a substantial amount of extra mathematical baggage.

2.6.5.4   Comparative Statics

Tipping games have made two major contributions to the study of collective action. First, they have brought to the fore the role of expectations, perhaps with more rigor than focal points. Second, they have offered an illustration of the possibility and the benefits of looking not just at equilibria, but also at the behavior of a game out of equilibrium. The method of stability sets I introduce in Chapter 3 draws heavily on these two ideas.

In a tipping game, mutual expectations among the players shape the outcome of their interaction. But it is mistaken to conclude from this that only expectations matter, to the detriment of the external circumstances represented by the payoffs. The opposite is true: tipping models, if specified rigorously, can be a tool to understand the interaction between the players' beliefs and the payoffs they face.

Let me go through a few examples to illustrate this point. Figure 2.6 represents two curves of one of Schelling's original examples (Schelling, 1978, pg. 106), in which he uses the narrative of a seminar. Suppose that the seminar's announcement says that it will be led by an obscure professor (one Medina), only known for being boring and hard to follow. We might represent this situation with Curve A which, as Schelling says, exemplifies a dying seminar, and predict that after a few sessions it will be gone, forgotten. But suddenly, just before the term starts, Medina takes a leave, for unspecified reasons, and immediately, the department manages to have Professor Thomas Schelling accept the invitation to lead this same seminar. As the news is inscribed in big, bold, red letters over the old posters, we can expect something to change. Curve A might have been an accurate representation for the seminar's fate under Medina but not under a world-renowned scholar, famous for the depth of his contributions and for the wit with which he makes them. Most people in the department, rationalists, structuralists, post-modernists, the undergraduate students who have not yet taken courses on collective action, and even Medina himself, will think that Curve B is now the right model to forecast what will happen to the seminar: everyone will be willing to attend even if no one else goes and, as these attendance expectations become self-fulfilled, the seminar will be a glowing success. The people involved in this situation do not assume that only collective expectations matter. For them, more than the actual attendance, what goes on inside the seminar determines the shape of the diagram's curve.

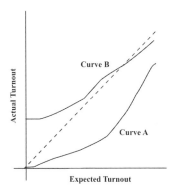

Figure 2.6: Schelling's Seminar Example

Alternatively, we can use a similar diagram (Figure 2.4) to think about the Eastern European revolutions of 1989, following Karklins and Petersen (1993), who explain the collapse of the Eastern European regimes in 1989 by appealing to the notion that different groups reach the tipping point, thus setting the stage for others to upgrade their expectations about turnout. Similarly, albeit thinking about an entirely different phenomenon, Laitin (1998) bases much of his prognosis about different languages in the former Soviet Union on the fact that their users may reach a tipping point beyond which they will enter into a self-sustaining dynamics of increased adoption.

This approach is plausible and intuitive. But when we try to make it systematic, it runs into difficulties. Left to their own devices, levels of aggregate turnout should always move *away* from the tipping point: levels of expectations below the tipping point lead to even lower turnout and levels above it validate even higher expectations. Thus, any displacement toward the tipping point occurs defying the model's logic. In a model that "reaches" the tipping point, there is some exogenous factor, say, motivation or conviction, so powerful that it can go against the implicit forces of tipping. But then, if this factor is so powerful, one suspects that it is it, not tipping, that does the real causal work. Tipping may, in fact, be playing a very minor role, if any at all. Just the fact that collective action succeeds would not constitute any evidence whatsoever in favor of tipping models.

If we suspect that a particular interaction is an instance of a tipping model, we can, however, resort to additional information. The pattern with which collective action occurs in the presence of tipping seems unmistakable: whatever increase in turnout levels there is before the tipping point, it will accelerate greatly once the tipping point is reached in much the same way that a rock that has been pushed uphill accelerates once it reaches the summit. If we study, say, a social movement, as we trace the evolution of its participation levels, we should be able to recognize the moment when it attained the critical mass level.

But this empirical exercise can only be conducted with examples that we already know are successful: it cannot be put to use for any predictive purposes and, by the same token, it selects on the dependent variable (to use the language of King, Keohane and Verba (1994)). Since this kind of analysis can only get off ground with respect to successful cases, it must wait for them to be over and it cannot include in its sample instances of failure. Claims pertaining the empirical validity of tipping models should be discounted accordingly.

There is another way to interpret tipping games, more consistent with their internal mechanisms. Instead of using tipping games as the basis for plausible, but ultimately problematic, statements about changes in expectations, this interpretation brings to the fore the interaction between expectations and payoffs. Here I will give a very loose explanation of this point, but a full formalization will be provided in Chapter 4.

In keeping with the popularity of tipping arguments to analyze the Eastern European revolutions of 1989, let's consider the analytic exercise of Antonin and Gustav, a few weeks before Prague's "Velvet Revolution."

> ANTONIN: (*Putting down his battered and heavily annotated samizdat copy of* Micromotives and Macrobehavior) I think this is it. The regime's days are numbered.

> GUSTAV: How can you be so sure?

> ANTONIN: This diagram (*showing a napkin where he draws Curve A of Figure 2.4*) shows it all. For a long time people have accepted the regime simply because they do not expect others to join them if they speak up. If you protest, nobody comes to your help, you are arrested and, for everyone else, life goes on as before. But now these expectations are going to change. Gorbachev has signaled that the Soviet Union will not intervene, we will not have a repeat of 1968. Before we were to the left of the unstable equilibrium, now we are fast moving to some point to the right of it and, once we reach it, things will snowball. The government will not be able to contain protests with millions of people in the streets. It will simply melt away.

> GUSTAV: I'd like to believe you're right. But I don't understand what Gorbachev has to do with what people in Prague expect from each other.

> ANTONIN: C'mon! Don't you think that without the threat of Soviet tanks the regime is much more fragile than before?

> GUSTAV: Yes, I think it is. But I'm not convinced that expectations have much to do with it. I've been in the clandestine opposition for years. I've been meeting with lots and lots of people, trying to convince them to join us and I know how hard it is to deal with their incredulity. They just don't believe that, when

push comes to shove, enough people will support us. If we in the opposition have failed to change people's expectations after years of long, long meetings, with all kinds of speeches and booklets and what not, what makes you think that reading the news will change the way they see each other?

ANTONIN: You sound skeptical. I can't understand how you can believe what you just said and still say that the regime is now weaker. If changed expectations haven't weakened it, then what?

GUSTAV: Let me put it this way: do *you* expect more people now to join the opposition?

ANTONIN: Absolutely.

GUSTAV: Why?

ANTONIN: Because this time around they won't be shot. There won't be Soviet tanks rolling in.

GUSTAV: My point exactly! I do believe that people are more likely to join the opposition now than before. I do believe that this might bring down the regime. But I believe that they will protest not because of what they expect others will do, but because of what they expect will happen to them or, more precisely, what they expect won't happen, namely, that they won't be rolled under the Soviet tanks. Can I have the napkin with the diagram? (*Antonin gives him the napkin, where Gustav draws Curve B*. (Figure 2.7.)) This is the way I see Gorbachev's gestures. Before we were in a point to the left of the unstable equilibrium, agreed. But most likely we are still there because I don't think that people change their expectations about others in a matter of weeks.

Your Curve A depicts the distribution of minimum levels of turnout that people find enough to justify their cooperation. But as your master Schelling says, "everybody has his own definition of how many is 'enough'," and we still need to give a definition of what "enough" is, not only for you and me as we chat here, but also for the people out there. I submit that this level of "enough turnout" is a function of what happens to people when they try to engage in any type of collective action. In this particular case, it is a function of how likely it is that they will get shot, arrested, etc. So, Gorbachev has not changed people's expectations. What he has changed is the definition of "enough," he has made it so that those levels of "enough turnout" are now in Curve B. He has pushed the curve upwards. So, notice that there are some points in the horizontal axis that are to the left of Curve A's unstable equilibrium but to the *right* of Curve B's unstable equilibrium. If we happen to be in one of those points, then the regime will collapse. Are we there? I don't know but it's likely. Now, although deep down I am optimist, I'm still not popping out the champagne because events may change and Curve B may again go down if, for instance, Gorbachev changes his mind, or the CPSU votes him down and gives him the "Malenkov treatment," sending him to manage a kolkhoz in Turkmenistan. Summing up: if we really want to overthrow the government, we better get moving before that Curve B falls again. And now, if you excuse me, I have to go. My underground cell has called an emergency meeting.

Antonin's analysis is couched in terms of changes in expectations. But as we saw before, this is problematic because

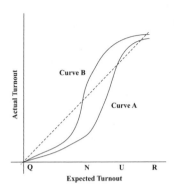

Figure 2.7: A Comparison of Antonin's and Gustav's Tipping Models

it raises the question of what force, external to the model, could be driving such change. Instead, Gustav's analysis tries to spell out the way in which the parameters of the model, especially the S-shaped curve, depend on the external payoffs the players face. In graphical terms, whereas Antonin sees the effect of Gorbachev's statements as producing a displacement along the horizontal axis, Gustav sees them as producing a vertical shift of the curve.

Despite their similarities, there are important differences between these approaches. For Antonin, Gorbachev's pronouncements are a *sufficient* condition for the regime's downfall whereas Gustav sees them as a window of opportunity (a change in the "opportunity structure," to use the terminology of McAdam, Tarrow and Tilly (2001)). Windows of opportunity are neither necessary nor sufficient. They are not necessary to the extent that the same outcome could have been accomplished, albeit with a much reduced likelihood, through another sequence of events. They are not sufficient to the extent that they create conditions that still have to be capitalized.

Whose analysis was correct? This may be a tricky question because now we know that the Czech government did indeed collapse and we do not have a control experiment, a Czechoslovakia$_1$, identical in every respect to the real one except that, propped up by a Soviet occupation, its regime did not collapse, something that would substantiate Gustav's reasoning. Antonin may point out that even though such Czechoslovakia$_1$ does not exist, all the similar regimes in Eastern Europe suffered the same fate. In turn, Gustav may argue that conditions that seem sufficient in retrospect were not so when events were unfolding: the window of opportunity could have closed and Antonin's 1992 article on tipping phenomena in Eastern Europe, which he ultimately published in a prestigious Czech journal of social sciences, would have never been written.

For all its shortcomings, Gustav's approach already illustrates that tipping games are indeed tools to analyze the impact of changes in the payoff structure of collective action over its outcomes. In other words, tipping models can offer support to a theory of collective action that assigns a central explanatory role to structural conditions. The sketchy analysis I have presented thus far is no substitute for such a theory, but is a start.

Loose ends remain. Thus far I have not offered a systematic construction, consistent with the fundamentals of game theory, to support this reading of tipping games. The method of stability sets does that. Neither have I offered an explicit account of how exactly changes in the game's parameters change the location of the tipping curve. That will require a model that is more carefully specified and the exact account will differ from one model to the next. In the concrete examples developed in Chapters 5 and 6 I will show how this can be accomplished.

It is worth recording that developers and users of tipping models are now making efforts at incorporating the role of objective circumstances in determining the distribution of thresholds, Yin (1998) and Wood (2002) (especially in her formal appendix) being two recent examples. The results these authors obtain do not differ much from the ones I will prove later although, I claim, the method I adopt is more firmly anchored in microfoundations and easier to generalize on several directions.

2.7   Which Is It, Then?

I opened this chapter with a general model of collective action and then proceeded to show that two major paradigms in this field are particular cases of this model. But there are substantial differences between these paradigms. One views collective action as a game with a unique equilibrium that does not depend at all on the mutual expectations that agents may develop. The other sees it as a game with multiple equilibria where these mutual expectations play a fundamental role in determining the outcome. For the purposes of Chapter 4, it is irrelevant which model is the right one. The method of stability sets works for both, although, of course, the conclusions reached differ. But in the second part of the book, where I develop applications of the general theory, I will rely on multiple-equilibria models. I cannot avoid taking sides.

First, the circumstantial evidence. Whatever its logical coherence the public goods model offers a portrait of collective action that misses fundamental aspects of real-life collective action problems. If we believe that collective action problems have a unique equilibrium, we are saying, like it or not, that mutual expectations are inconsequential for the end result. To be consistent, we must say that political organizations have no business in trying to create expectations of success among their members or expectations of defeat among their rivals.

Opposition leaders engaged in overthrowing a regime might find this shocking. It means that they do not need to maintain morale among the members of their organization, that they should not care at all about trying to generate the feeling that the effort might succeed, that they should not even bother to engage in the shadowboxing of preliminary demonstrations and other displays of power just to send the message to their supporters that success is at hand. Rulers might also be shocked to discover that they need not worry about dissident propaganda or about the opposition putting a million demonstrators on the streets (ostensibly because they are not aware of the public goods model) because, although the demonstration's numbers affect the opposition's beliefs in its chances of success, strategic dominance makes such beliefs irrelevant.

I do not know of any defender of the public goods model that is willing to take these implications to heart and argue that, in fact, in a collective action problem expectations of success do not matter. There simply is too much evidence that they do matter and it is incumbent upon believers in this model to formulate a version that accommodates this fact.

Some readers may not find this critique compelling. It could be argued that the right procedure in social sciences is to lay down a set of axioms and reason from them, come what may. A critical reader of an earlier, much weaker, version of this book expressed in despair the view that: "I have trouble even *defining* a collective action problem in terms that do not make it sound like a PD."

This does not seem an unrepresentative stance but I believe that the preceding arguments prove it wrong. It is easy to confuse PDs with collective action problems in general. After all, PDs are special models that share the basic properties of any collective action problem. In fact, in a PD the collective goal is desirable for all players, the individual acts of cooperation are costly and their effects on success is negligible. It satisfies all the conditions of Model 0. But to defend PDs we must be willing to defend much more than these assumptions. We must also rule out the possibility of different costs of cooperation, one when it succeeds, another when it fails. We must also rule out the possibility of benefits that are contingent on success. Introduce any of these possibilities, and the collective action problem at hand becomes a model with multiple equilibria. In sum, PDs are a very narrow case of collective action, and a particularly fragile one at that.

Ultimately, the choice between a model of strategic dominance and a model with multiple equilibria turns on the payoff structure. From the study of tipping games we have learned that a model of collective action can only have multiple equilibria if $w_{1i} > w_{2i}$ for at least some players. Is this a plausible modeling choice?

I believe it is, but I understand there are difficulties. The main reason to doubt this assumption is that, after all, cooperating is an act that requires some effort. This simple realization is at the core of much of the discussion on free-riding. It is a powerful point and if there were no offsetting considerations, we could pronounce this an open-and-shut case in favor of the public goods model. But there are offsetting considerations.

The difference between terms w_{1i} and w_{2i} represents the gain (or loss) for an individual that cooperates in a successful collective endeavor. Such an act of cooperation may be the source of "psychic benefits," something that both Olsonians and Schellingeans have acknowledged. As we already discussed, the public goods model has difficulties dealing with such benefits because it needs to explain why they would compensate for the cost of cooperation both when it succeeds and when it fails. But strategic models do not have this difficulty, precisely because they already allow for differential costs that depend on the outcome.

On top of purely psychic benefits, there is also the role of organizations. To its credit, the public goods approach prompted rational-choice scholars to think seriously about organizations as facilitators of collective action. It is easy to overdo this point; ultimately, public goods models conclude that only organizations matter when it comes to explaining collective action. But the basic point remains true: whereas collective action could, in theory, arise without any previous organizational work, in practice this is a rarity barely worth studying.

In the public goods model, an organization's task is to provide selective incentives, something that, as we have seen, is shot through with conceptual difficulties. But organizations may well be in charge of offering and delivering contingent benefits, not unlike firms that issue stock to levy the necessary capital during their start-up period. We see this all the time. Serious political organizations have rules of seniority and promotion that demand from their members sacrifices to be compensated for after success. The costs of engaging in successful collective action may go from negligible to staggering, from just the time spent in a demonstration on a sunny day to years of clandestine activity and long night marches in the jungle. But organizations that succeed in their collective endeavor can compensate their members for their efforts.

There are two objections worth discussing. First, it could be argued that in real life participants are often not rewarded, but instead punished by the organization they helped bring to victory. But this misses the point. An agent makes her decisions on the basis of the information available at the time she makes it. In other words, she evaluates the ex ante benefits. Whether the ex post benefits, the ones that will ultimately obtain, are greater or smaller is not relevant for the strategic calculations. Consider, for instance, the investment in a risky asset. At the time the decision is made, the investor, if he knows something about what he is doing, is aware that the asset may lose value. But if at that point he thinks that, all things considered, the expected profit, that is, the ex ante benefit, is positive, he will make the investment. If, down the road, the asset does indeed lose all its value, this does not mean that the original decision was irrational. It simply means that new information has become available. Going back to collective action, it is true that, like Chronos, many revolutions devour their children. Zinoviev did not get the deal he wanted when he joined the Bolsheviks, but ex ante, when it was relevant for his decision-making, he had good reasons to believe that it was worth it, whether his motivations were selfish (which I doubt) or not.

A second objection is that, given that the rewards necessary to ensure that $w_{1i} > w_{2i}$ are made contingent on success, they may be plagued by credibility issues. This is a good point, but there is a risk of reading too much into it. Organizations have enforcement mechanisms to ensure that their past commitments are honored, at least to some extent. A party leader, fresh from a resounding victory, can double-cross some of his followers, especially if that is needed to give more to others. But it is unlikely that he will defraud all of them; that would spell the end of the organization. Some of those enforcement mechanisms can be every bit as binding as the mechanisms that enforce the distribution of profits to stockholders in a firm. Just like firms, organizations have internal constitutions and systems of control. The credibility problems that may arise in a situation of collective action are, like those that arise in stock markets, serious but not insurmountable.

In trying to understand the costs of cooperation, we should notice a fundamental difference between the comparison of w_3 and w_4 and that of w_1 and w_2. The first one refers to what happens in case of failure, something the agents do not control and is, instead, decided by those they wish to challenge or, at least, dictated by the circumstances they wish to change. In contrast, w_1 and w_2, the payoffs from success, are well within their reach: it is up to the players to decide how to compensate themselves for their work. Ultimately, an organization that cannot overcome its credibility issues, that cannot propose a course of action that will generate the right non-material benefits for its members, that, in sum, cannot convey clearly to its members that they can look forward to some kind of compensation of whatever type, such that $w_{1i} > w_{2i}$, is not a serious contender for collective action. In a way, the model where $w_2 > w_1$ does not capture, to paraphrase Olson, the logic of collective action, but the logic of inept organizations.

2.8   Infinitely Repeated Prisoners' Dilemmas

Much of the vast literature on collective action as an iterated game borrows from the model of infinitely repeated PDs (Bendor and Mookherjee, 1987; Abreu, 1988; Taylor, 1987). As tools for the study of collective action, infinitely repeated PDs owe their popularity to two important properties: (a) they make explicit the dynamic structure of a game and (b) they have equilibria with cooperation.

At first glance, it may seem that these two properties make infinitely repeated PDs a much better tool for the study of collective action than the games we have discussed thus far. But this would be a misperception. Repeated games are a powerful tool. They offer valuable insights on the structure of human interactions. But it would go too far to say that they render the other models unnecessary. Each approach has strengths and weaknesses and we ought to investigate how they complement each other.

Most real-life instances of collective action unfold through time, often measured in years, rather than weeks. One could conclude, then, that a dynamic, extensive-form game, such as an infinitely-repeated PD, is the only possible model of collective action. This conclusion is unwarranted. It is possible to use one-shot games to represent interactions that take place over time because the strategies of a one-shot game can be as elaborate as we wish. If I want to study a situation that requires two players to act on Monday, Tuesday and Wednesday, for instance, I can use a one-shot game where "Do A on Monday, B on Tuesday and C on Wednesday" is one strategy and "Do A' on Monday, B' on Tuesday, C' on Wednesday" is another. This is simply an instance of the basic principle of equivalence between extensive-form games and normal-form games.

Apart from convenience, the only reason to prefer the dynamic representation of a game over its one-shot version is that the former can represent contingent strategies that depend on previous moves of the game. The folk theorems of repeated games exploit such property in studying the large variety of "sticks and carrots" that populate this literature.

In essence, these mechanisms of threats and punishments transform a one-shot PD into a game with multiple equilibria, not unlike the ones we have already encountered. In that sense, repeated games have the same potential and face the same challenges as the collective action models discussed above.

I will not offer a detailed mathematical study of repeated games in this book similar to the one I will present for one-shot games. But discussing a simple example will help us see the implications of this point.

Let's study what happens to the canonical PD when we no longer assume that it is played only once. Although we have already seen the original payoff matrix, I reproduce it here once again for the reader's convenience (Figure 2.8):

2

		C	D
1	C	1,1	$-1,2$
	D	$2,-1$	0,0

Figure 2.8: Prisoners' Dilemma

Suppose that the two players of this PD are a baker (Player 1) and a customer (Player 2). The baker has two possible strategies: he can give the customer a croissant (C) or decide not to (D). In turn, the customer can give the baker one dollar in cash (C) or decide not to (D). There is no external enforcement of this exchange so that the players face the exact payoff matrix of a PD: if Player 1 gives the cash and Player 2 gives the croissant, both parties are better off than if they both choose D. But for Player 2 it is even better if the baker gives her the croissant and she does not give him the cash. Likewise, the baker is better off if the customer gives him the cash and he does not have to give her the croissant. It may seem odd that I choose a fable that has nothing to do with collective action as we commonly understand it, but it helps the later analysis and shows, at least to those of us who are skeptical of the PD as a model of collective action, that its real purview may be elsewhere.[11]

Absent any external enforcement, these two players may still arrive at mutually beneficial exchanges if the game is infinitely repeated or, more realistically, if after any given round, with some positive probability, there will be another one. The folk theorems of repeated games show this formally. To get to that point, though, we still need some preliminary steps. Since the potential number of interactions is infinite, we need to postulate a discount rate δ so that the infinite streams of

---

[11]In unearthing the story behind the Prisoners' Dilemma, Russell Hardin makes the following comment about its origins in the experiments of Merrill Flood: "Oddly, two of the games with which Flood experimented before the prisoner's dilemma involved simple exchanges – of old cars for money. He seems not to have seen that his prisoners' dilemma game was a simplification and generalization of such exchanges" (Hardin, 1995, pg. 32). The example in the main text brings out this same point.

payoffs add up to finite net present values. Alternatively, we can interpret δ as the probability of the game being continued after each round. Both interpretations are common in the literature and the mathematical study of repeated games is the same under either of them.

There is already a long list of analytical results pertaining this situation but, to fix ideas, I will focus only on the first and best-known ones: the first and second folk theorems of infinitely repeated games. Let's reproduce their standard formulation; their respective proofs can be readily found in any modern textbook of game theory.

Theorem 2 (First Folk Theorem) *If a game with a finite strategy space is infinitely repeated and its players have intertemporal discount rates δ, then:*

- *All the vectors of (discounted) payoffs inside the convex hull of the original vectors of (discounted) payoffs can be attained through some strategy profile, and*

- *There exists a discount rate $\bar{\delta}$ such that if $\delta > \bar{\delta}$, then every strategy profile that results in a vector of payoffs that dominates the vector of* minmax payoffs *of the original game can be supported as a* Nash equilibrium *of a repeated game where the players choose their* minmax strategy *from round $T+1$ on if they observe a deviation in round T.*

The second folk theorem is almost identical to the first, except for the emphasized parts:

Theorem 3 (Second Folk Theorem) *If a game with a finite strategy space is infinitely repeated and its players have intertemporal discount rates δ, then:*

- *All the vectors of (discounted) payoffs inside the convex hull of the original vectors of(discounted) payoffs can be attained through some strategy profile, and*

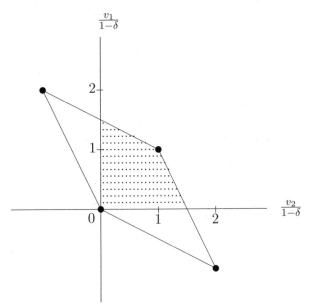

Figure 2.9: Convex Hull of the (Discounted) Payoffs of the Infinitely Repeated Prisoners' Dilemma. The shaded area represents the set of payoffs that dominate the Nash equilibrium.

- *There exists a discount rate $\bar{\delta}$ such that if $\delta > \bar{\delta}$, then every strategy profile that results in a vector of payoffs that dominates the vector of* payoffs of the Nash equilibrium *of the original game can be supported as a* subgame perfect equilibrium *of a repeated game where the players choose their* Nash equilibrium strategy *from round $T+1$ on if they observe a deviation in round T.*

In the case that concerns us here, the PD, these two theorems come to the same conclusion but I reproduce both to show how general the subsequent analysis is. Figure 2.9 illustrates both theorems in the case of the PD.

Each axis measures the net present value of infinite streams of payoffs for each player: Player 1's payoffs on the horizontal axis and Player 2's payoffs on the vertical axis. The polygon is the convex hull of the payoffs from the original game so that the first statement of both theorems is that any payoff in that region can be attained through some combination of strategies in the infinitely repeated version of the game. The shaded area is the region of payoffs that can be supported as an equilibrium, given the punishments players can inflict on each other in case of a deviation. In the PD, the minmax payoffs and strategies and the payoffs and strategies of the Nash equilibrium are the same so the region supported by each theorem is the same.

Any point in the convex hull of the original payoff vectors (Figure 2.9) can result from a combination of both players' strategies over time. Player 1 may give the croissant today while Player 2 brings one dollar for the next five days without getting anything in return or, alternatively, Player 1 may give Player 2 croissants for three days while only on the fourth day does Player 2 bring one dollar. In other words, any given point in the convex hull represents a contract: we could read off from it how the contract stipulates the amount of trade and the price of the croissants.

The second part of the folk theorems tells us which contracts are possible as an equilibrium, in other words, which contracts are self-enforcing. To interpret correctly the folk theorems, we need to pay special attention to their circuitous formulation and their silences. The theorems do *not* say that if the game is infinitely repeated the players will cooperate. They say that, *if* the players have the right intertemporal discount factors and *if* they use "trigger" strategies to punish each other (minmax in one case, Nash in the other), then *any* combination of strategies whose payoff is higher than the "punishment payoffs" can be supported as an equilibrium. If we neglect all these caveats, we miss the main point of the folk theorems.

Trade is self-enforcing in this case because each player can threaten the other with suspending trade altogether if the contract is breached. The folk theorems tell us that, given such threat, there are infinitely many possible contracts. But this leaves three questions open: (*a*) will the players trade? (*b*) for how long? and (*c*) at what price?

Question *b* is the easiest one to answer, which is not to say much. If trade is mutually beneficial, no player should interrupt it arbitrarily, without a breach of contract. Graphically, this means that the players will not choose contracts below the convex hull's outer border. If they will trade at all, they will enter a contract to trade forever, obtaining the maximum benefits possible. Intuitive as this conclusion is, the folk theorems are not even enough to ensure it. In fact, the folk theorems say that, if players decide to trade for just a few sessions and leave it at that, thus choosing a point inside the convex hull, that will also be an equilibrium. To restrict our attention to the optimal contracts at the border we need to invoke arguments external to the folk theorems themselves.

There are many possible answers to Question c because infinitely repeated games are afflicted by distributive conflicts. To each point on the convex hull's border corresponds a price for croissants and all these prices can result from an equilibrium of the iterated PD. The only constraint imposed by the folk theorems is that each player can recoup the costs of obtaining the croissant or the cash in the first place. But a move from one equilibrium on that line to another represents a transfer of payoffs between the players. The players can attain mutual gains from cooperation but they face then the problem of how to distribute those gains. Once again, we must resort to considerations beyond the folk theorems to answer this question.

Bargaining theory is one option. We could start by imposing a set of normative restrictions that a price should have in this situation until we narrow the set of possible prices to one. The Nash bargaining solution is one such example, arguably the most famous one. This is not the place to discuss it in detail; suffice it to say that, when applied to this case, the Nash bargaining solution selects the payoff vector $(1/(1 - \delta), 1/(1 - \delta))$: at every round players must exchange one croissant for one dollar.

The folk theorem's answer to Question a is: "Maybe." This may seem counterintuitive at first glance because trade is mutually beneficial. But on closer inspection, things are more complicated. "Self-enforcing" is something of a misnomer. Such contracts have clear enforcers, the parties themselves who must bear all the costs and risks this entails. If a breach occurs, the harm is done and the aggrieved party has no one to resort to for compensation. All he can do is to make violations less attractive ex ante, but that will not eliminate them entirely.

To see this more clearly, suppose that the baker and the customer ask themselves if they should accept a contract according to which every day they will trade one croissant for one dollar, the Nash bargaining solution, under penalty of suspending trade indefinitely if one of them walks away with the other party's goods without giving anything in return. They must consider what the likely outcomes are. Denote by C the decision of each one to enter and honor the contract from now on and by N the decision not to do so. So, if both parties honor the contract, the baker will receive the following stream of payoffs:

$$
\begin{aligned}
v_1(C_1, C_2) &= 1 + \delta + \delta^2 + \cdots \\
&= \frac{1}{1 - \delta}.
\end{aligned}
$$

If the baker does his part but the customer cheats, this leads to a breakdown of trade but the baker has incurred in a one-period loss:

$$
\begin{aligned}
v_1(C_1, N_2) &= -1; \\
v_2(C_1, N_2) &= 2.
\end{aligned}
$$

If both players decide not to contract, there is no trade:

$$
\begin{aligned}
v_1(N_1, N_2) &= 0; \\
v_2(N_1, N_2) &= 0.
\end{aligned}
$$

Let's arrange all these payoffs in a matrix (Figure 2.10):

From the folk theorems we know that there exists an intertemporal discount rate δ enough to support the contract as an equilibrium. In terms of this payoff matrix, this means that

$$2$$

		C	N
1	C	$\frac{1}{1-\delta}, \frac{1}{1-\delta}$	$-1, 2$
	N	$2, -1$	$0, 0$

Figure 2.10: Will They Trade?

there is a δ high enough to make unilateral cheating unattractive. We can calculate that value with the following inequality:

$$v_1(C_1, C_2) \ \geq \ v_1(D_1, C_2),$$
$$\frac{1}{1-\delta} \ \geq \ 2,$$
$$\delta \ \geq \ 1/2.$$

But now we have a problem. If $\delta < 1/2$, the payoff matrix is analogous to that of the original PD: N will be the dominant strategy for both players. If instead $\delta > 1/2$, the payoff matrix becomes analogous to that of assurance games; although (C, C) is an equilibrium, (N, N) is also an equilibrium: we cannot be sure which one will be played.

No matter how much we repeat the game, no matter what discount rates the players have, no matter what contracts they offer each other, not to trade remains an equilibrium. We already knew this from the statement of the folk theorems: in the original PD, (N, N) is the game's Nash equilibrium and therefore is, by definition, a subgame perfect equilibrium of the iterated version.

Intuitively, if we want trade to get off the ground in this game, there is an irreducible component of trust needed. Since the parties are simultaneously beneficiaries from the possible contracts and responsible for enforcing them, they can only enter into such transactions if they believe the other player's honorable behavior will make it worthwhile to run the risk of been defrauded.

We have already encountered this situation: it is the same as the coordination games studied above. If the players have the right beliefs about each other, they can interact in mutually beneficial ways. Otherwise they will get stuck with an inferior outcome that is, nevertheless, an equilibrium.

There is, then, a deep connection between one-shot coordination games and infinitely repeated games. They are different ways of looking at the same problem. While the one-shot coordination games emphasize the role of beliefs in allowing players to take advantage of their opportunities for mutual betterment, infinitely repeated games explain how, in some contexts, such opportunities emerge in the first place. It is pointless to claim that one approach is superior to the other without knowing exactly the question we want to address.

Folk theorems show that the issue of multiple equilibria is, if anything, much more relevant for repeated games than for coordination games. Even the simplest 2×2 game generates a continuum of equilibria once it is repeated and the same reasoning followed above could be replicated for any other possible contract. As theorists of collective action we cannot hope to simply walk away from the difficulties of multiple equilibria by embracing repeated games. Without a systematic approach to the problem, this will only make matters worse.

2.9   Bayesian Games

Just like infinite repetition, games with incomplete information generalize the study of one shot, normal-form games, thus having become the subject of a large literature, for instance, (Lohmann, 1994, 1993; Kuran, 1991). These studies on collective action under informational asymmetries rightly point out that, in coordinating with somebody, I have to guess how my counterpart sees the external world, knowing that her choices may depend on private elements to which I have no access. This is a source of important insights but, for my purposes, there is no important loss from assuming that there is no asymmetric information. The intuition I want to formalize refers to the effect of objective payoffs on outcomes of coordination games. Being objective, those payoffs are known by everybody through public, symmetric information. Going back to the example at the beginning of the book, we want to study things such as the impact of increased water fees over the stability of a regime. Water fees are an objective fact of the world, not emotional states that only their bearer can know fully, and they affect every member of this hypothetical country in ways potentially accessible to everybody.

2.10   Conclusions

I wrote this chapter in the belief that, when a research field has grown too profusely for a long while, it is time to look for a unified theory. There are already various approaches to collective action and often it may seem that it is hard to state succinctly and rigorously the reasons for preferring one over the next.

Here I have tried to go some way toward solving this problem. Starting with a general model of collective action it is possible to see how different approaches to the topic come down to specific versions of it, an exercise that leads to several findings.

First, public goods models of collective action are not robust in the face of tiny changes in their payoff structure. Simply by introducing costs of and rewards from cooperation that depend on its outcome, the strategic dominance of non-cooperation disappears and multiple equilibria emerge.

Second, any use of tipping games or focal points implicitly assumes that, in a collective action problem, cooperators can expect a reward sufficient to compensate for the cost of cooperation, provided that the endeavor succeeds. It is not possible to attack this assumption and use a multiple-equilibria model at the same time.

These two claims are independent of any individual researcher's preferences for one model or another: they result from working through the mathematical properties of a generalized model of collective action and, as such, they are what they are. But mathematics is not enough. In developing and using models of social interactions there are many judgment calls that a researcher must make. Although these mathematical results do not substitute for such judgment calls, I hope they can improve their quality.

By virtue of their broad applicability and plausible assumptions, strategic models of the focal point effect and tipping games hold promise for a general theory of collective action and my approach will use some of their insights. But these models need to be formulated with greater precision before we can use them as a source of comparative statics. Absent such precision, they are reduced to act as simple placeholders for whatever comparative statics we desire to impose without further justification.

By using a payoff structure with multiple equilibria, where no player has a dominant strategy, the focal point models identify correctly the structure of the collective action problem. When these models claim that the "focalness" of an equilibrium is not related to the game's payoff structure, they acknowledge that the players' beliefs and expectations determine the outcome of a game with multiple equilibria. But without an explicit mechanism connecting the relative salience of an equilibrium with its payoffs, we cannot transform this insight into a source of comparative statics results. Consequently, focal points arguments are often used to rationalize ex post whatever outcomes can be observed in a collective action problem, but cannot serve as guides ex ante.

Tipping games offer a suggestive way of generalizing the focal points approach by considering the possibility that beliefs and expectations do not need to be always in equilibrium, but can, instead, converge to one. In the next chapters, I will make abundant use of this crucial insight. But tipping models leave without microfoundations their most critical component: the threshold levels above which players cooperate. This failure obscures the connection between the benefits of cooperation and the players' willingness to coordinate. The ambiguities that surround tipping models have led to a situation where they are, much like arguments about focal points, mere rationalizations of previous outcomes but not tools for systematic, testable predictions. It does not have to be that way and in the next chapter I will propose what I believe is a better treatment.

Whatever its merits, the unified model I offered in this chapter does not succeed at covering all the important approaches to collective action problems. Two types of models cannot be considered special cases of Model 0: repeated games and games with incomplete information.

Although different in many ways, repeated games share some crucial properties with the one-shot coordination games presented above: they also present multiple equilibria and, crucially, they can also result in non-coordination. In this regard, it is likely that repeated games will benefit from being subjected to the type of analysis I will develop in the next chapter. Although I have not proved a general theorem to that effect, I will have the chance to study in detail one example that suggests how this could come about.

Though sources of valuable insights, games with incomplete information do not speak to the effects of changes in the publicly-known payoffs. Bayesian games formalize the impact of private individual traits over collective action and as such, they do not contribute to the specific questions I want to address in this book. Chances are that a more elaborate version of the method of stability sets can be applied to these games as well.

2.A   Proof of Theorem 1

First, I will prove that $\gamma^* = 0$ is always an equilibrium. Since $F(0) = 0$, then $(1 - F(0))/F(0) = \infty$ and since individual benefits are always finite $(b_i < \infty)$, then $G(\infty) = 1$. Therefore, we obtain that:

$$1 - G\left(c\frac{1 - F(0)}{F(0)}\right) = 0$$

which proves that $\gamma = 0$ is an equilibrium. Any equilibrium γ^* is stable if departures from it are self-correcting. Formally, this means that:

$$\frac{\partial}{\partial \gamma}\left(1 - G\left(c\frac{1 - F(\gamma)}{F(\gamma)}\right) - \gamma\right)\bigg|_{\gamma = \gamma^*} < 0. \qquad (2.13)$$

If, instead, the inequality sign of 2.13 is reversed, the equilibrium is unstable: it is a tipping point. When evaluated at $\gamma = 0$, this condition becomes:

$$g\left(c\frac{1-F(0)}{F(0)}\right)c\frac{f(0)}{F(0)^2} - 1.$$

This expression is negative as far as $g(x), f(x)$ are finite, which they are because they are derivatives of continuous, everywhere differentiable, distribution functions.

The same stability condition, evaluated at $\gamma = 1$ gives:

$$\begin{aligned} g\left(c\frac{1-F(1)}{F(1)}\right)c\frac{f(1)}{F(1)^2} - 1 &= g(0)cf(1) - 1 \\ &= -1. \end{aligned}$$

This means that whatever the highest equilibrium is, it will be stable.

The question now is how many equilibria will there be. Usually, tipping games deal with S-shaped functions, something that guarantees that the game will have either one or three equilibria. The assumptions concerning F, G are sufficient for that purpose.

To see why, we need to define precisely what is an S-shaped function. In this context, we say that a function $y(x)$ is S-shaped if, for some value x, $y(x_0)$ is convex for all $x < x_0$ and concave for all $x > x_0$. The assumptions about f', g' imply that F, G are S-shaped. Now we need to prove that $1 - G(c(1 - F(\gamma))/F(\gamma)) - \gamma$ is also S-shaped.

The first step is to notice that $(1 - F(\gamma))/F(\gamma)$ is a convex function. In fact, the second derivative of this function is:

$$\frac{\partial^2}{\partial\gamma^2}\frac{1-F(\gamma)}{F(\gamma)} = -\frac{F(\gamma)^2 f'(\gamma) - 2F(\gamma)f(\gamma)^2}{F(\gamma)^4}.$$

This expression is positive if and only if:

$$f'(\gamma) < \frac{2f(\gamma)^2}{F(\gamma)}.$$

Since F is concave the left-hand side of this inequality is negative and, since F is also increasing and positive, the right-hand side will be positive. We conclude, then, that the function $(1 - F(\gamma))/F(\gamma)$ is convex.

Knowing that $(1 - F(\gamma))/F(\gamma)$ is convex, we can now prove that the entire function is S-shaped. Assume that G's mean is $\mu > 0$. Since $G(x) = \Phi(x)$, then it is convex for all values $x < \mu$ and concave for $x > \mu$. Define a value γ_0 such that:

$$\frac{1 - F(\gamma)}{F(\gamma)} = \mu.$$

Since $(1 - F(\gamma))/F(\gamma)$ is decreasing in γ, for any value $\gamma > \gamma_0$, $(1 - F(\gamma))/F(\gamma) < \mu$. That is, for every value $\gamma > \gamma_0$, $G((1 - F(\gamma))/F(\gamma))$ is a convex function of a convex function and so is itself convex. In turn, this implies that $1 - G((1 - F(\gamma))/F(\gamma))$ is concave.

When $\gamma < \gamma_0$, the result is a concave function of a convex function so that to determine its curvature we need extra assumptions about G. In particular, $G = \Phi$ is sufficient. In particular, to ensure concavity, we need that:

$$\frac{\partial^2}{\partial \gamma^2} G\left(\frac{1 - F(\gamma)}{F(\gamma)}\right) \quad < \quad 0,$$

$$g\left(\frac{1 - F(\gamma)}{F(\gamma)}\right) \frac{F(\gamma)^2 f'(\gamma) - 2F(\gamma)f(\gamma)^2}{F(\gamma)^4} \quad < \quad g'\left(\frac{1 - F(\gamma)}{F(\gamma)}\right) \frac{f(\gamma)^2}{F(\gamma)^4}.$$

Upon substituting and solving, this becomes:

$$F(\gamma)^2 f'(\gamma) - 2F(\gamma)f(\gamma)^2 \quad < \quad \frac{1}{\sigma^2}\left[\frac{1 - F(\gamma)}{F(\gamma)} - \mu\right] f(\gamma)^2.$$

Since F is concave, the left-hand side of this inequality is negative and when $\gamma < \gamma_0$, $(1 - F(\gamma))/F(\gamma) > \mu$ and the right-hand side is positive. This ensures that the compound function is concave and so, $1 - G((1 - F(\gamma))/F(\gamma))$ is convex in the relevant interval.

Putting these results together, we conclude that the function $1 - G((1 - F(\gamma))/F(\gamma))$ is S-shaped. Since there is already a stable equilibrium at $\gamma = 0$, this proves that either there is exactly one equilibrium or exactly three (although see Footnote 10).

Chapter 3

The Method of Stability Sets

3.1   Introduction

In this chapter I will introduce, extend and apply the method of stability sets, the technique that will allow us to extract comparative statics results from games with multiple equilibria. The method is not new: its fundamental concepts were developed more than twenty years ago by John Harsanyi and Reinhardt Selten (Harsanyi and Selten, 1988), albeit with a different purpose. But its potential has gone largely unappreciated and it has been relegated to the study of very specific games.

Although the method of stability sets uses little known mathematical arguments, its intuitive basis will sound familiar to students of focal points and tipping games. Both arguments recognize that in a game with multiple equilibria, beliefs and expectations among players determine the final outcome. Tipping games generalize the equilibrium analysis of focal points by offering a description of how a game arrives at an equilibrium starting from belief profiles that are not already one. The method of stability sets uses these same notions, formalizing them and making explicit how they relate to the game's payoff structure.

Rather than searching for an elusive and perhaps arbitrary deterministic prediction, or opting for total agnosticism about the final outcome, the method of stability sets allows the analyst to assess the relative likelihood of a game's different equilibria. Such probabilistic assessments are more than mere educated guesses: they are firmly based on game-theoretic microfoundations and display systematic patterns connected to the game's payoffs. These probabilities are, then, an adequate basis for comparative statics.

In the interest of expository clarity, I will step back momentarily from the stage attained in the previous chapter. I will first introduce the basic notions of stability sets in 2×2 games and will then extend the analysis to large games. Once this is done, we will be in a position to see what happens when we apply the method to the games of the previous chapter.

3.2   The Method of Stability Sets in a 2×2 Coordination Game

All the formal results of this book are consequences of a basic insight that can be exemplified in the simplest possible games: 2×2 games. So, let's go back to the case we have been analyzing, the collective action game with 2 players that I reproduce here for convenience (Figure 3.1):

$$2$$

		C	D
1	C	1,1	$-1,0$
	D	$0,-1$	0,0

Figure 3.1: Collective Action

We already know that this game has three Nash equilibria: (C,C), (D,D) and a mixed strategy Nash equilibrium in which both players use randomizations over their pure strategies. If α_1 denotes the probability of Player 1 choosing C, α_2 the probability of Player 2 choosing C, this mixed strategy equilibrium is $\alpha_1^* = 1/2, \alpha_2^* = 1/2$.

Mixed strategy equilibria have become a source of many debates (and much confusion), some of which will be rehearsed later. To clarify them, let's go back to the basic concept from which all the Nash equilibria of a game, pure and mixed, are derived: the best-response correspondence.

A best-response correspondence is a mapping that tells us the optimal strategy (or strategies) of each player, as we change the other players' strategy profile. Best-response correspondences play an important role in motivating my approach so they deserve special care.

In this example, $\alpha_1^*(\alpha_2)$ represents Player 1's optimal strategy given Player 2's choice and $\alpha_2^*(\alpha_1)$ represents Player 2's optimal strategy given Player 1's choice. In classical game theory, we say that Player 1 will choose strategy C when its expected payoff is higher than that of choosing D and that she will only randomize between both strategies if she is indifferent between them. In game theory the payoffs from any strategy typically depend on the other players' choices so here I represent Player 1's payoff as a function of α_1 and α_2: $v_1(\alpha_1, \alpha_2)$ where

$$\begin{aligned} v_1(\alpha_1, \alpha_2) &= \alpha_1(\alpha_2 - (1 - \alpha_2)) \\ &= \alpha_1(2\alpha_2 - 1). \end{aligned} \tag{3.1}$$

This equation results from the weighted average of all the possible payoffs Player 1 may obtain in the game, where their respective weights are given by their probability, which, in turn, is a function of the players' strategies. So, for example, the cell C, C in the payoff matrix gives Player 1 a payoff of 1 and, if the players' strategies are α_1, α_2 respectively, it will occur with probability $\alpha_1\alpha_2$, which explains the first term of the first equation.

When $\alpha_2 < 1/2$, the payoff v_1 is a negative and decreasing function of α_1 so that, if Player 1 wants to maximize it, she must choose $\alpha_1^* = 0$. Likewise, when $\alpha_2 > 1/2$, v_1 is increasing in α_1 so that the optimal choice is now $\alpha_1^* = 1$. Finally, if $\alpha_2 = 1/2$, then $v_1 = 0$ for any choice of α_1 so that any possible randomization is equally optimal: $\alpha_1^* = [0, 1]$. We

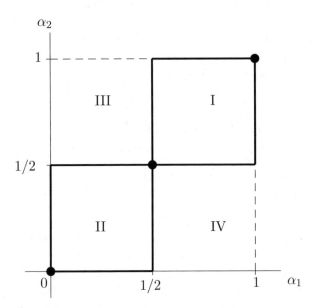

Figure 3.2: Best-response Correspondences of the Collective Action Game

can put all these results together in Player 1's best-response correspondence:

$$\alpha_1^*(\alpha_2) = \begin{cases} 1 & \text{if} \quad \alpha_2 > 1/2, \\ [0,1] & \text{if} \quad \alpha_2 = 1/2, \\ 0 & \text{if} \quad \alpha_2 < 1/2. \end{cases}$$

With the same procedure, we can calculate Player 2's best-response correspondence $\alpha_2^*(\alpha_1)$, which is entirely analogous. In Figure 3.2 I plot these two best-response correspondences on a plane that contains both α_1 and α_2. The Nash equilibria are represented by dots.

   Player 1's best-response correspondence represents her optimal choice for every possible value of α_2. If, for some reason, Player 1 believes that the probability of Player 2 cooperating is less than $1/2$ ($\alpha_2 < 1/2$), her best strategy is not to cooperate ($\alpha_1^* = 0$). If, instead, $\alpha_2 > 1/2$, then Player 1's optimal choice is C ($\alpha_1^* = 1$). The same is true for Player 2 which allows us to partition the strategy space into four regions, as shown in

Figure 3.2. If the beliefs players hold about each other are in Region I, their optimal choice is C whereas beliefs in Region II will lead them to choose D.

We will need a specific term to refer to those beliefs and this raises a bit of a problem. In the work where they developed this analysis, Harsanyi and Selten (1988) referred to them as *priors*. In principle this choice is as good as any other. But over time, in no small part thanks to Harsanyi's own work on games with incomplete information, the term "priors" has come to be associated with an entirely different notion. In general, I have tried to stick as close as possible to the original work of Harsanyi and Selten, mainly for two reasons. First, although not perfect, their formalization is outstanding and hard to improve upon. Second, given that this area is not as well-known as others in game theory, there is an advantage in allowing precedents to sediment, especially when they have been laid down by authors of such stature. But this is one instance where I will depart from the conventions adopted by Harsanyi and Selten. Using the term "priors" to refer to these beliefs that have only an oblique connection with beliefs in games with incomplete information may be the source of much confusion. Thus, from now on I will refer to them as *initial belief conditions*.

In an intuitive sense, initial belief conditions in Regions I and II gravitate toward the pure-strategy equilibria of the game. This property makes them, in the terminology introduced by Harsanyi and Selten (1988), *stability sets* of the equilibria to which they gravitate: Region I is the stability set of equilibrium (C, C) and Region II is the stability set of equilibrium (D, D).[1] In contrast, Regions III and IV are unstable.

---

[1] A lengthy but necessary remark on terminology: There are five concepts that ought to be kept separate, although there are similarities among some of them: stability sets, source sets, stable sets of cooperative games, stable sets of non-cooperative games and basins of attraction of evolutionary games. The stable sets of cooperative games (a.k.a. von Neumann-Morgenstern stable sets) have nothing in common with the rest and are of no direct relevance to this book, which deals exclusively with non-cooperative game theory. I only mention them to caution the reader about yet another source of terminological confusion. The stable sets of non-cooperative games (a.k.a. Kohlberg-Mertens stable sets) are closer

Initial belief conditions in these sets are self-defeating: if players' beliefs belong to one such region, their optimal strategies
will belong to some other region.[2] For purely expository reasons, I will simply ignore Regions III and IV while discussing
the basic notions of stability sets. That is not true of the
subsequent formal analysis.

---

to the area of interest of this book but are refinements of sequential equilibria and, as such, pertain to the connections between games in extensive
form and games in normal form. Here I focus only on normal-form games
so we shall not deal with these problems. Furthermore, the Kohlberg-
Mertens stable sets are sets of equilibria, whereas the stability sets are
sets of strategies. The stability sets are formalized by Harsanyi and Selten in the development of the tracing procedure. The source sets, also
introduced by Harsanyi and Selten, generalize the concept of stability
sets in a sense that will be explained below. For the most part, I refrain
from using the term "source sets" for the most relevant concept because
the way I generalize the tracing procedure blurs some of the distinctions
between these concepts. In addition, "stability sets" better conveys the
basic intuition than does "source sets," which seems something of an infe-
licitous coinage, no doubt induced by the proliferation of game-theoretic
concepts putting a strain on terminology. Unencumbered by terminological constraints, I would have used here my favorite label: "basins of
attraction." This name conveys better what stability sets are about. But
"basins of attraction" is a concept with wide currency in evolutionary
game theory so this could be considered an infraction. A minor one, I
should add, because there are very close connections between stability
sets and basins of attraction. (See, for instance, Binmore and Samuelson
(1999); Young (1998).) In fact, clarifying and formalizing this connection
would be a very interesting avenue of further research. But the group of
users of evolutionary game theory has grown so much both in quantity
and quality that one should engage it with special care. So, I adopt here
the term "stability sets" which, although not my preferred one, has the
advantage of having been introduced by the very creators of the tracing
procedure.

   [2]This is the heart of the distinction between "stability sets" and
"source sets." The way Harsanyi and Selten use these concepts, Regions I and II are stability sets whereas, through the tracing procedure,
initial belief conditions in Regions III and IV can be mapped onto one
of the pure-strategy equilibria of the game, not unlike what happens in
Regions I and II. In this case, the mapping will differ somewhat from the
one that can be obtained for initial belief conditions in I and II. The set
of initial belief conditions mapped onto equilibrium (C, C), be it because
they belong to Region I, or because of the other properties of the tracing
procedure, are its "source set."

Stability sets are closely related to the focal points and tipping effects of the previous chapter. An equilibrium, say (C, C) is focal if each player attaches to it some special property that leads him to expect the other player to choose C. This analysis can be couched in the language of stability sets by saying that Player 1's initial belief conditions about Player 2 are $\alpha_2 = 1$ while Player 2's initial belief conditions about Player 1 are $\alpha_1 = 1$. A focal point equilibrium is an equilibrium such that its strategy profile coincides with the players' initial belief conditions.

But stability sets generalize this analysis. Differing from focal point arguments, and resembling tipping models, stability sets do not assume that the only possible initial beliefs are already equilibrium profiles. In this example, the pair of initial belief conditions $(1/3, 1/3)$ is part of the stability set of (D, D), without itself being an equilibrium. In Figure 3.2, Regions I and II are akin to a two-person Schelling diagram: for every possible set of expectations, they tell us to which equilibrium the players will "tip." For example, if we restrict our attention to initial belief conditions such that $\alpha_1 = \alpha_2 = \bar{\alpha}$, then we conclude that players "tip" toward the equilibrium (D, D) when $\bar{\alpha} < 1/2$ and toward (C, C) when $\bar{\alpha} > 1/2$. A "two-person Schelling diagram" may seem like an oxymoron because, by definition, tipping models imply many agents. But to make it precise, we will have to wait until the formal analysis for large games is developed.

A key property of stability sets, one that I will exploit throughout the entire book, is that they are a continuous function of the game's payoffs, thus offering a clear connection between the structure of the game and its outcomes. To see this point more clearly, modify the collective action game presented above by introducing selective incentives, worth 0.5, that the players receive if they cooperate. Now the game is represented by Figure 3.3.

Now the mixed strategy equilibrium is $\alpha_1^* = 1/4, \alpha_2^* = 1/4$ and the best-response correspondences are:

$$\alpha_1^*(\alpha_2) = \begin{cases} 1 & \text{if } \alpha_2 > 1/4, \\ [0, 1] & \text{if } \alpha_2 = 1/4, \\ 0 & \text{if } \alpha_2 < 1/4. \end{cases}$$

		2	
		C	N
1	C	1.5,1.5	−0.5, 0
	N	0, −0.5	0,0

Figure 3.3: Collective Action with Selective Incentives

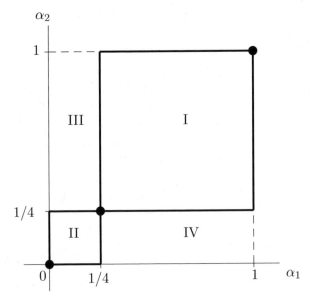

Figure 3.4: Best-response Correspondences of the Collective Action Game with Selective Incentives

Player 2's best-response correspondence $(\alpha_2^*(\alpha_1))$ is exactly analogous. Both can be portrayed in a graph as in Figure 3.4.

This game, like the previous one, has three equilibria, two in pure strategies $((C, C)$ and $(D, D))$ and one in mixed strategies $(\alpha_1 = 1/4, \alpha_2 = 1/4)$. With the new parameters, Region I grows and Region II shrinks: the "tipping point," in this case $(1/4, 1/4)$, moves toward $(0, 0)$; but, the players' preferences being the same as before, this move results from a change in the payoffs that shifts the game's mixed strategy equilibrium.

This is the cornerstone of all the comparative statics results that follow: *The size of an equilibrium's stability set is directly proportional to its probability and in a game with multiple equilibria, the relative size of the different stability sets, and hence their relative likelihood, is a continuous function of the game's payoffs.*

As an example, consider initial belief conditions $(1/3, 1/3)$. In the previous game, these initial belief conditions belonged to Region II because, without selective incentives, if a player believes her counterpart will choose C with probability $1/3$, she should not choose C. But in the game with selective incentives, $(1/3, 1/3)$ is now part of Region I: given the prospect of a payoff of 1.5, and facing a punishment of only -0.5, each player considers that, if the other one is willing to cooperate with probability $1/3$, it is worth participating.

Introducing selective incentives makes coordination more likely: the set of initial belief conditions that lead to cooperation is now larger. Suppose that we want to remain absolutely agnostic about the initial belief conditions these players hold and we represent this agnosticism by assuming that all the points of Regions I and II are equally likely; we may call this a Laplacian assumption.[3] In that case, the areas of both regions are the probability of each equilibrium. In the first case, since both regions are equal, both with area $1/4$, we say that the probability of collective action (equilibrium (C, C)) is 50%. In the second case, Region I is nine times larger than Region II (their respective areas are: $9/16$, $1/16$), then we say that the probability of collective action is 90%. If we believe that only equilibrium points are possible initial belief conditions, as the focal point models do, then none of this holds because we are implicitly assuming that the Regions I and II are empty and their size is immaterial. But this is an unnecessary restriction and tipping games routinely relax it. Accordingly, if we suppose that players may have initial belief conditions out of equilibrium, changes in the relative size of the stability sets are changes in the set of possible states of beliefs that will lead to each equilibrium. As social scientists observing

---

[3]I owe this christening to John Ferejohn.

this game, we can say that, whatever the players' initial belief conditions are, selective incentives increase the likelihood of coordination because now the players do not need to have the same high expectations as before to conclude that it is worthy to cooperate.

If we are not entirely ignorant about the initial belief conditions of these two players, the Laplacian assumption may be too timid and we may want to abandon it. We may, for example, know something about their previous interactions in other instances. Since we know better, we can improve our forecast by assuming a distribution that places higher probability on those initial belief conditions we know to be more likely. If, say, we have evidence that these individuals consider each other unreliable, we may adopt a distribution that places more probability to initial belief conditions around $(0,0)$ than to those around $(1,1)$. But, whatever we do, it will not alter the fundamental issue: changes in the game's payoffs change the areas of Regions I and II.

Consider now the two-player version of the generalized collective action game we have been analyzing. Previously we found that the mixed strategy equilibrium of this game was $(1/(w + 1), 1/(w + 1))$. The best-response correspondences of this game have the same shape as those of Figure 3.4, only their intersection is not at $(1/4, 1/4)$ but at $(1/(w + 1), 1/(w + 1))$. Following the logic of the previous example the probability of successful collective action is given by the relative sizes of Regions I and II. In turn, this relative size is equal to $w^2/(w^2 + 1)$. Under this procedure, we conclude that increases in the payoff of collective action (w) increase the likelihood of its success, just as LPT claims. (The reader should compare this result with the ad hoc LPT result postulated in Section 2.6.4 (pg. 48).)

An example from the physical world may further illustrate this point. Suppose that we want to drop a ball on a very bumpy field, full of holes, and that we are interested in forecasting where the ball will stop. Since the field is so uneven, we know that the ball's final position depends on the exact location where it first touches the ground. If we know the surface of the field, we can even provide a forecast conditional on that location. Now imagine that to drop the ball we use an unreliable mechanism, perhaps a jittery cannon. Then, the ball might touch down anywhere, but we can still devise an imperfect but informative forecast considering the relative size of the field's different basins of attraction. Each hole in the field is a basin of attraction, and gravity will pull to its bottom any ball that lands there. If our field has hundreds of holes, but one of them covers 99% of the field, with very high likelihood, its bottom will be the ball's final location no matter how unreliable our cannon. Once we know the exact shape of the field, the only way to improve our forecast is to learn more about how the cannon jitters.

The field is a good metaphor for the approach I advocate here for collective action problems. The bottom of each hole in the field is an equilibrium: once the ball reaches it, it will not move any further. Once the ball is in the basin of attraction formed by a hole, we can be confident that it will reach that hole's equilibrium point because the only forces that act on it, send it in a downward trajectory. These basins of attraction are equivalent to the stability sets of a game's equilibria. Just as if we know the exact location where the ball touches the ground, we can predict where it will stop, if we know the exact initial belief conditions of the players in a game, we can know the equilibrium they will play. But we do not know what the initial belief conditions are, any more than we know the exact touchdown point of a ball thrown by a jittery cannon. Although this uncertainty makes it impossible to predict exactly the final equilibrium, we can still make informed probabilistic predictions by comparing the size of the stability sets. With more information about the distribution of initial belief conditions, gleaned through, say, detailed ethnographic accounts of the players, we can improve our forecast. This would be the equivalent to learning more about the cannon's tremulous pattern. But this knowledge is a complement of, not a substitute for, the knowledge about the field's shape. Whatever the distribution of initial belief conditions, equilibria with larger stable sets are more likely. This would not be true, however, if we were to assume that a particular stability set has 0 probability so its size would be irrelevant. This is the assumption that users of focal points make, but its wisdom is dubious.

A by-product of the notion of stability sets is that it brings mixed strategy equilibria under a new light. It shows how problematic it is to use such equilibria as a basis for comparative statics. Just as in real life randomized choice is a rarity, so is it in game theory. Players choose mixed strategies in response to a razor-thin condition: exact indifference between pure strategies. Any tiny advantage of one strategy over the other and a player will no longer randomize among them. Players almost never choose mixed strategies, where I use "almost never" in the technical sense of probability theory meaning "with probability 0." In a mixed strategy equilibrium, each player chooses a mixed strategy because he is indifferent among his pure strategies and he is indifferent, in turn, *because* the other player is also choosing a mixed strategy. Analysts willing to ascribe predictive powers to the mixed strategy equilibrium must defend the view that, when making their choices, individuals do not try to maximize their payoff but instead try to make the other players indifferent among their respective strategies.[4]

To see how misguided this is, notice that the mixed strategy equilibrium's stability set is only the equilibrium itself. Players only play it if it is common knowledge among them that this is the equilibrium being played. Any tiny deviation, any mismatch in beliefs, will send players away from this equilibrium. To persist with the metaphor of the field, using the mixed strategy equilibrium as a prediction of the game's outcome would be like predicting that the ball in that example will stop at precisely the ridge that divides the basins of attraction, a location that could only happen if, miraculously, it were to be the touchdown point.

---

[4]An analytical exercise that regards mixed strategy equilibria as possible predictions of the model is carried out by Palfrey and Rosenthal (1983) in their strategic model of voting. This is interesting because the authors, both extremely competent game theorists, are entirely aware of the arguments I make here but do not seem to see them as objections to such a procedure.

While rigorous, the conclusions obtained with the aid of stability sets are compatible with common sense, something to which our everyday parlance attests. When describing collective action problems from an standpoint untrained by the social sciences, we say things such as: "it would take a lot of trust from all parties to do that," or "these difficult conditions would have tried any group's confidence," etc. With expressions of this kind we convey that, while players coordinate according to what they expect from each other, their success depends in part on the objective circumstances they face.

3.2.1 Stability Sets of the Prisoners' Dilemma

The PD has been such an influential game that no analysis of collective action is complete without it. This book's main results come from applying the tracing procedure to games with multiple equilibria and this may give the impression that the PD is beyond the method's purview. This is wrong. It is possible and, in fact, very easy, to study the PD's stability sets. The results, though, do not add anything to our knowledge because PDs have a unique equilibrium and, so, the method of stability sets puts all the probability on that result. Consider the following game (Figure 3.5):

$$
\begin{array}{cc|c|c|}
 & & \multicolumn{2}{c}{2} \\
 & & C & D \\
\cline{3-4}
1 & C & 1,1 & -1,2 \\
\cline{3-4}
 & D & 2,-1 & 0,0 \\
\cline{3-4}
\end{array}
$$

Figure 3.5: Prisoners' Dilemma

Since this game has dominant strategies, we already know how the best-response correspondences look like. But, in the interest of illustration, let's calculate them. Just as before, denote by α_1 the probability that Player 1 chooses C and by α_2 the probability that Player 2 chooses C. We then have the following expected payoffs:

$$
\begin{aligned}
v_1(\alpha_1, \alpha_2) &= \alpha_1\alpha_2 - \alpha_1(1 - \alpha_2) + 2(1 - \alpha_1)\alpha_2 \\
&= 2 - \alpha_1;
\end{aligned}
$$

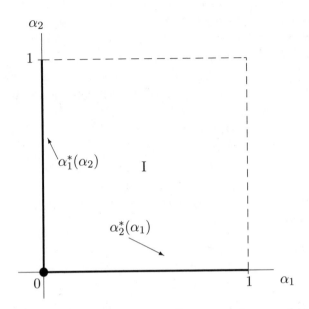

Figure 3.6: Best-response Correspondences of the Prisoners' Dilemma

$$v_2(\alpha_1, \alpha_2) = \alpha_2\alpha_1 - \alpha_2(1 - \alpha_1) + 2(1 - \alpha_2)\alpha_1$$
$$= 2 - \alpha_2.$$

So, the best-response correspondences, depicted in Figure 3.6, are:

$$\alpha_1^*(\alpha_2) = 0;$$
$$\alpha_2^*(\alpha_1) = 0.$$

Because of strategic dominance, these best-response correspondences do not partition the strategy space into different regions, like the other ones did. Regardless of what players believe about each other, their optimal strategy is always D. In other words, the stability set of the equilibrium (D, D) is the entire strategy space. If we were to apply to this game the same idea applied to the other ones and find the probability of its equilibrium by measuring the size of said equilibrium's stability set, we would conclude that (D, D) occurs with probability 1.

Although somewhat trivial, this example already shows that the method of stability sets is more general, not less, than the standard equilibrium analysis, a point we will revisit later. For any game, every conclusion that we obtain from equilibrium analysis can be expressed as a special case of the analysis of its stability sets.

Thus we complete the first examples of games where the analysis of stability sets makes it possible to find the probability of each equilibrium as a continuous function of the payoffs, at once intuitive and consistent with the basic postulates of rational-choice theory. Obviously, this is not enough. Systematic, general results of comparative statics in collective action must cover games with many players. Before presenting the solution to this problem, I will clarify some issues pertaining to stability sets and their connection with the rest of game theory.

3.3 Stability Sets and Other Related Concepts

The concept of stability sets is relatively unknown but it does not appear out of the blue. It has a history going back to the joint effort of Harsanyi and Selten, and it is connected to other concepts and research agendas in game theory. When these connections are clarified, stability sets lose their exotic character and appear in a more familiar light. Although this familiarity may seem disappointing and even suggest that stability sets have nothing new to contribute, it is a good thing: it means that stability sets are part of a broader inquiry in game theory and that we can benefit from their study without having to reject the progress made in other areas.

3.3.1   The Distribution of Initial Belief Conditions and the Problem of Infinite Regress

Stability sets and initial belief conditions form part of the theory of equilibrium selection proposed by Harsanyi and Selten (1988) and they have ever since remained very controversial among game theorists. Given their crucial role in my theory, this controversy must be engaged explicitly.

Much of the debate has to do with the role of rationality and knowledge in games. Suppose that you and I are playing a coordination game like the ones in the previous section and that you need to decide your optimal strategy. To calculate it, you need to know my strategy but this leads to a problem of circularity: while you need to know my strategy, to compute it I need to know yours. You cannot infer my choice unless you compute yours, something you can only do if you know mine ...

Equilibrium analysis is intended to short-circuit this circularity, and its potential for infinite regress, by making it moot. Players could just make up any guess about the other players' choices and compute their optimal strategy according to that guess. If, and only if, all those guesses are an equilibrium profile, circularity will not be a problem: all the guesses will be self-validating.

In a Nash equilibrium, when each player forms a conjecture about the other players' strategies, she assumes they are rational so that their strategies will be the optimal response to whatever she chooses. Formally, this means that a Nash equilibrium supposes common knowledge of rationality, meaning that not only players are rational, they also know this to be true, know all the other players know this, know all players know that all players know this, and so on.

Stability sets broaden the inquiry to include beliefs that are not already equilibrium strategies. To take the example of the first collective action game studied in this chapter, if we say that the players' initial belief conditions are $(1/3, 1/3)$ (which is not an equilibrium point of that game), we are implicitly assuming that none of them is considering the other as a fully rational agent. After all, why would Player 1 believe that Player 2 is choosing the randomization 1/3? It is not an optimal response to any strategy Player 1 may choose, except for 1/2. And in that case, 1/3 is not strictly optimal; it is just as good as any other strategy. When Player 1 attributes a probability of 1/3 to Player 2's choice of C, she is not thinking of Player 2 as an optimizing agent.

It may seem as if this more general approach to common knowledge might lead to a theory without any predictive power because, if accepted, there is no longer any reason to privilege equilibrium profiles over any other outcome of the game. Since equilibria are only a handful of all the possible guesses players can make, players are unlikely to feed their computational procedure with precisely the input that will support them. But, with their development of the tracing procedure (to be discussed below) Harsanyi and Selten have shown that this fear is misplaced at least most of the time. For very large families of games, including all the games considered in this book, it is possible to feed the process with guesses out of equilibrium and still be assured that the simultaneous computations of all the players will arrive at an equilibrium profile. Even if players start off by holding beliefs about each other that are not themselves equilibria, equilibrium outcomes remain relevant predictions of the game because players will react to their initial belief conditions in ways that push them toward an equilibrium.

As any other attempt to relax the assumptions of common knowledge of rationality, the method of stability sets opens the Pandora box of infinite regress. If initial belief conditions are not confined to equilibrium profiles, where are they? Here I adopt the response known as "Harsanyi's doctrine," to wit, that initial belief conditions are themselves common knowledge. Harsanyi's doctrine represents the current orthodoxy in game theory but seems gratuitous.[5] If we are willing to accept that beliefs are not common knowledge, it is not clear that their prior distributions should be. We could just as well assume that those prior distributions are not common knowl-

---

[5]This is a view hinted at by Kreps (1990).

edge but instead come from, say, a meta-prior, that, not being common knowledge, comes from a meta-meta-prior that, in turn, comes from ...

This is a good criticism of the method of stability sets but orthodox game theorists are the least indicated to make it. Strictly speaking, stability sets do not open the Pandora box of infinite regress: such box has always been open in game theory, except that our standard notions of equilibrium pretend otherwise. Stability sets do not make extraneous assumptions about common knowledge; they generalize the ones made by normal solution concepts. All the results of standard game theory follow from assuming, restrictively, that initial belief conditions are concentrated on the equilibria of the game, and not distributed over the entire strategy space. This book's technique simply exposes and generalizes assumptions that are often kept hidden. To reject it on these grounds is to shoot the messenger.

The initial belief conditions correspond to what we call in everyday parlance a group's collective mood: they represent the predispositions to coordinate that the group has attained through some exogenous mechanism. For example, if we believe that a group's members are already highly motivated, and reliable partners for coordination, we can represent this with initial belief conditions heavily concentrated around a probability of choosing C equal to 1, say a beta distribution with very low variance and mean 1.

The exact way in which the size of stability sets translate into probabilities of the different equilibria depends on the distribution we assume. But this does not change the fundamental principle of this book's technique: anything that increases the size of a stability set, increases the probability of its equilibrium. A spatial metaphor may be useful. Suppose I want to calculate the relative volume, as opposed to simply the area, of a room in a house. The exact answer will depend on the ceiling's shape. If the ceiling is flat, areas in the floor plan will translate directly into volumes simply by multiplying them by the ceiling's height. But if the ceiling is not flat, just knowing the floor plan is not enough. At any rate, regardless of the ceiling, I know that any changes in the floor plan that increase the room's area will also increase its volume. The probability of an equilibrium is the analogue of the room's volume; the size of its stability set corresponds to the room's area and the prior distribution to the ceiling's shape. If I take a Laplacian stance, I assume that the ceiling is flat. But I do not need to if I have some extra knowledge about the distribution of the initial belief conditions. The exact distribution is not a fundamental assumption of the model but a degree of freedom that the modeler can change without altering the comparative statics results.

The distribution of initial belief conditions, it should be acknowledged, does not depend on the game's structure and is, as it were, beyond the reach of game theory. Game theory studies the effects of beliefs, not their causes. These causes are the subject matter of other disciplines. Understandably, as game theorists we cringe at being forced to state explicitly our assumptions about the players' initial belief conditions. But we can transform this problem into an opportunity: the resulting clarity on how a group's shared understandings determine its actions allows us to benefit from the knowledge acquired in other social sciences.

3.3.2 Equilibrium Selection and Probabilistic Predictions

Disturbed by the many possible solutions of collective action problems, many game theorists have launched the research program of equilibrium selection, imposing further constraints on the game's equilibria until only one survives. Focal points are special instances of equilibrium selection but, as we have already seen, they are not a systematic theory. If two analysts of a game disagree on the focal point mechanism they prefer, there is no way of settling the matter.

Theories of equilibrium selection replace such mechanisms, derived from the analyst's whims, with other ones based on rigorous microfoundations. But, as much as I borrow from them, especially the version of Harsanyi and Selten, I disagree with their ultimate goal. That is, I agree with the premise, but

not the conclusion, of the following statement of the program
of equilibrium selection, formulated by one of the paramount
game theorists:

> In general, a given game may have several equi-
> libria. [...] Nash equilibrium makes sense only if
> each player knows which strategies the others are
> playing; if the equilibrium recommended by the
> theory is not unique, the players will not have this
> knowledge. Thus it is essential that for each game,
> the theory selects one unique equilibrium from the
> set of all Nash equilibria. (Robert Aumann in his
> *Introduction* to Harsanyi and Selten (1988), pg.
> xi)

In equilibrium, players have self-fulfilling theories about
their counterpart's play; they choose strategies that are optimal given what they believe others will choose. Being self-
fulfilling, these theories are consistent with the rationality
postulates of the game and, as social scientists, we have no
grounds for discriminating among them.

The program I propose acknowledges that in a society individuals may hit upon different belief systems, but tries to
explain how they succeed as guides for navigating life in society. Such program does not need an argument of equilibrium
selection. To the contrary, it retains all the possible equilibria
of a game and then makes sense of that diversity in systematic
ways.

Confronted with the multiplicity of equilibria, many theorists of collective action think it prudent to stop the analysis
at the point of reporting all the possible solutions. Hence,
scholars who invoke focal points and tipping games are reluc-
tant to privilege one solution over the other. In their view,
only history can decide what happens and, as scientists, we
are reduced to writing narratives after the facts. While those
theorists seeking an equilibrium-selection argument want to
suppress the diversity of predictions, these scholars are showing it full deference. I take an intermediate position. I also
believe that when we acknowledge and preserve the multi-

plicity of solutions, we do justice to the nature of the problem. But I do not believe that we should just passively report these solutions, abstaining from any statement about their relative likelihood. We could use the seemingly mundane device used by doctors and meteorologists, who also deal with systems that lack a unique solution: a probability distribution over the possible end-states of the system. Doctors routinely speak about chances of survival; meteorologists routinely speak about chances of rainfall. Their theories are consistent with many possible outcomes, but provide elements to tell which are more likely. Neither profession would exist if their practitioners could only tell their customers that "anything can happen."

These professions remain viable thanks to such probabilistic statements that improve upon a wild guess, that draw from a coherent knowledge of how external forces change the systems they deal with. I believe that, with its knowledge of the impact of payoffs and beliefs over actions, game theory can make equally useful probabilistic statements.

3.3.3   Stability Sets and Evolutionary Games

The analysis of stability sets bears such a close resemblance to the analysis of evolutionary equilibria that the latter will not be discussed here with all the rigor it deserves. Both evolutionary games and stability sets pertain to the game's behavior outside of an equilibrium. Evolutionary arguments offer a detailed temporal dynamic that makes off-equilibrium conditions converge to an equilibrium. Stability sets do not deal with the specifics of the adjustment process although the tracing procedure, the method used to compute them, can serve as one. This is a difference of emphasis and purpose, rather than of conceptual basis. Inside an equilibrium's stability set, any sensible dynamic process, be it based on evolutionary arguments or the tracing procedure, will converge to said equilibrium. Furthermore, as Young (1998) notices, in evolutionary games with the same structure as the ones analyzed here, mixed strategy equilibria are unstable, just as the method of stability sets would conclude.

3.4   The Tracing Procedure

The tracing procedure is a method developed by Harsanyi and Selten (1988) for games with perfect information that characterizes the stability sets and the source sets of the pure-strategy equilibria. Although they introduced it as a stepping stone for their theory of equilibrium selection, I will follow them in this first step and then part company, since I believe that a method of equilibrium selection would do more harm than good by imposing unnecessary blinders. As introduced by its authors, the tracing procedure is of limited scope because they only discuss two-player games and assume Nash play which, as I will show later, is not a fruitful assumption for collective action problems. Their focus on two-player games is only a expository device as Harsanyi and Selten prove powerful theorems that show the applicability of the tracing procedure to large games. Their assumption of Nash play is more substantive but can be relaxed, something I will do later.

Previously I used the metaphor of a field to illustrate the basic principles of the method of stability sets (pg. 96). The same metaphor can be useful to understand the role of the tracing procedure.

In the method of stability sets we are interested in the relative sizes of different basins of attraction in a field. But before we can make measurements on a field we need to know its shape. The tracing procedure is the method that helps us determine it.

Going back to our analogy of a field, imagine that our task is to determine the size and distribution of holes in it but that we only have access to its two-dimensional projection on a screen. Visual inspection of the field, which would have otherwise been the obvious way of determining its shape, is not an option under these circumstances. But there is something else we can do: we can drop balls on different points of the field and watch where they end up going. By carefully recording where we drop the balls and where they stop, we can get a reading of the field's shape.

This is not unlike the procedure followed in many computational simulations and it may well be that in more complex games we can only find sizes of stability sets by intensive use of computers.[6] But that is not necessary for the simple games discussed here. In fact, the characterization of stability sets here leads to tight analytical expressions. This is one of the main reasons I adopted it.

Intuitively, the tracing procedure consists on choosing an arbitrary value of initial belief conditions (the equivalent to a touchdown position for a ball in our metaphor) and follow the behavior of the game's equilibria as the players attain common knowledge of rationality under those initial conditions. This is the same as following the path of a ball until it reaches a stopping point. The method of stability sets uses the tracing procedure to calculate such stopping point, that is, the equilibrium the game reaches, for each possible value of the initial belief conditions. In other words, if the tracing procedure follows the path of each initial touchdown point, the method of stability sets aggregates the results for all those points.

The tracing procedure requires more mathematical reasoning than what is usual in basic game theory (though not by much). Understandably, some readers will thus prefer not to dwell too much on it. In what follows, I will structure my presentation to help those readers move faster. But while they can dispense with the mathematical details, they may benefit from seeing the tracing procedure in action at least once. So, I will offer here a simple example, solved with the aid of a diagram. By necessity, this will leave some technicalities out of the picture because there is no point in trying to imitate the mathematical depth and rigor that earned Harsanyi and Selten their privileged place in game theory.

We already saw that if the initial belief conditions in the stability set of, say, equilibrium (C, C) become common knowl-

---

[6]Such a computational method has been used, for instance, in several applications of game theory to political science. Although not directly related to this book's purpose, there are two examples so prominent that they deserve special mention: the procedure used by Shepsle and Laver (1996) to determine the size of "winsets" in a cabinet-formation game and the procedure used by Roemer (2001a) to determine the region of "party unanimity Nash equilibria" in a game of electoral competition with multi-dimensional policy spaces.

edge, players will realize that their rational response is (C, C). But this vague intuition does not deal rigorously with common knowledge, a deficiency that the tracing procedure remedies.

The tracing procedure gradually phases in common knowledge and traces the reactions of the players along the process. Imagine that you are Player 1 and have to decide what to do in any of the 2×2 games presented above. You have two pieces of information about Player 2: you know that Player 2 is a rational agent, much like you, and you assess at $1/3$ the probability that he chooses C, so that this value of $1/3$ is your initial belief about him. These two bits of information are inconsistent as we already saw, because if Player 2 is rational, he has no reason to choose the randomization $1/3$. Either one is true, but not both, and you cannot know which is it; in making your final decision, it would be prudent to keep in mind how confident you are in each of them. If you are very confident on your initial belief conditions, you trust your gut-feeling as we often say, you can assign to them a probability of, say, $4/5$ and base your decision on the combination of both statements, each weighted by its respective probability.

Such is the method Harsanyi and Selten propose to phase in common knowledge of rationality. They let the players' belief in their initial belief conditions vanish gradually, something they accomplish by generating a family of games, called **auxiliary games**, associated with the original game and parameterized by a scalar $0 \le \lambda \le 1$. All the games in this family share the same basic structure, viz. the strategy space, but differ on the way their payoff functions are defined. When $\lambda = 0$, each player's payoff function depends only on her strategies and her initial belief conditions about other players (as opposed to those players' strategies). When $\lambda = 1$, the payoff functions depend fully on every player's strategies: this is just the original game. In contrast, $\lambda = 0$ represents the players' decision problem when they guess what the other players will do solely on the basis of their impressions about those players and without even assuming that they are rational. At $\lambda = 0$, players respond to what they believe about other players, beliefs that may come from any source, their own prejudices, previous experiences with similar players, etc. In general, those beliefs do not need to be consistent with any principle of rationality. Rationality will come in later as λ increases. If A_i denotes Player i's strategy set and B_{-i} his set of initial belief conditions about the remaining players, i's payoff is a function of her strategy α_i and her specific beliefs β_{-i}, $v_i(\alpha_i, \beta_{-i})$ when $\lambda = 0$ and $v_i(\alpha_i, \alpha_{-i})$ when $\lambda = 1$. As the parameter λ moves from 0 to 1, the payoff function of the player is defined as:

$$v_i^\lambda(\alpha_i, \alpha_{-i}) = (1 - \lambda)v_i(\alpha_i, \beta_{-i}) + \lambda v_i(\alpha_i, \alpha_{-i}).$$

The tracing procedure computes the equilibria of all the λ games for any given profile of initial belief conditions, generating several paths of equilibria, possibly with ruptures and ramifications. A profile of initial belief conditions β is mapped into an equilibrium α^* of the game if there is a continuous path leading from the equilibrium of the game when $\lambda = 0$ to α^* when $\lambda = 1$. For a game with $\lambda = 0$ and initial belief conditions in a stability set, the path will lead to this stability set's equilibrium without branching out. Thanks to this principle, the tracing procedure gives us a rigorous rule to compute the stability set of each pure-strategy equilibrium. Knowing the stability sets, we can calculate their size and probability in much the same way as we did in the previous 2×2 examples.

3.4.1   A Numerical Example

An example may help. Consider the game represented in Figure 3.1 (pg. 88). When I introduced verbally the notion of stability sets, I showed that while initial belief conditions $(1/4, 1/4)$ belong to the stability set of equilibrium $(0, 0)$, the initial belief conditions $(3/4, 3/4)$ belong to that of $(1, 1)$. Let's see how the tracing procedure formalizes this.

Just as I denoted with α_1, α_2 the players' strategies, β_1, β_2 will now denote the initial belief conditions. Equation 3.1 represents the expected payoffs of Player 1 as a function of both players' strategies. We can create a similar function in which Player 1's payoff depends on her strategy and her initial beliefs about Player 2: that would be the payoff function when $\lambda = 0$.

The solution of the game when $\lambda = 0$ will differ in two important ways from the solution when $\lambda = 1$. First, as Harsanyi and Selten proved, there will be only one equilibrium even if the original game has more than one. Second, the strategies of said equilibrium will depend on the value of the initial belief conditions chosen.

These two properties are what make the method suitable for the purpose of characterizing stability sets. The equilibrium when $\lambda = 0$ is the beginning of the tracing path. In keeping with our field metaphor, it is the first point the ball will reach after touching down and, if our procedure of recording the endpoints is to work, we need that such endpoints depend on the specific touchdown point. The tracing procedure satisfies these two properties.

In this particular game, if we let $\lambda = 0$, we obtain the payoff functions:

$$
\begin{aligned}
v_1^0(\alpha_1, \beta_2) &= \alpha_1(2\beta_2 - 1); \\
v_2^0(\beta_1, \alpha_2) &= \alpha_2(2\beta_1 - 1).
\end{aligned}
$$

A linear combination of these new functions and the one of Equation 3.1 will give us the payoff function for any auxiliary game (and the corresponding analogue for Player 2):

$$
\begin{aligned}
v_1^\lambda(\alpha_1, \alpha_2, \beta_1, \beta_2) &= \lambda\alpha_1(2\alpha_2 - 1) + (1 - \lambda)\alpha_1(2\beta_2 - 1); \\
v_2^\lambda(\alpha_1, \alpha_2, \beta_1, \beta_2) &= \lambda\alpha_2(2\alpha_1 - 1) + (1 - \lambda)\alpha_2(2\beta_1 - 1).
\end{aligned}
$$

To see the tracing procedure at work, consider first initial belief conditions $(1/4, 1/4)$. That is, let $\beta_1 = \beta_2 = 1/4$ so that the payoff functions become:

$$
\begin{aligned}
v_1^\lambda(\alpha_1, \alpha_2, 1/4, 1/4) &= \lambda\alpha_1(2\alpha_2 - 1) - (1 - \lambda)\alpha_1/2 \\
&= \alpha_1\left[\lambda(2\alpha_2 - 1) - \frac{1 - \lambda}{2}\right]; \\
v_2^\lambda(\alpha_1, \alpha_2, 1/4, 1/4) &= \lambda\alpha_2(2\alpha_1 - 1) - (1 - \lambda)\alpha_2/2 \\
&= \alpha_2\left[\lambda(2\alpha_1 - 1) - \frac{1 - \lambda}{2}\right].
\end{aligned}
$$

From this we can obtain the following best-response correspondences:

$$\alpha_1^*(\alpha_2) \;=\; \begin{cases} 1 & \text{if} \quad \alpha_2 > \frac{1+\lambda}{4\lambda}, \\ [0,1] & \text{if} \quad \alpha_2 = \frac{1+\lambda}{4\lambda}, \\ 0 & \text{if} \quad \alpha_2 < \frac{1+\lambda}{4\lambda}, \end{cases}$$

with an entirely analogue expression for $\alpha_2^*(\alpha_1)$.

For any value $\lambda < 1/3$, these best-response correspondences can only be satisfied by $\alpha_1^* = \alpha_2^* = 0$. Crucially, this same equilibrium exists for any other value of λ. But, when $\lambda = 1/3$, $(1 + \lambda)/4\lambda = 1$ and a new equilibrium becomes feasible: $\alpha_1^* = \alpha_2^* = 1$. For values of λ larger than $1/3$ this equilibrium will always exist and, likewise, a mixed strategy equilibrium becomes now feasible: $\alpha_1^* = \alpha_2^* = (1 + \lambda)/4\lambda$.

3.4.2 An Illustrative Diagram

Since the game is symmetric and we are considering initial belief conditions that are also symmetric, we can summarize the information about the equilibria of the different auxiliary games in Figure 3.7.

The horizontal axis represents λ and the vertical axis represents $\alpha^* = \alpha_1^* = \alpha_2^*$. Thanks to the game's symmetry we can represent in two dimensions what would be in all rigor a three-dimensional graph. The thick solid line along the horizontal axis represents that $\alpha^* = 0$ is an equilibrium for any value of λ. Instead, the other two equilibria of the game only exist for values of λ larger than $1/3$. In the words of Harsanyi and Selten, with initial belief conditions $\beta_1 = \beta_2 = 1/4$, the only **feasible path**, that is, the only continuous path of equilibria as we vary λ, is $\alpha^* = 0$.

Conceptually, this means that, as we phase in common knowledge of rationality, the players will move continuously along the feasible path.[7] Instead, it would take a sudden, unexplained shift in their strategies for the players to move

---

[7]In this particular case, they will not change their strategies at all. This is typical of stability sets, but not of source sets.

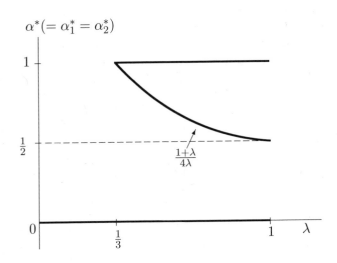

Figure 3.7: Tracing Paths for the Collective Action Game with Initial Beliefs $\beta_1 = \beta_2 = 1/4$

to any of the other equilibria. If players start off with initial belief conditions $(1/4, 1/4)$, as they attain common knowledge of rationality they will react in ways that lead them to choose $(0, 0)$ but they will have no reason to jump to any other paths.

Let's look briefly at the case with priors $(3/4, 3/4)$. If we repeat the calculations above, we obtain the following best-response correspondences:

$$\alpha_1^*(\alpha_2) \;\; = \;\; \begin{cases} 1 & \text{if } \alpha_2 > \frac{3\lambda-1}{4\lambda}, \\ [0,1] & \text{if } \alpha_2 = \frac{3\lambda-1}{4\lambda}, \\ 0 & \text{if } \alpha_2 < \frac{3\lambda-1}{4\lambda}, \end{cases}$$

with an entirely analogue expression for $\alpha_2^*(\alpha_1)$.

Now the situation is reversed. The only equilibrium that exists for every value of λ is $\alpha_1^* = \alpha_2^* = 1$. The equilibria $\alpha_1^* = \alpha_2^* = 0$ and $\alpha_1^* = \alpha_2^* = (3\lambda - 1)/4\lambda$ are only feasible for values $\lambda \geq 1/3$. This results in the diagram in Figure 3.8.

This diagram tells us that the tracing procedure maps initial belief conditions $(3/4, 3/4)$ onto the equilibrium $(1, 1)$.

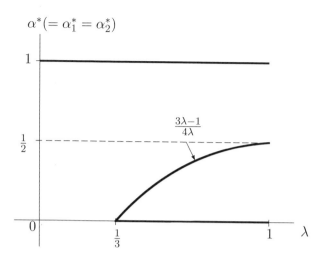

Figure 3.8: Tracing Paths for the Collective Action Game with Initial Beliefs $\beta_1 = \beta_2 = 3/4$

This confirms our initial claim that those priors belong to the stability set of cooperation.

3.5 Nash Play in Collective Action Problems with Large Numbers of Players

While stability sets are straightforward in 2×2 examples, some difficulties arise when we extend them to large games. One such case has to do with the choice of the appropriate equilibrium concept.

Nash equilibrium is the standard solution concept in much of game theory and it is already taken for granted in most of the literature on collective action. But Nash equilibrium does not deal adequately with some aspects of coordination among large groups.

Our everyday talk about collective action and the rational-choice models of focal points and tipping games recognize the need of behavioral statements that apply to all the members of a group, or at least to a significant part of them. We often say that the masses are "apathetic," or "worked up," or "reaching the boiling point" and all the other expressions that observers, journalists and secret informers use to describe a situation involving the potential for collective action. Likewise, the analyses based on focal points and tipping models rest on the idea that groups can have "high" or "low" expectations about themselves. Cooperation is focal if, when thinking about other players, each individual in the game expects them to cooperate. Tipping phenomena depend on the confidence players place on high (or low) turnout levels.

According to the theory of focal points, an equilibrium is focal if players can discern in it some special property and thereby be prompted to recognize that the remaining players will coordinate around it. Implicitly, this assumes that players are not choosing their strategies independently of each other. Consider a three-player version of Schelling's famous example of choosing a meeting time and place at random in New York. In his analysis, if there is something focal about "noon at Grand Central," the players' strategies are not statistically independent. If Player 1 knows that Player 2 will choose "noon at Grand Central," this allows him to infer something about Player 3's strategy. This violates the assumption of Nash play because if players are choosing their strategies independently, knowing the choice of one tells us nothing about the choice of others.

Something similar happens with tipping levels. Analyses of collective action often claim that the expectations of a group move toward a tipping point.[8] If we claim that expectations about a group's behavior can tip, we are implicitly assuming that individuals do not choose their strategies independently because knowing that some members of the group are more likely to cooperate tells us something about the likelihood of other members' cooperation.

---

[8] This is, for example, Laitin's interpretation (Laitin, 1998) about the survival prospects of the Russian languages in the former Soviet Union.

In any society, individuals have shared experiences of their environment, experiences that shape their beliefs and actions. Technically, this implies that such actions are statistically correlated across individuals. In that case, the statistical independence assumed by Nash equilibrium is simply incorrect. Critics of rational-choice theory often claim that individuals are not isolated computers of optimal decisions. Perhaps unwittingly, this claim objects to the assumption of Nash play, that is, the assumption that players' strategies are always statistically independent.

But this is a self-imposed constraint that game theory does not need. The framework of Nash play can be generalized: as Robert Aumann (1974) proved with his work on correlated equilibria, it is possible to compute solutions for a game that, while entirely consistent with individual optimizing behavior, do not assume strict independence among all the players' strategies. Such solutions are known as correlated equilibria.

Although not as popular as Nash equilibria, correlated equilibria are well-understood in the game-theoretic literature, are often simpler to compute and are already considered the necessary starting point for the analysis of games with communication, where players can affect each other's choices in extra-strategic interactions.[9] Correlated equilibria are more general than Nash equilibria: every Nash equilibrium of a game is a correlated equilibrium, but not vice versa. Thus, the results I will obtain would also hold, albeit in a less interesting form, if they were applied to Nash equilibria.

Such statistical correlation does not require any deliberate attempt at coordination among the agents. Even if everyone is forming beliefs and choosing actions independently, just the fact that such beliefs and actions stem from publicly available information makes them statistically correlated.

Let's make this precise. To fix ideas, imagine that we are told by a perceptive journalist that Ruritania's dispossessed peasants are becoming restive. He has travelled through Ruritania's countryside witnessing how entire families of squat-

---

[9]See, for instance, Myerson (1991); Heath (2003); Johnson (1993).

ters, indentured laborers, small landowners flood the villages, expelled by the landed oligarchy as it clears the land in preparation for the imminent bonanza in cattle-growing. He has interviewed peasants, heard the stories of loan sharks, burned huts, hired thugs, corrupt judges and so on.

Determined to verify firsthand reports about an incipient peasant insurgency, we go to one of Ruritania's villages to talk to the locals about the support such a movement may enjoy. We are given the following statistical information: 10% of the village's population is made up by peasants who have arrived there fleeing the abuses in the countryside; the other 90% are lifelong town dwellers. Among the peasants, sympathy for the insurgency is at a level of 30% whereas among the town dwellers it is 5%. This means that, for any individual chosen at random, the probability of her being an insurgency sympathizer is 7.5% and that, in addition, the probability of her being both a peasant and a sympathizer is 3%.

For any two members of the same category (peasants, town dwellers), even if they are total strangers, who are not aware of each other's existence, their opinions are statistically correlated. More precisely, they are *conditionally independent* given their category, but not entirely independent.

Consider, for instance, Citizens 1 and 2, two peasants, and use $P(\cdot|\cdot)$ to express conditional probabilities. The probability of Citizen i being a sympathizer of the insurgency (denoted by s_i) given that she is a peasant (p_i) is $P(s_i|p_i) = 0.3$. Since 1 and 2 are total strangers, we surmise that their opinions are chosen independently. In fact, they are conditionally independent: if we know that they are peasants, knowing the opinion of one is of no help in forecasting the opinion of the other. More rigorously:[10]

$$P(s_1|p_1, p_2, s_2) = P(s_1|p_1, p_2).$$

Applying the definition of conditional probabilities, we can verify that:

---

[10]This definition of conditional independence follows the work of Dawid (1979).

$$P(s_1|p_1, p_2, s_2) = \frac{P(s_1, p_1, p_2, s_2)}{P(p_1, p_2, s_2)}$$

$$= \frac{0.03 \cdot 0.03}{0.1 \cdot 0.03}$$

$$= 0.3,$$

$$P(s_1|p_1, p_2) = \frac{P(s_1, p_1, p_2)}{P(p_1, p_2)}$$

$$= \frac{0.03 \cdot 0.1}{0.1 \cdot 0.1}$$

$$= 0.3.$$

But, their opinions are not entirely independent. If both citizens are peasants, but all we know is that they belong to the same group (an event that, in terms of set functions is: $p_1, p_2 \cup \neg p_1, \neg p_2$), knowing the opinion of one contains information about the other's. Formally: $P(s_1|s_2, (p_1, p_2 \cup \neg p_1, \neg p_2)) \neq P(s_1|(p_1, p_2 \cup \neg p_1, \neg p_2))$:

$$P(s_1|p_1, p_2 \cup \neg p_1, \neg p_2) = \frac{P(s_1, (p_1, p_2 \cup \neg p_1, \neg p_2))}{P(p_1, p_2 \cup \neg p_1, \neg p_2)}$$

$$= \frac{0.03 \cdot 0.1 + 0.045 \cdot 0.9}{0.1^2 + 0.9^2}$$

$$\approx 0.053,$$

$$P(s_1|s_2, (p_1, p_2 \cup \neg p_1, \neg p_2)) = \frac{P(s_1, s_2, (p_1, p_2 \cup \neg p_1, \neg p_2))}{P(s_2, (p_1, p_2 \cup \neg p_1, \neg p_2))}$$

$$= \frac{0.03^2 + 0.045^2}{0.03 \cdot 0.1 + 0.045 \cdot 0.9}$$

$$\approx 0.067.$$

This is nothing new. Serious pollsters use this fact to design representative samples; instead of surveying individuals at random, they make sure that different categories in their polls are represented with adequate weights, lest they draw spurious conclusions about opinions in one group from opinions in another.

This example illustrates that, as long as individuals have a common observational basis for their opinions, preferences and strategies (in this case, being a peasant, as opposed to being a town dweller), those opinions, preferences and strategies, although arrived at independently by each individual, will display statistical correlation. The notion of correlated equilibrium formalizes this for the case of strategic choices. Just as in Nash equilibrium, in a correlated equilibrium, each player is choosing her strategy optimally given what the other players are doing. The only difference is that a correlated equilibrium recognizes that there is no reason for those strategies to be statistically independent, given that they result from a set of common observations.

3.6   An Example of Correlated Equilibria[*]

Correlated equilibria are not very popular in game-theoretic applications so some readers might benefit from seeing an example fully worked out. To that end, consider the collective action game we have been studying throughout these chapters, represented in Figure 3.9:

Figure 3.9: Collective Action

Previously we studied the solution to this game assuming that each player chooses her strategy independently of the others. Now suppose that a central authority solves this game and issues non-binding suggestions to each player in isolation. Each set of orders results in a probability distribution over all the possible outcomes of the game and, being unenforceable, the only suggestions the authority can consider are those that players find in their own interest. Let's denote as μ_{CC} the probability of outcome (C, C), as μ_{DD} that of (D, D), and so on. This authority's task is to find values of all these μ's such that they all add up to 1, none of them is negative (both conditions are needed to have a real probability distribution),

---

[*]Technical section.

and every player has incentives to follow the suggestion they embody (incentive-compatibility constraints).

For example, Player 1 will be instructed to play C with probability $\mu_{CC} + \mu_{CD}$. So, the incentive-compatibility constraint for this particular strategy says that for Player 1 the expected value of obeying the suggestion is larger than the expected value of deviating:

$$\mu_{CC}(w-0) + \mu_{CD}(-1-0) \geq 0. \tag{3.2}$$

Extending this reasoning to all strategies and players, we obtain the remaining incentive-compatibility constraints:

$$\mu_{DC}(0-w) + \mu_{DD}(0--1) \geq 0, \tag{3.3}$$
$$\mu_{CC}(w-0) + \mu_{DC}(-1-0) \geq 0, \tag{3.4}$$
$$\mu_{CD}(0-w) + \mu_{DD}(0--1) \geq 0. \tag{3.5}$$

To these we add the probability constraints μ_{CC}, μ_{CD}, μ_{DC}, $\mu_{DD} \geq 0$ and $\mu_{CC} + \mu_{CD} + \mu_{DC} + \mu_{DD} = 1$.

Every Nash equilibrium of this game is a correlated equilibrium. For example, the equilibrium in pure strategies (C, C) sets $\mu_{CC} = 1$ and the remaining values at 0. This assignment of values satisfies Inequalities 3.2 - 3.5 and the probability constraints. The reader can verify that the same is true with equilibrium (D, D) (where $\mu_{DD} = 1$) and with the mixed strategy equilibrium where each player randomizes with probability $1/w$ of choosing C.[11]

But there are many other correlated equilibria that are not Nash equilibria. One example is: $\mu_{CC} = p$, $\mu_{DD} = 1 - p$ for any $0 < p < 1$. These probabilities cannot be accomplished if both players choose their strategies independently but it is easy to verify that they fulfill the incentive-compatibility constraints. One way of interpreting these equilibria would be if the central authority tosses a coin with probability p of heads and suggests both players choose C when heads comes

---

[11]In this latter case, the values are: $\mu_{CC} = \frac{1}{w^2}, \mu_{DC} = \frac{w-1}{w^2}, \mu_{CD} = \frac{w-1}{w^2}, \mu_{DD} = \left(\frac{w-1}{w}\right)^2$.

up. The incentive-compatibility constraints constitute a set of linear inequalities so that there is a continuum of correlated equilibria, even for 2×2 games.

Nash play is an unsatisfactory assumption for the analysis of collective action, and an appropriate model should assume that players correlate their decisions with one another. Correlated equilibria are, then, the right formalism. Regretfully, even very simple games have a continuum of correlated equilibria, making the task of obtaining comparative statics very difficult.[12]

3.7 Correlated Equilibrium: A Formal Definition*

The appropriate solution concept for collective action problems is the correlated equilibrium, introduced by Aumann (1974). Correlated equilibria can be usefully visualized as equilibria of a game with a communication system where players have no incentive to deviate from the strategy recommended by a mediator (Myerson, 1991), a property that helps us characterize them in a convenient manner.

Whereas Nash equilibria are strategy profiles, correlated equilibria are probability distributions over strategy profiles. This is yet one more demonstration that correlated equilibria are more general than Nash equilibria; we can retrieve all the Nash equilibria of a game by focusing only on those correlated equilibria that put all the probabilistic weight on one specific profile.

---

[12]Perhaps not completely impossible. Tsebelis (1990), one of the few applications of correlated equilibria to political science that I have encountered, uses an ingenious graphical procedure to obtain results similar in spirit to the kind of comparative statics I want to develop here. But he studies applications to two-player games so it remains to be seen how that approach could be extended to large games. I submit that the theory developed in this book generalizes the method used by Tsebelis.

*Technical section.

A probability distribution μ defined over the strategy set A is a **correlated equilibrium** of game Γ if:

$$\sum_{a_{-i} \in A_{-i}} \mu(a) \sum_{\omega \in \{0,1\}} u(a_i, g(a, \omega)) \pi(\omega \mid a)$$

$$\geq \sum_{a_{-i} \in A_{-i}} \mu(a) \sum_{\omega \in \{0,1\}} u(a_i', g((a_i', a_{-i}), \omega)) \pi(\omega \mid a_i', a_{-i})$$

for every player $i \in N$ and for every pair of strategies $a_i, a_i' \in A_i$.

Since our goal here is analytical, we shall impose some assumptions on the probabilistic distributions to make them easier to describe and compute. From now on, we shall consider distributions that satisfy the following conditions:

Assumption 5 (Anonymity) *A probability distribution ν is said to be* anonymous *if for any permutation $\langle i \rangle$ of the players,* $\nu(a_1, \ldots, a_N) = \nu(a_{\langle 1 \rangle}, \ldots, a_{\langle N \rangle})$.

Assumption 6 (Convergence) *A probability distribution ν is said to be* convergent *if there exists a constant γ_ν such that:*

$$\lim_{N \to \infty} \sum_a \nu(a) \gamma(a) = \gamma_\nu.$$

Anonymity means that the probability distribution assigns weight to the different action profiles considering only the actions themselves and not on the players performing them. Convergence means that, as the number of players goes to infinity, the variance of the aggregate turnout goes to zero. Not only these two assumptions greatly simplify the task of computing equilibria, they are also natural for the analysis of large games. Although I will not show this explicitly, the reader can verify that the distributions considered in this analysis include the standard symmetric Nash equilibria typical of the study of large games.

These two assumptions have an implication that is important in its own right. If ν is anonymous and convergent, the probability with which a player is called upon to cooperate is the same for all players and converges to the asymptotic level of aggregate turnout. To formalize this, introduce indicator random variables $I(C_i|a)$ defined to be 1 if $a_i = C_i$ and 0 otherwise. In other words, $I(C_i|a)$ indicates whether Player i is cooperating in the strategy profile a. The following lemma provides a technical and convenient summary of this implication. Because the lemma is a straightforward by-product of anonymity, I omit its proof.

Lemma 1 *If ν is anonymous, then, for any two players i and j:*

$$\lim_{N \to \infty} \sum_a \nu(a)I(C_i|a) = \lim_{N \to \infty} \sum_a \nu(a)I(C_j|a) = \gamma_\nu.$$

3.8   Tracing Correlated Equilibria[*]

The tracing procedure formalizes how different priors lead to different equilibria as they become common knowledge. The following framework generalizes that of Harsanyi and Selten.

While they define the tracing procedure for Nash equilibria, here I extend it to cover the case of correlated equilibria. It is easy to verify that the definitions given in this section coincide with those of Harsanyi and Selten for Nash equilibria.

Let $B_i, \Delta(B_i)$ be replicas of $A_i, \Delta(A_i)$ respectively. Define a **separable version** of game Γ as a game identical to Γ in every respect except that the Bernoulli utility functions are defined as: $u_i : A_i \times_{j \neq i} B_j \times \Omega \to \Re$ so that:

$$u_i((a_i, b_{-i}), \omega) = u_i(a_i, g((a_i, b_{-i}), \omega)$$

and the outcome function is $g : A_i \times_{j \neq i} B_j \times \Omega \to \mathcal{O}$. Consequently, the probability of ω is conditioned on (a_i, b_{-i}) so that we can write: $\pi_i(\omega \mid (a_i, b_{-i}))$.[13]

Introduce a parameter $0 \leq \lambda \leq 1$. The parameterized game Γ^λ is a game identical to Γ in every respect except that the Bernoulli utility functions are:

---

[*]Technical section.

[13]Strictly speaking, π_i varies across players. However, in large games these discrepancies vanish and play no substantial role.

$$u_i^\lambda(a, b, \omega) = \lambda u_i((a_i, a_{-i}), \omega) + (1 - \lambda)u_i((a_i, b_{-i}), \omega).$$

Accordingly, we need to redefine the expected utility conditional on state ω. To that end, define the function $E(u_i^\lambda(a \mid \omega))$ as:

$$E(u_i^\lambda(a, b, \omega)) = \lambda u_i(a, \omega)\pi(\omega \mid a) + (1 - \lambda)u_i((a_i, b_{-i}), \omega)\pi(\omega \mid a_i, b_{-i}).$$

Let $\eta : B \to [0, 1]$ be a probability distribution over B (i.e., $\eta(b) \geq 0, \sum_{b \in B} \eta(b) = 1$). This distribution is called the **initial belief condition** of Γ. The tracing procedure computes the solutions for all the members of the family of games Γ^λ. When $\lambda = 0$, each player's payoff function depends only on her priors and not on the other players' strategies so the equilibrium results from solving each player's decision problem separately. When extended to correlated equilibria, this method finds correlated strategies such that the mediator's instruction to each player are incentive-compatible given this player's prior beliefs over the behavior of others, as captured by η. A distribution μ will be called a **correlated equilibrium of Γ^λ** if:

$$\sum_{a_{-i} \in A_{-i}} \sum_{b_{-i} \in B_{-i}} \mu(a)\eta(b) \sum_{\omega \in \{0,1\}} E(u^\lambda(a, b, \omega))$$

$$\geq \sum_{a_{-i} \in A_{-i}} \sum_{b_{-i} \in B_{-i}} \mu(a)\eta(b) \sum_{\omega \in \{0,1\}} E(u^\lambda((a_i', a_{-i}), b, \omega)), \quad (3.6)$$

for every player $i \in N$ and every pair of strategies $a_i, a_i' \in A_i$.

Let E^λ be the set of correlated equilibria of Γ^λ. $X(\Gamma, \eta)$ is the graph of the correspondence $\lambda \to E^\lambda$. It will be called the **tracing graph** of Γ, given η.

Each member of the tracing graph will be of the form (λ, μ) where λ is the value of the tracing parameter and μ is an equilibrium of Γ^λ. If graph X contains a path L connecting $x(0, \mu^0)$ and $x(1, \mu^1)$, then L is called a **feasible path**. Finally, the set of priors η belongs to the **stability set** of equilibrium μ if every feasible path in $X(\Gamma, \eta)$ has μ as its endpoint.

Thus far, we have been involved in purely definitional work. It is now time to put the method of stability sets to work. In this section I will apply the method to the general structure laid out in Chapter 2 (Model 0) and in the next chapter I will show how the different assumptions of each model of collective action lead to different implications.

We can decompose the inequality defining the correlated equilibria (Inequality 3.6) into inequalities pertaining each of the strategies. So, μ is a correlated equilibrium of game Γ^λ if the following two conditions hold simultaneously, for every player i.

$$\sum_{a_{-i} \in A_{-i}} \sum_{b_{-i} \in B_{-i}} \mu(a)\eta(b)I(C_i|a) \sum_{\omega \in \{0,1\}} E(u^\lambda((C_i, a_{-i}), b, \omega))$$

$$\geq \sum_{a_{-i} \in A_{-i}} \sum_{b_{-i} \in B_{-i}} \mu(a)\eta(b)I(C_i|a) \sum_{\omega \in \{0,1\}} E(u^\lambda((D_i, a_{-i}), b, \omega));$$

$$\sum_{a_{-i} \in A_{-i}} \sum_{b_{-i} \in B_{-i}} \mu(a)\eta(b)(1 - I(C_i|a)) \sum_{\omega \in \{0,1\}} E(u^\lambda((D_i, a_{-i}), b, \omega))$$

$$\geq \sum_{a_{-i} \in A_{-i}} \sum_{b_{-i} \in B_{-i}} \mu(a)\eta(b)(1 - I(C_i|a)) \sum_{\omega \in \{0,1\}} E(u^\lambda((C_i, a_{-i}), b, \omega)).$$

Using the definitions of expected utility and the game's parameters, we can now introduce the following substitutions:

$$\sum_{\omega \in \{0,1\}} E(u^\lambda((C_i, a_{-i}), b, \omega)) = \lambda[(w_1 - w_3)F(\gamma(C_i, a_{-i})) + w_3] +$$
$$(1 - \lambda)[(w_1 - w_3)F(\gamma(C_i, b_{-i})) + w_3],$$

$$\sum_{\omega \in \{0,1\}} E(u^\lambda((D_i, a_{-i}), b, \omega)) = \lambda[(w_2 - w_4)F(\gamma(D_i, a_{-i})) + w_4] +$$
$$(1 - \lambda)[(w_2 - w_4)F(\gamma(D_i, b_{-i})) + w_4].$$

Since we are dealing with convergent measures, in the limit, as the number of players grows to infinity, these expressions can be simplified even further so that the inequalities that describe the correlated equilibrium become:

$$\gamma_\mu(\lambda[(w_1 - w_3)F(\gamma_\mu) + w_3] + (1 - \lambda)[(w_1 - w_3)F(\gamma_\eta) + w_3])$$
$$\geq \gamma_\mu(\lambda[(w_2 - w_4)F(\gamma_\mu) + w_4] + (1 - \lambda)[(w_2 - w_4)F(\gamma_\eta) + w_4]),$$
$$(1 - \gamma_\mu)(\lambda[(w_2 - w_4)F(\gamma_\mu) + w_4] + (1 - \lambda)[(w_2 - w_4)F(\gamma_\eta) + w_4])$$
$$\geq (1 - \gamma_\mu)(\lambda[(w_1 - w_3)F(\gamma_\mu) + w_3] + (1 - \lambda)[(w_1 - w_3)F(\gamma_\eta) + w_3]).$$

These inequalities allow us to compute the equilibria of all the auxiliary games during the tracing procedure. I will immediately simplify them somewhat more, but that simplification should not be buried in a purely technical section.

3.9   Tracing Equilibria in Large Games

The preceding section discussed the mathematical details behind the tracing procedure in large games. It may well be the part of the book with the highest mathematical requirements. But it results in two inequalities that will reappear over and over again: even readers not interested in the previous discussion might benefit from seeing them.

Let's consider the case where all players have identical payoffs (e.g., $w_{1i} = w_1$ for every player i). Later I will relax this assumption but in the meantime it greatly simplifies matters. Then, we can define the following function of the game's payoff structure:

$$W \equiv \frac{w_4 - w_3}{(w_1 - w_3) - (w_2 - w_4)}.$$

The analysis of the previous section concludes that, subject to the simplifying assumptions stated:

- It is possible to summarize the relevant information regarding initial belief conditions in an aggregate level of expected turnout γ_η, a share of expected cooperators, defined between 0 and 1.

- It is possible to represent any equilibrium of a collective action game by an aggregate level of turnout γ_μ, that also varies between 0 and 1.

- An equilibrium of any given auxiliary game along the tracing path must satisfy the following inequalities:

$$(\lambda F(\gamma_\mu) + (1 - \lambda)F(\gamma_\eta))\gamma_\mu \; \geq \; \gamma_\mu W, \qquad (3.7)$$

$$(\lambda F(\gamma_\mu) + (1 - \lambda)F(\gamma_\eta))(1 - \gamma_\mu) \; \leq \; (1 - \gamma_\mu)W. \qquad (3.8)$$

With these inequalities we can compute the stability sets of the different collective action games already analyzed.[14] Let me describe briefly the procedure.

The first step is to describe the equilibria of the original games. This can be done by finding the values γ_μ that satisfy Inequalities 3.7 and 3.8 when $\lambda = 1$. Keep in mind that, when $\lambda = 1$, the initial belief conditions η play no role whatsoever.

Second, given the initial belief conditions η, we need to calculate the (unique) equilibrium of the auxiliary game Γ^0. This will be the starting point of the tracing path and can be computed by solving the same inequalities when $\lambda = 0$. The reader will notice that, when the original game has multiple equilibria, the solution to this auxiliary game will depend on η (more exactly, on γ_η).

The final step might be the trickiest and consists on finding, for any initial belief condition, the continuous path that joins the equilibrium of Γ^0 with one of the equilibria of Γ^1. When this is done, we can assign each initial belief condition to the stability set of one of the game's multiple equilibria. This requires us to look at the sequence of solutions as λ changes between 0 and 1. In the next chapter I will use this technique in the study of the games presented before.

3.10   In Lieu of a Conclusion

In this chapter I have presented the method of stability sets, the technique that will serve as the foundation for this book's

---

[14]In following this analysis, the reader must resist the temptation of "cancelling out" the value γ_μ, which appears on both sides of the inequalities. In several instances, doing so would amount to a division by zero and would inadvertently suppress one of the possible solutions of the game.

subsequent analysis of collective action problems. In essence, the method of stability sets calculates the relative likelihood of a game's different equilibria, likelihoods that are continuous functions of its payoffs. This is the analytical counterpart of LPT. When not influenced by rational-choice theory, analyses of the collective action problem posit a connection between their outcomes and the structural conditions where they occur. Both lay accounts and social-scientific studies of collective action processes are replete with statements to the effect that material changes (e.g., economic downturns, emergence of new trade patterns, technological changes) have consequences over a polity's functioning because of what they do to promote or inhibit its member's options of collective action. The method of stability sets shows that such statements are not incompatible with game theory but that, instead, can be formalized with game-theoretic tools by going beyond standard equilibrium analysis.

Thus far we have only seen 2×2 examples of this, not enough to mount a theoretical justification. But the pieces for a general analysis are already in place. In the next chapter I will put these pieces together and show what they enable us to do in the study of the models of collective action developed in Chapter 2.

Chapter 4

The Comparative Statics of Collective Action Problems

The time has come to put together all the theoretical elements developed in the previous chapters. In this chapter I will apply the method of stability sets to the games presented in Chapter 2 to see what new insight results.

This chapter will prove one conclusion: in general, in a collective action problem, the likelihood of cooperation is a continuous function of the game's payoffs. The exception to this occurs when the model is a single-equilibrium game because then outcome is deterministic and does not respond to changes in the payoffs. In light of the preceding analysis, this may not come as a surprise, but without a rigorous mathematical proof, this statement cannot be used to develop applications such as the ones in this book's second part. To prove this central claim, I will analyze the different models discussed in Chapter 2 with the aid of the method of stability sets.

4.1 Single-equilibrium Models

Since the goal of the method of stability sets is to calculate the relative likelihood of the different equilibria in a game, when that game has only one equilibrium the method is largely redundant: this unique equilibrium will be the only outcome with a positive probability. Applying the method to these models will not tell us anything we do not already know. But it is worth spending some time on these cases given their prominence in the scholarship on collective action. Additionally, when using unfamiliar methods, it is a good idea to test them first in the familiar cases where we already know what the solution should be.

4.1.1   The Public Goods Model

Let's start by reviewing the payoffs of the standard Olsonian model. This is the same model already studied in Section 2.4.1:

$$
\begin{aligned}
w_1 &= B - c, \\
w_2 &= B, \\
w_3 &= -c, \\
w_4 &= 0.
\end{aligned}
$$

With these payoffs we obtain $W = \infty$. If we fix $\lambda = 1$ in Inequalities 3.7 and 3.8, we can retrieve the game's Nash equilibrium. It is clear that the only value γ_μ that can satisfy these conditions is $\gamma_\mu = 0$. (This makes Inequality 3.7 hold because it becomes $0 \geq 0$.) This is Olson's free-riding result: the only solution is a turnout of zero.

Now let's turn to the computation of the stability set. In Section 3.2.1 I showed with the aid of a 2×2 example that, when a game has dominant strategies, the entire strategy space is the stability set of the game's unique equilibrium. The framework developed here comes to the same. To see why, consider first the case $\lambda = 0$. Just as when $\lambda = 1$, the only solution is $\gamma_\mu = 0$. In other words, regardless of what players initially believe about each other, they will always free-ride.

Under these conditions, checking for the entire tracing path is rather superfluous, but the reader can see that, regardless of the value of λ, the only solution for both inequalities is always the same: $\bar{\gamma}_\mu = 0$. This proves that, just as we had already established, in an Olsonian public goods problem, the only possible outcome, which occurs with probability 1, is universal defection.

4.1.1.1 The Public Goods Model with Selective Incentives

This is also a case we have already studied exhaustively (Section 2.4.2) but that can help illustrate the tracing procedure. The payoff structure of this model is:

$$
\begin{aligned}
w_1 &= B - c + s, \\
w_2 &= B, \\
w_3 &= s - c, \\
w_4 &= 0.
\end{aligned}
$$

If, as Olson claims it must, the selective incentive takes values $s > c$, then $W = -\infty$. This becomes the mirror image of the previous case. Now the only solution to Inequalities 3.7 and 3.8 is $\gamma_\mu = 1$, regardless of the value of λ or the value of γ_η. This game is, just as the previous one, dominance-solvable. The only difference is that now the dominant strategy is to cooperate. As a result, the only equilibrium is for every player to cooperate ($\gamma_\mu = 1$) and the stability set of this equilibrium is the entire strategy space, so that this result happens with probability 1.

4.1.1.2 Generalizing Strategic Dominance

The analysis of these first two cases would have achieved the same results for values of W different from ∞ and $-\infty$. In fact, the results would have been the same had W been > 1 in the first case and < 0 in the second. This suggests that strategic dominance can occur in payoff structures more general than the one of the original Olsonian model.

In any model in which $W < 0$ cooperation will be a dominant strategy. Likewise, in any model in which $W > 1$ defection will be the dominant strategy. This latter case gives us the implicit assumptions of the public goods model and, by contrast, allows us to see also the implicit assumptions of the multiple-equilibrium approach. If $w_4 > w_3$, that is, if participating in a failed attempt at collective action entails a cost, then $W > 1$ is true if and only if $w_2 > w_1$. In Section 2.6.5.2 (pg. 53) I stated that any model of collective action that relies on focal points, tipping, or any other concept tied to the existence of multiple equilibria is, wittingly or unwittingly, assuming that players who participate in a successful instance of collective action are compensated, at least ex ante. Here we see a more formal proof of that same statement. If there is no such compensation, that is, if $w_2 > w_1$, the collective action problem does not have multiple equilibria and invoking tipping mechanisms or focal points becomes plainly nonsensical.

While the method of stability sets does not add anything we did not already know to the study of single-equilibrium models, it does not do any harm either. The same standard conclusions about universal free-riding that result from the typical equilibrium analysis are also true here. This was to be expected: the method of stability sets is more general, not less, than equilibrium analysis.

4.2   A Basic Model with Multiple Equilibria

In Chapter 2 I presented several variants of the collective action problem that had multiple equilibria (e.g., the model with differential costs or the "stock-option" model). Here I will subsume most of them under one general structure and will analyze it thoroughly.

I will simplify the analysis by assuming that all players have identical payoffs. This is the assumption made in Sections 2.6.1 - 2.6.4. What these models have in common, from the point of view of their payoff structure, is that $0 < W < 1$. As we have just seen, if this condition is violated, the game has only one equilibrium. It is now time to study the multiple-equilibria case.

The procedure I will follow here is the same as the one already shown for 2×2 games although, of course, the notation and the mathematical arguments involved may be a bit intimidating for some readers. So, let's describe it in essence:

Step 1: Compute the Equilibria of the Original Game. This step is to some extent redundant because we already computed these equilibria in Chapter 2. But the analysis will be tighter if we have all the results together and coming from the same place. Inequalitites 3.7 and 3.8 give us the equilibria of any game along the tracing procedure, including the original one. All we have to do is to adapt these inequalities to the game at hand and let $\lambda = 1$. Once this is done, whatever value of γ_μ that satisfies both inequalities simultaneously is an equilibrium.

Not surprisingly, we will find the same equilibria: one equilibrium where nobody cooperates, another one where everyone does so and a third equilibrium with an intermediate level of turnout of W ($\gamma_\mu = 0$, $\gamma_\mu = 1$ and γ_μ such that $F(\gamma_\mu) = W$). It may be useful for the reader to verify that this equilibrium coincides with the mixed strategy equilibria computed in Sections 2.6.1 - 2.6.4 and that it is also the same as the unstable equilibrium of the tipping game in Section 2.6.5 if we assume identical payoffs. This is an instructive way of verifying that the analysis in this chapter truly generalizes the conventional equilibrium arguments. In light of what has already been discussed, it should come as no surprise that the first two equilibria will have sizeable stability sets, while the latter one will be a razor-edge equilibrium.

Step 2: Compute the Equilibrium of Game Γ^0. In this step we compute the equilibrium of the game when players base their decisions on their initial beliefs only. This is the equilibrium with which the tracing path starts. Just as in the examples already studied, the solution here will differ in two important ways from the solution obtained in the first step: there will be only one equilibrium and its strategies will depend on the initial belief conditions chosen.

Step 3: Compute the Tracing Path.   This step generates the tracing path for any set of initial belief conditions. It will tell us all the equilibria of the game as λ varies from 0 to 1. The single most important information we need from this step is which of the equilibria at $\lambda = 1$ is continuously connected to the equilibrium at $\lambda = 0$. This will give us, for each initial condition, the stability set to which it belongs.

Step 4: Characterize the Stability Sets.   Once we know how to assign each possible vector of initial belief conditions to a stability set, all we need to do is to put together the information. In the cases studied below, the tracing procedure will result in a rule that tells us what kind of initial belief conditions are mapped onto what equilibrium. In fact, the final result is not entirely surprising.

4.2.1   The Main Result

This section presents the main result that culminates the tracing analysis of the preceding chapters. Let W be defined, following pg. 127, as:

$$W = \frac{w_4 - w_3}{(w_4 - w_3) + (w_1 - w_2)}.$$

If the mutual expectations players have are summarized by initial belief conditions with expected aggregate turnout $\gamma_\eta < W$, those expectations belong to the stability set of noncooperation $(\gamma_\mu = 0)$. If, instead, the initial belief conditions are such that $\gamma_\eta > W$, they belong to the stability set of cooperation $(\gamma_\mu = 1)$.

Intuitively, levels of expected turnout below W are not enough to persuade players that it is worthwhile to cooperate. Just as successful collective action results in benefits for the participants, failed collective action results in a cost. If the expected turnout is too low, viz. below W, the risk of failure outweighs the prospects of success. Thus deterred, players opt out of cooperation and collective action does not take off. In contrast, if the expected turnout level is above W, players find the risk worth taking and, as these expectations are validated, they reach the cooperative equilibrium.

This is the cornerstone of the comparative statics of collective action. With this result, if we want to compute the probability of cooperation, all we need is to specify our assumptions about the distribution of initial belief conditions.

The method of stability sets is just that, a method. It does not legislate what conclusions we must obtain from the study of a game with multiple equilibria but simply gives us a rigorous language in which to state our conclusions and sheds light on the connection between beliefs and payoffs in a game. The method of stability sets does not debunk any theory of collective action but clarifies its assumptions so that we can decide on its merits.

For example, if we want to cling to the notion that collective action problems are inherently unpredictable, that their outcome depends so much on human agency that no a priori statement makes sense, that knowing their structure tells us nothing about their result, we can simply disregard the information contained in the stability sets. Such extreme agnosticism implicitly assumes that any knowledge we may have about initial belief conditions is of no use in inferring anything about the prospects for coordination in a group. This is an entirely consistent stance but I do not see its rationale. Stability sets are mathematical objects, just the way equilibria are. In both cases it is up to the model's user to interpret their meaning in ways relevant to understand human interactions. I do not see how we can regard equilibria as meaningful constructs for the study of social coordination while at the same time denying that status to their stability sets.

The above type of agnosticism has some further difficulties. In the analysis of a game with multiple equilibria, just as in the analysis of any system that may arrive at different outcomes, there comes a point when we need to spell out our conjectures about its behavior. Given that country A's currency entered a free fall, should we expect the risk of regime collapse to go up or down? Given that country B granted more autonomy to province B1, should we expect the risk of civil war to go up or down? Given that country C signed a free-trade agreement with D, should we expect union membership to go up or down? Given that country F is now producing good G at a lower price, should we expect the membership of the "Protect Domestic G Producers" lobby in country H to go up or down?

Without knowing the details, it is pointless to try to answer these questions. In all these instances the answer may well be "up," "down" or "stay roughly the same." But whatever answer we give, it must be preceded by a statement of how likely we believe these outcomes are. Those of us who believe that game theory offers a good way to represent some aspects of human interactions, will be inclined to answer these questions with the aid of a model and if this model turns out to have multiple equilibria, our final assessment will depend on the probability we assign to each of them. At that point we face a choice: either we assign probabilities without microfoundations to support our judgment, or we try to come up with probabilities that in some way respond to the underlying game-theoretic logic that we adopted from the start. The first choice strikes me as inconsistent: if, when push comes to shove, we are willing to give up the search for microfoundations, maybe we should have not used game theory in the first place. The method of stability sets formalizes the second choice.

Another option is to cling to the standard arguments of focal points. Suppose that, in analyzing a collective action problem, we are convinced that cooperation is focal. Then we simply postulate that the distribution of initial belief conditions is concentrated on $\gamma_\eta = 1$.

The analysis just developed is entirely compatible with such an argument. But its wisdom seems dubious. Unless we have overwhelming evidence, it is hard to justify the assumption that initial belief conditions are fixed at any single level. The advocate of focal points claims to know that under no circumstance could there be initial belief conditions in a stability set different from the one he is defending. In making that claim, he is invoking some added insight beyond game theory because the analysis of a game does not tell us anything about focality. Those of us who take a more skeptical stance are entitled to ask where that added insight comes from.

It seems more reasonable to hedge, allowing that initial belief conditions may, in fact, be at different levels. This is what tipping games do. But we do not have to stop there and simply conclude that many equilibria are possible. If we have some knowledge about initial belief conditions, which can be very vague and does not have to be as absolute as that claimed by defenders of focal points, we can translate our knowledge about stability sets into probabilities of the different equilibria.

Suppose, for example, that in this particular case we want to remain absolutely agnostic about the exact location of the initial belief conditions. Then we can adopt the Laplacian stance and represent that agnosticism by assuming that γ_η is uniformly distributed over $[0, 1]$. Now, the border between the two stability sets of this collective action problem is given by $F(\gamma_\eta) = W$. So, we can put together our results about the stability sets and our probabilistic assessment of the initial belief conditions to say that the probability of cooperation $(P(\gamma_\mu = 1))$ is such that:

$$P(\gamma_\mu = 1) = F^{-1}(W) = F^{-1}\left(\frac{w_4 - w_3}{(w_1 - w_3) - (w_2 - w_4)}\right).$$

For illustrative purposes, let's assume that $F(x) = x$. That is, let's assume that the probability of success of collective action given any level of turnout is equal to that level of turnout. Then, the probability of cooperation would be:

$$P(\gamma_\mu = 1) = \frac{w_4 - w_3}{(w_1 - w_3) - (w_2 - w_4)}.$$

Although the exact algebraic expression for the probability depends on our assessment of the initial belief conditions, the qualitative properties will not. The value W *is* the border between the stability sets of the game's equilibria regardless of the probability distribution we want to use to represent γ_η. We are free to assume any other distribution over those initial belief conditions. But, unless we take an extreme assumption such as the one of the focal points model, changes in W will change the resulting probability of cooperation.

At long last, we are in a position to enter the water fees debate with which this book opens. The method of stability sets allows us to pronounce General B's analysis as essentially correct but lacking nuance. Here is a way to formalize the intuition he had in mind. Suppose that the citizens of country X understand that, were they to engage in collective action, they could overthrow this odious regime. If there is some insurgent organization waiting on the wings, it faces the task of offering prospective rewards to the would-be participants. In the terminology adopted here, this organization, if it is to be taken seriously, must see to it that, at least ex ante the potential members believe that $w_1 > w_2$. In other words, they believe that, if the organization were to take control, it would arrange the state of affairs so that direct participants receive w_1 and those who remained on the fence receive a smaller benefit w_2. The regime, instead, controls the variables w_3 and w_4: it determines the status quo payoff for the citizens as long as the regime survives and the payoff that awaits those who challenge the regime but fail to bring it down (w_3). By his own reckoning, General B, who is an expert in w_3, feels that, as much as he can raise it with his ruthless secret police, there is only so much he can do. In formal terms, he worries about the effect that the Finance Minister's proposal will have over w_4. A gratuitous increase in water fees, without any visible benefit for the citizenry will depress w_4 and, as a result, will reduce the value of W. We know that as W decreases, this means that the stability set of collective quiescence decreases. In more pedestrian terms, the ones that General B would understand, a decrease in W means that the population is more restive, more likely to coordinate and revolt.

Of course, he cannot be sure that the insurrection will happen. He simply expressed his gut feeling that the water fees plan would be the straw that would break the camel's back. There have been several straws heaped on this particular camel in the past so it is tricky to say that this is the decisive one. He may be wrong and the only way he could prove his argument is if he knew exactly the values of W before and after the water fees increase and the level γ_η representing the aggregate initial belief conditions of this collective action problem. If he could, say, prove that $\gamma_\eta = 0.6$ and that currently $W = 0.7$ but the water fees increase would bring it down to 0.5, he would be entitled to conclude that this scheme will spell the regime's demise. But he does not know these values and it is dubious that he could ever know them.

From a conceptual point of view, however, it is irrelevant whether he is exactly right or wrong. What matters is that his entirely untrained insight into the citizens' collective action problem is compatible with what we know about rational decision making, both individual and collective, as codified by game theory with the help of the method of stability sets. It would be wrong to rebuke him for being inconsistent with rational-choice theory because he is not. To claim, as the advisors in that story do, that water fees are irrelevant for the regime's survival, one would have to be ready to defend the restrictive assumptions of the Olsonian framework, or to claim that the initial belief conditions among the populace happen to be just so that an increase in water fees will not increase the likelihood of insurgent coordination.

The lengthy theoretical and mathematical exercise that has brought us here would be pointless if all it accomplished was to bring support to General B's uncouth views. But with a solid formalism we can go beyond that. For instance, suppose that we now abandon the stance of the security chief of an odious regime (a stance many of us might find uncomfortable) and instead adopt the viewpoint of social scientists who want to understand how the economic transformations ravaging Country X shape its political process.

At first glance, we would surmise that a five-fold increase in water fees has a larger impact over the likelihood of massive revolt than, say, a tax on jewelry. The preceding analysis of collective action confirms this because, on average, the effect of a tax on jewelry over the w_4 of this country's citizens is smaller than the effect of water fees. But we do not need to stop there. We can use this theoretical framework to bring together deeper and more extensive findings about Country X's economic and social structure. The bare-bones formula of page 136 is simply a tool; it is up to us to put it to use in fruitful ways by developing plausible accounts of the forces shaping the value W. Changes in Country X's export performance will affect the statu quo and may be mapped into effects over w_4. Increases in the share of public-sector employment, unaccompanied by modern civil-service legislation, might increase the power of the government to threat dissenters, something that will impact w_3. (I present a more detailed example of this line of thought in Chapter 5.) This is not the place to describe in detail the possible uses of this chapter's main result. Instead I just want to claim, much more modestly, that this result offers promise in our search for comparative statics results about politico-economic processes, given how much those processes are shaped by collective action, be it actual or potential.

Not only does the method of stability sets give us probabilities of the game's outcomes; it also gives us probabilities that depend functionally on its payoff structure. In other words, it gives us comparative statics of the game. With the previous result in hand we can study how changes in the payoffs (the w's) affect the probability of cooperation. I submit that this type of study cannot be conducted with the conventional methods. At the end of the day, focal points and tipping games are not tools to investigate the effect of structural changes upon outcomes of collective action.

In essence, this is the analysis I will carry out in the second part of this book. I will make explicit the collective action problem that agents in a polity face, be this in wage bargaining (Chapter 5) or in a clientelistic regime (Chapter 6). Then, I will show that the severity of those collective action problems depend on the politico-economic structure in which they are embedded. To prove this, I will appeal to the results I have obtained in this part of the book from using the method of stability sets. In other words, the method will help us generate predictions about the comparative statics of the collective action problems analyzed in these chapters.

In this sense the method of stability sets provides the game-theoretic foundations of a structural analysis of collective action. Rational-choice approaches have shown that mutual beliefs and expectations shape the outcomes of collective action and that those beliefs can be, in turn, shaped by organizations, institutions and leaders. But although beliefs are fundamental, so are payoffs. The method of stability sets shows that there is no analytic reason to reject this point and that, on the contrary, game theory has the right tools to transform it into a source of testable hypotheses.

4.2.2 Computing Stability Sets in a Generalized Collective Action Game[*]

Now I will offer the mathematical proof behind the results just discussed. To that end, let $\lambda = 0$ to compute the unique equilibrium of Γ^0 as a function of the initial belief conditions η. In this case, Inequalities 3.7 and 3.8 become:

$$
\begin{aligned}
F(\gamma_\eta)\gamma_\mu &\geq \gamma_\mu W, \\
F(\gamma_\eta)(1 - \gamma_\mu) &\leq (1 - \gamma_\mu)W.
\end{aligned}
$$

So, if $F(\gamma_\eta) < W$, the only solution is $\gamma_\mu = 0$. Likewise, if $F(\gamma_\eta) > W$, then the equilibrium is $\gamma_\mu = 1$. If $F(\gamma_\eta) = W$, then any value γ_μ is an equilibrium.

Now we need to know which equilibria will exist for each value of λ. This will depend on the initial belief conditions.

Consider first the aggregate turnout level $\gamma_\mu = 0$. It can only be an equilibrium if:

$$
\begin{aligned}
\lambda F(\gamma_\mu) + (1 - \lambda)F(\gamma_\eta) &\leq W, \\
\lambda F(0) + (1 - \lambda)F(\gamma_\eta) &\leq W, \\
(1 - \lambda)F(\gamma_\eta) &\leq W, \\
F(\gamma_\eta) &\leq \frac{W}{1 - \lambda}.
\end{aligned}
$$

If $F(\gamma_\eta) \leq W$, this inequality holds for every value of λ. This already means that for initial belief conditions that

---

[*]Technical section.

satisfy this inequality there is a continuous tracing path to equilibrium $\gamma_\mu = 0$.

If, instead, $F(\gamma_\eta) \geq W$, this inequality holds only for values such that:

$$\lambda \geq \frac{F(\gamma_\eta) - W}{F(\gamma_\eta)}.$$

If the level of turnout $\gamma_\mu = 1$ is to be an equilibrium of an auxiliary game, it must be that:

$$
\begin{aligned}
\lambda F(\gamma_\mu) + (1 - \lambda) F(\gamma_\eta) &\geq W, \\
\lambda F(1) + (1 - \lambda) F(\gamma_\eta) &\geq W, \\
\lambda + (1 - \lambda) F(\gamma_\eta) &\geq W, \\
F(\gamma_\eta) &\geq \frac{W - \lambda}{1 - \lambda}.
\end{aligned}
$$

In a mirror image of the previous case, if the initial belief conditions are such that $F(\gamma_\eta) \geq W$, then the equilibrium $\gamma_\mu = 1$ exists for every value of λ. Otherwise, it will exist only if:

$$\lambda \geq \frac{W - F(\gamma_\eta)}{1 - F(\gamma_\eta)}.$$

What about the equilibrium with randomized play $0 < \gamma_\mu < 1$? This equilibrium only exists if:

$$\lambda F(\gamma_\mu) + (1 - \lambda) F(\gamma_\eta) = W.$$

If $F(\gamma_\eta) < W$, there is no possible solution to this equation unless $\lambda \geq (W - F(\gamma_\eta))/(1 - F(\gamma_\eta))$. In that interval, the solution will be a level of turnout γ_μ that is a decreasing function of λ. Analogously, if $F(\gamma_\eta) > W$, any solution to this equation can only exist if $\lambda \geq (F(\gamma_\eta) - W)/F(\gamma_\eta)$. Then the equilibrium γ_μ will be an increasing function of λ.

4.2.3   A Diagrammatic Presentation

The graphs in Figures 4.1 and 4.2 summarize all the results thus far:

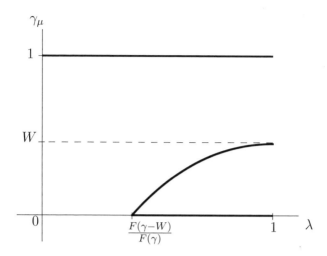

Figure 4.1: Tracing Path for Initial Belief Conditions $\gamma_\eta > W$. The only continuous path corresponds to the equilibrium with cooperation.

Conceptually, this means that initial belief conditions with an expected turnout such that $F(\gamma_\eta) < W$ belong to the stability set of noncooperation ($\gamma_\mu = 0$) and that, conversely, those initial belief conditions for which $F(\gamma_\eta) > W$ belong to the stability set of cooperation ($\gamma_\mu = 1$). Just as we expected, the randomized equilibrium has a measure-zero stability set.

As already explained, once we have described the stability sets of a game's equilibria, it is up to us to translate them into probabilities. The final result will depend on the assumptions we want to make about the distribution of initial belief conditions.

4.2.4 A "Simple" Tipping Game[*]

In Chapter 2 I showed that, starting from Model 0, we could obtain the structure of a tipping game if we allow payoffs to differ across agents. There are very good reasons to do so. Most collective action problems differently affect people in different stations of life. We may want to analyze the prospects

---

[*]Technical section.

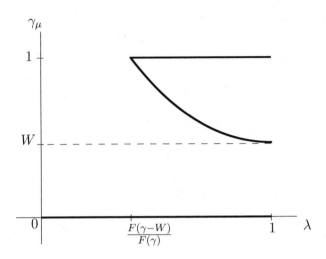

Figure 4.2: Tracing Path for Initial Belief Conditions $\gamma_\eta < W$. The only continuous path corresponds to the equilibrium with no cooperation.

of collective action aimed at, say, income redistribution in a group that includes blue-collar and white-collar workers, or the prospects of collective action aimed at trade reform in a group that includes producers of tradeables and nontradeables, or of labor-intensive goods and capital-intensive goods, and so on.

Proving a general result for any conceivable tipping game is beyond the scope of this book. But for the purposes of a full-blown agenda of structural analysis of collective action, differences in payoffs are crucial, as the examples in the previous paragraph attest. So, I will offer here an illustration of how to handle this issue. To that end, I will study a "simple" tipping game in which there are only two possible payoff vectors.

Consider a version of Model 0 in which there are two groups of players: Group 1 with size ρ and Group 2 with size $1 - \rho$. The payoffs for any member of Group 1 are $w_{11}, w_{21}, w_{31}, w_{41}$ and, likewise, the payoffs for any member of Group 2 are $w_{12}, w_{22}, w_{32}, w_{42}$. In keeping with the previous notation, we shall introduce values:

$$W_1 \equiv \frac{w_{41} - w_{31}}{(w_{11} - w_{31}) - (w_{21} - w_{41})};$$

$$W_2 \equiv \frac{w_{42} - w_{32}}{(w_{12} - w_{32}) - (w_{22} - w_{42})}.$$

Without loss of generality, I will assume that $W_1 < W_2$. Notice that this can come about if, for instance, Group 1 stands to gain more from success or to lose more from failure. All else being equal, members of Group 1 will be more prone to cooperate. From our previous discussion of tipping games we know that each player's threshold value, that is, the expected aggregate turnout that will lead each to cooperate, depends on the payoffs faced. In this case, we have two such threshold values. Not coincidentally, the threshold values computed in Chapter 2 are exactly the same as the W values introduced here.

In this game with two possible threshold values, the distribution G is a discrete distribution with the following form:

$$G(x) = \begin{cases} 0 & \text{if} & x < W_1, \\ \rho & \text{if} & W_1 \le x < W_2, \\ 1 & \text{if} & W_2 < x. \end{cases}$$

Depending on the values ρ, W_1 and W_2 we will have either two or three equilibria in pure strategies. This is somewhat anomalous for a tipping game: it is an artifact of having only two threshold values.

But the standard tipping diagrams focus only on pure strategies while, as we have shown, there is much to be learned about the game by looking at the entire set of equilibria. The preceding analysis retrieves not only the pure-strategy equilibria that the tipping diagram shows but also those that involve mixed strategies.

In this case, we need to satisfy Inequalities 3.7 and 3.8 for both sets of payoffs. Once we introduce the assumption $F(x) = x$ we conclude that an equilibrium of this game will be described by turnout levels γ_μ^1 and γ_μ^2 for Group 1 and Group 2 respectively that satisfy the following conditions:

$$\gamma_\mu^1[\lambda(\rho\gamma_\mu^1 + (1-\rho)\gamma_\mu^2)$$
$$+ (1-\lambda)(\rho\gamma_\eta^1 + (1-\rho)\gamma_\eta^2)] \;\;\geq\;\; \gamma_\mu^1 W_1, \qquad (4.1)$$
$$\gamma_\mu^2[\lambda(\rho\gamma_\mu^1 + (1-\rho)\gamma_\mu^2)$$
$$+ (1-\lambda)(\rho\gamma_\eta^1 + (1-\rho)\gamma_\eta^2)] \;\;\geq\;\; \gamma_\mu^2 W_2, \qquad (4.2)$$
$$(1-\gamma_\mu^1)[\lambda(\rho\gamma_\mu^1 + (1-\rho)\gamma_\mu^2)$$
$$+ (1-\lambda)(\rho\gamma_\eta^1 + (1-\rho)\gamma_\eta^2)] \;\;\leq\;\; (1-\gamma_\mu^1)W_1, \qquad (4.3)$$
$$(1-\gamma_\mu^2)[\lambda(\rho\gamma_\mu^1 + (1-\rho)\gamma_\mu^2)$$
$$+ (1-\lambda)(\rho\gamma_\eta^1 + (1-\rho)\gamma_\eta^2)] \;\;\leq\;\; (1-\gamma_\mu^2)W_2. \qquad (4.4)$$

These inequalities show that there are five possible equilibria of the original game (when $\lambda = 1$):

- $\gamma_\mu^1 = \gamma_\mu^2 = 0$. This equilibrium exists for any values W_1, W_2 and ρ.

- $\gamma_\mu^1 = \gamma_\mu^2 = 1$. This equilibrium also exists for any set of parameters.

- $\gamma_\mu^1 = 1, \gamma_\mu^2 = 0$. This equilibrium exists only if $W_1 < \rho < W_2$.

- $0 < \gamma_\mu^1 < 1, \gamma_\mu^2 = 0$. This equilibrium exists only if $\rho < W_2$.

- $\gamma_\mu^1 = 1, 0 < \gamma_\mu^2 < 1$. This equilibrium also requires $\rho < W_2$.

Let's now calculate the starting points of the tracing paths by calculating the equilibrium of each auxiliary game Γ^0 for a given set of initial belief conditions. To that end, let's fix $\lambda = 0$ and we obtain the following solutions to Inequalities 4.1 - 4.4.

- $\gamma_\mu^1 = \gamma_\mu^2 = 0$. This equilibrium exists only if $\rho\gamma_\eta^1 + (1-\rho)\gamma_\eta^2 < W_1$.

- $\gamma_\mu^1 = \gamma_\mu^2 = 1$. This equilibrium exists only if $\rho\gamma_\eta^1 + (1-\rho)\gamma_\eta^2 > W_2$.

- $\gamma_\mu^1 = 1, \gamma_\mu^2 = 0$. This equilibrium exists if $W_1 < \rho\gamma_\eta^1 + (1 - \rho)\gamma_\eta^2 < W_2$.

To map out the tracing paths it will be useful to find the smallest value of λ for which a given equilibrium exists. This gives us the following results:

- Equilibrium $\gamma_\mu^1 = \gamma_\mu^2 = 0$ exists for values of $\lambda \geq (\rho\gamma_\eta^1 + (1 - \rho)\gamma_\eta^2 - W_1)/(\rho\gamma_\eta^1 + (1 - \rho)\gamma_\eta^2)$.

- Equilibrium $\gamma_\mu^1 = \gamma_\mu^2 = 1$ exists for values of $\lambda \geq (W_2 - \rho\gamma_\eta^1 - (1 - \rho)\gamma_\eta^2)/(1 - \rho\gamma_\eta^1 - (1 - \rho)\gamma_\eta^2)$.

- Equilibrium $\gamma_\mu^1 = 1, \gamma_\mu^2 = 0$ exists for values of $(W_1 - (\rho\gamma_\eta^1 + (1 - \rho)\gamma_\eta^2))/(\rho - (\rho\gamma_\eta^1 + (1 - \rho)\gamma_\eta^2)) \leq \lambda \leq (W_2 - (\rho\gamma_\eta^1 + (1 - \rho)\gamma_\eta^2))/(\rho - (\rho\gamma_\eta^1 + (1 - \rho)\gamma_\eta^2))$.

The same reasoning proves that the paths that lead to the equilibria where members of one of the two groups randomize branch out of the paths with pure strategies. More exactly, the equilibrium $\gamma_\mu^1 = 1, 0 < \gamma_\mu^2 < 1$ becomes feasible only when $\gamma_\mu^1 = 1, \gamma_\mu^2 = 0$ *stops* being feasible and the equilibrium $0 < \gamma_\mu^1 < 1, \gamma_\mu^2 = 0$ becomes feasible only when the equilibrium $\gamma_\mu^1 = 1, \gamma_\mu^2 = 1$ is also feasible.

Summing up, the stability sets of this tipping game's equilibria are the following:

For Equilibrium	the stability set is formed by priors such that	for size parameter ρ such that
$\gamma_\mu^1 = \gamma_\mu^2 = 0$	$\rho\gamma_\eta^1 + (1 - \rho)\gamma_\eta^2 < W_1$	$0 < \rho < 1$
$\gamma_\mu^1 = \gamma_\mu^2 = 1$	$\rho\gamma_\eta^1 + \gamma_\eta^2 > W_2$	$0 < \rho < 1$
$\gamma_\mu^1 = 1, \gamma_\mu^2 = 0$	$W_1 < \rho\gamma_\eta^1 + (1 - \rho)\gamma_\eta^2 < W_2$	$W_1 < \rho < W_2$
$\gamma_\mu^1 = 1, 0 < \gamma_\mu^2 < 1$	$W_1 < \rho\gamma_\eta^1 + (1 - \rho)\gamma_\eta^2 < W_2$	$\rho < W_2$
$0 < \gamma_\mu^1 < 1, \gamma_\mu^2 = 0$	$W_1 < \rho\gamma_\eta^1 + (1 - \rho)\gamma_\eta^2 < W_2$	$\rho < W_2$

In two of these equilibria, some players randomize their choice but they nevertheless do have stability sets. This does not contradict the conclusions obtained in our discussion of 2×2 games: the fact that some players use pure strategies is enough to precipitate the existence of a stability set with positive measure.

Since those equilibria have stability sets with positive measure they will form part of any final forecast. To sharpen the result, then, we can compute the aggregate turnout that each of them generates. This can be done by solving the following equations that describe them when $\lambda = 1$:

$$0 < \gamma_\mu^1 < 1, \gamma_\mu^2 = 0 \quad \Longleftrightarrow \quad \gamma_\mu^1 = \frac{W_1}{\rho};$$

$$\gamma_\mu^1 = 1, 0 < \gamma_\mu^2 < 1 \quad \Longleftrightarrow \quad \gamma_\mu^2 = \frac{W_2 - \rho}{1 - \rho}.$$

Just as in the examples above, once we have computed the stability sets, we can complement them with our knowledge (or ignorance) about the players' initial belief conditions to obtain a probabilistic assessment of the different equilibria which, in turn, will give us the probability of success as a function of the game's structure. The method of stability sets subsumes the focal point arguments because, if we want, we can postulate a distribution of the initial belief conditions such that, in the end, all the probability is assigned to the equilibrium we believe is focal. Under the approach taken in this book, such procedure would be entirely legitimate because the method of stability sets does not legislate the distribution of initial belief conditions. But, as the method makes clear, if we say that one equilibrium is focal we are implicitly restricting the distribution of initial belief conditions. However legitimate from a purely theoretical standpoint, this reasoning is questionable. Unless a theorist has powerful arguments in favor of a distribution of initial belief conditions restricted to justify a focal point, he is liable to the charge of simply assuming what he is supposed to prove.

If we maintain our assumption of a uniform distribution over initial belief conditions, we can arrive at a precise probabilistic assessment of this collective action problem: the stability sets map into probabilities of each equilibrium. So, we have to consider several cases depending on the groups' relative size, determined by the parameter ρ.

If $\rho < W_1$:

$$
\begin{aligned}
P(\gamma_\mu^1 = 0, \gamma_\mu^2 = 0) &= W_1, \\
P(\gamma_\mu^1 = 1, \gamma_\mu^2 = (W_2 - \rho)/(1 - \rho)) &= W_2 - W_1, \\
P(\gamma_\mu^1 = 1, \gamma_\mu^2 = 1) &= 1 - W_2.
\end{aligned}
$$

This translates into a probability of success:

$$
P(S) = \frac{W_2 - \rho}{1 - \rho}(W_2 - W_1) + (1 - W_2).
$$

If $W_1 < \rho < W_2$:

$$
\begin{aligned}
P(\gamma_\mu^1 = 0, \gamma_\mu^2 = 0) &= W_1, \\
P(\gamma_\mu^1 = 1, \gamma_\mu^2 = 0) &= W_2 - W_1, \\
P(\gamma_\mu^1 = 1, \gamma_\mu^2 = 1) &= 1 - W_2.
\end{aligned}
$$

Then, the probability of success is:

$$
P(S) = \rho(W_2 - W_1) + (1 - W_2).
$$

If $W_2 < \rho$:

$$
\begin{aligned}
P(\gamma_\mu^1 = 0, \gamma_\mu^2 = 0) &= W_1, \\
P(\gamma_\mu^1 = W_1/\rho, \gamma_\mu^2 = 0) &= W_2 - W_1, \\
P(\gamma_\mu^1 = 1, \gamma_\mu^2 = 1) &= 1 - W_2.
\end{aligned}
$$

In this case, the probability of success is:

$$
P(S) = \frac{W_1}{\rho}(W_2 - W_1) + (1 - W_2).
$$

Compared to the standard way of dealing with tipping games, this approach is much more laborious, especially when we consider that this was the "simple" case with only two types of payoffs. Given its immature state, the method of stability sets still needs to generate more powerful algorithms for more general cases. But I believe that the extra effort is well worth it. Had we settled for the conventional analysis of tipping, all we could have said about this collective action problem was that several outcomes were possible, depending on the location of the initial belief conditions. We could have even refined this idea and arrived at conclusions about how changes in those beliefs would map into changes in the outcome. But we could have not made any claim about the effect of the game's structure, viz. its payoffs and the size of the groups, upon such outcome.

With the method of stability sets, in contrast, we have expressions for the probability of cooperation that depend in a systematic way on the structural parameters. We can formulate deductive hypotheses about the game's comparative statics without eroding the theoretical foundations on which our analysis is based.

4.3 Toward an Analysis of Stability Sets in Repeated Games

In Chapter 2 (Section 2.8) we saw that infinitely repeated PDs do not differ much from the general structure we have been analyzing from the start. In fact, they have many more equilibria than the other games in this book and, as such, their study offers some possibilities for the method of stability sets. In this section I will illustrate this point by continuing the study of the example of a repeated game introduced above.

This same trading game plays a crucial role in the vast literature on trust so it is instructive to see, however tentatively, what the method of stability sets can add to this research.[1] Much of the research on trust games has focused on the endogenous emergence of trust. Considering a game such as the

---

[1] For a recent treatment of the problem similar in spirit to the one adopted here, see Yamagishi et al. (2005).

one studied here, this literature asks whether repetition itself will lead players to be more willing to trade, in other words, if cooperation leads to trust or if it is the other way around.

Cooperation and trust, one could argue, always depend on the context in which they occur. Just because two people trust each other enough to lend and borrow a pen while waiting in a line does not mean that they will also serve as each other's co-signer for a home loan. If we want to investigate the effects of trust as a facilitator of interactions in a society, one of the pillars of the research on social capital (in the tradition of Putnam, Leonardi and Nanetti (1993)), we cannot remain oblivious to the external circumstances, to the stakes involved. If trust is a scarce resource, like any material resource, we want to use it wisely and not require or expect people to trust each other in situations where their social capital is not up to the task.

Let's see what the method of stability sets can contribute to this topic. Not much can be expected at this stage because I will not present a complete analysis of the game but will instead focus on one of its parameters: the discount rate. For purposes of illustration this is at once easy and fruitful to study. One standard interpretation of the discount rate links it to a structural aspect of a repeated interaction: the probability with which it continues over time. A low discount rate in this situation represents the trade between two agents that know that there is a high likelihood of the game being cut short for some exogenous reason. The higher the discount rate, the more the agents can rely on there being another round of interaction.

Intuitively, we would expect that cooperation is more likely in a stable environment, where the players are confident that the opportunities for mutual benefit that cooperation gener- ates will not vanish on short notice, than in a volatile context where today's partner may tomorrow be gone for good. Inhab- itants of small villages often complain of how modernization and trade erode trust in their communities for precisely that reason: with new opportunities available, agents that were bound before for the long haul have now to take into account that their would-be partner may tomorrow move to the big city. A systematic study of trust and its social effects should be able to articulate this intuition and turn it into a solid basis for comparative analysis. With the method of stability sets we can do just that.

For convenience, I will reproduce here the game that captures the decision of both players to enter in a contract that is self-enforced through iteration. (This is the same payoff matrix as on page 78.) In the game in Figure 4.3, we can compute the mixed strategy equilibrium with the standard method. Let α_i denote the probability that Player i will choose C. Then, the expected payoffs become:

$$2$$

		C	N
1	C	$\frac{1}{1-\delta}, \frac{1}{1-\delta}$	$-1, 2$
	N	$2, -1$	$0, 0$

Figure 4.3: Will They Trade?

$$v_1(\alpha_1, \alpha_2) = \alpha_1 \left(\frac{\alpha_2}{1-\delta} - (1-\alpha_2) \right) + (1-\alpha_1)2\alpha_2$$

$$= \alpha_1 \left[\alpha_2 \left(\frac{\delta}{1-\delta} \right) - 1 \right] + 2\alpha_2;$$

$$v_2(\alpha_1, \alpha_2) = \alpha_2 \left[\alpha_1 \left(\frac{\delta}{1-\delta} \right) - 1 \right] + 2\alpha_1.$$

These equations give us the following best-response correspondences:

$$\alpha_1^*(\alpha_2) = \begin{cases} 1 & \text{if} \quad \alpha_2 > \frac{1-\delta}{\delta}, \\ [0,1] & \text{if} \quad \alpha_2 = \frac{1-\delta}{\delta}, \\ 0 & \text{if} \quad \alpha_2 < \frac{1-\delta}{\delta}, \end{cases}$$

with an analogous best-response correspondence for $\alpha_2^*(\alpha_1)$. If, just as before, we plot these best-response correspondences, we will see graphically the stability sets of the equilibria (Figure 4.4).

The stability sets of this game articulate formally the intuition discussed above: the higher the discount rate, that is, the

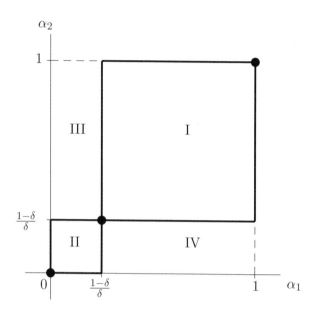

Figure 4.4: Best-response Correspondences of the "Contract game"

greater the likelihood of the interaction continuing into the future, the larger the stability set of the equilibrium where both parties enter and honor the contract, and so the more likely it is that the players will take the risks involved in the contract and attain the mutual benefits from trade. By the same token, the lower the discount rate, the more likely it is that the players will simply abstain from this self-enforcing contract, lest they misplace their trust.

The preceding analysis shows that the method of stability sets, far from being a competitor, could become a useful complement of the folk theorems often invoked in the study of repeated interactions. By their very nature, the folk theorems of repeated games leave many crucial questions open. All they tell us is that mutually beneficial exchange is possible in a repeated PD, but they cannot guarantee that such exchange will occur nor can they tell the exact terms under which it will. Several strands of literature have worked on this topic, notably the theory of bargaining solutions, and each of them has made worthy contributions to it.

As regards the overarching problem of trust and cooperation in mutually beneficial exchanges, the method of stability sets could conceivably clarify the role external circumstances play in facilitating these types of interactions. After all, as social scientists we are interested in how different societies, facing different conditions, arrive at different answers to similar predicaments. The method of stability sets can help us isolate the role of material conditions so that we can understand better how all the other ingredients (e.g., social beliefs, traditions, institutions) combine.

Much work remains to be done. All I have shown here is how to calculate the stability sets of two narrowly defined equilibria, one with symmetric exchange and one with no exchange whatsoever. But we know from the folk theorems that a repeated game has a continuum of equilibria: the result presented in this section is no substitute for a general theorem and can only count as an indication, a clue that the method's reach is much more general than what its current version suggests.

4.4   Conclusions

This chapter culminates the theoretical analysis of Chapters 2 and 3 and sets the stage for the politico-economic models of Chapters 6 and 5. It is, then, appropriate that we take stock of what has been accomplished thus far.

We began with a general model of collective action that unifies the Olsonian and the Schellingean paradigms. According to that model's fundamental result, the difference between these approaches turns on their assumptions regarding the cost of successful collective action: if we believe that players can recoup the cost of participating whenever their collective endeavor succeeds, we are implicitly using a model with multiple equilibria. If we deny this, then our model is, of necessity, a single-equilibrium model.

After showing that these two main paradigms are special cases of a general model, we studied a method, the method of stability sets, that can be applied to the general framework to calculate the relative probabilities of all the equilibria in a game. That method is not incompatible with standard equilibrium analysis and in fact generalizes it. It is also closely related to other approaches in game theory, such as evolutionary games and quantal-response equilibria.

Although the formal calculations of stability sets are not well-known, the underlying intuition is not entirely unfamiliar. Tipping games offer a good but informal template. When studying a tipping game, we begin by postulating different possible levels of expected turnout as an input for the model. Unlike standard analysis, tipping games do consider expectations out of equilibrium and study how the game itself sets in motion an adjustment process that pushes them toward an equilibrium. In a typical tipping game there are multiple equilibria and so different levels of expected turnout may be mapped into different equilibria.

The method of stability sets formalizes this reasoning and goes beyond it. Rather than simply determining that some initial beliefs lead to coordination and others to defection, the method transforms this insight into a basis for probabilities of coordination that depend on the game's payoffs. In short, the method gives us the key element for comparative statics of collective action.

The third step, the one taken in this chapter, was to apply the method of stability sets to collective action problems, something that results in crisp, analytical expressions for the probabilities of cooperation and defection. In a collective action problem, if we assume that all players face the same payoffs, the size of the stability set of the noncooperative equilibrium is $W = (w_4 - w_3)/[(w_1 - w_3) - (w_2 - w_4)]$. This expression covers both the single-equilibrium and the multiple-equilibria versions and tells us that in games with strict dominance, players will either cooperate with probability 1 (with selective incentives $W > 1$), or will defect with probability 1 (without selective incentives $W < 0$) and that in games without dominant strategies, that is, Schellingean games where $w_1 > w_2$, the probability of collective action varies as the payoffs of the game vary.

This line of reasoning can be extended to other games and I have illustrated how to do this in two simple cases: an iterated PD and a collective action game with nonidentical payoffs. In the first case, if we fix the terms of trade, by virtue of, say, the Nash bargaining solution, the method of stability sets tells us how changes in the external environment (e.g., the probability of iteration) affect the likelihood of trade. In the second case, the method arrives at an expression more complex than the one above, where now the probability of the cooperative equilibrium depends not only on the payoffs but also on the relative size of the groups.

From a technical point of view, this is all there is to these three chapters. A set of long-winded mathematical steps, covering pages and pages of definitions and graphs, boils down to a one-line equation. But these technical details mask important issues about the research agenda I want to launch here and how it relates to other lines of inquiry.

The method of stability sets offers us a way to deal with the lack of predictive power of game theory when it comes to games with multiple equilibria. Instead of leaving the game's outcome entirely indeterminate, and instead of imposing on it a set of arbitrary restrictions, the method obtains the relative likelihood of different outcomes, a relative likelihood entirely derived from the game's microfoundations.

I believe this technical solution has far-reaching implications for the way we study collective action problems. In its early stages, rational-choice theory's involvement with collective action was perceived by friends and foes alike as a calculated attack on what, for lack of a better word, I will call "structuralism," that is, the belief that instances of collective action, or the lack thereof, are responses to external, objective circumstances.

Game theory, the argument would go, had taught us that the real triggers of collective action are internal to the agents themselves, be it their organization responsible for offering selective incentives or the mutual beliefs they cultivate about each other and that determine their ability to coordinate in the pursuit of a common goal. With these variables doing all the explanatory work, it would seem that there is no room in a coherent theory of collective action for the kind of structural, especially socioeconomic, variables that studies of an earlier generation had privileged.

The method of stability sets throws this received wisdom into question. Once we generalize the standard methods and look not only at a game's equilibria but at their stability conditions, we see that exogenous parameters, the payoffs, *do* play a role in shaping the game's outcome. They certainly do not determine the result, but they make some results more likely than others.

History is replete with instances where agents have been able to overcome the most formidable barriers imposed by their external circumstances. Countless tales of treason and courage are based on this. After all, structural conditions do not exert any deterministic causal impact over collective action: they are just enablers or impediments that cannot substitute for human agency. But as social scientists, we care about enablers and impediments. Quite often those are the ones we can affect. We may never find a way to prevent a decent democratic regime from collapsing under massive protests. After all, focal points of coordination may emerge in the most unexpected places. But if it turns out that helping such regime avoid the worst effects of a drought forestalls such instability, social scientists should take notice of this whenever their analysis and advice is required.

Institutions, ideas and often sheer individual resolution drive collective action but always in a context given by objective circumstances. We cannot claim to understand a particular instance of collective action if we ignore this context.

This suggests that research about collective action should try to integrate the study of external, structural factors with the study of institutions, organizations and mutual expectations, rather than belittling the impact of either of these. The method of stability sets offers a way to do this. In a game with multiple equilibria, the likelihood of the different outcomes depends on two main types of factors: the payoffs and the initial belief conditions. The payoffs are exogenous parameters that constitute the context where collective action occurs, whereas the belief conditions are shaped by the shared ideas and interactions of the agents concerned.

If we knew exactly what the belief conditions in a group are, we would not need any extra inputs, we could make a deterministic and accurate prognosis in any collective action problem. But as social scientists, most of the time we cannot know exactly what the belief conditions are. At best, we can surmise what they could be. In the technical framework developed above, this is what the distribution of initial belief conditions does: it captures the analyst's information, or ignorance, about the expectations agents have about each other.

Stability sets capture the other side of the problem: payoffs. The payoffs inform us which initial belief conditions are conducive to coordination and which are not. Combining the stability sets and the distribution of beliefs brings together the structural context where agents operate and the expectations they have when they act. This avoids two types of one-sidedness: that of attributing all the explanatory role to structural conditions and that of ignoring them altogether.

Structural accounts of collective action have been criticized within the tradition of rational-choice theory so often that there is hardly any need to rehearse the criticisms in a book that relies so much on it. Perhaps it is more salutary to spend some time discussing the drawbacks of the other extreme and what the method of stability sets can do to overcome them.

If we focus entirely on belief conditions, on the work of the organizations, institutions and ideas that shape them, we forgo the possibility of analyzing them from a systematic comparative perspective. Let's call this the "exceptional-people bias." Collective action requires mobilizing strategies, but the strategy that succeeds famously in one context may fail in another. It is tempting to conclude that this is a matter of talent: some people are simply more gifted than others when it comes to mobilizing large groups. It would be obtuse, however, to deny that part of this erratic pattern of success and failure has to do with exogenous circumstances, some of which affect the payoffs of collective action.

Part of the job of a good political entrepreneur consists of finding the right time and place, the right combination of external factors, in a word, the right context, to operate. Many activists that would otherwise be considered masterful mobilizers have seen their enterprise blow up in their face, often costing them their life, for having been cavalier about the context, for choosing as a base a town where their opponents had co-opted vast parts of the population, for beginning their mobilizing efforts when other alternatives were already gathering momentum, for overestimating the impact of the upcoming economic crisis, and so on. Context is not everything, but politicians ignore it at their peril. In fact, most of the time, they do not. Any organization serious about collective action spends time and effort getting a good reading of its context. The social scientists that study them must do the same.

For those of us who use the language of game theory to analyze social phenomena, the method of stability sets offers a tool with which to keep in mind the objective conditions that surround collective action without reifying them into an iron law of determinacy, recognizing the scope of human agency. Changes in payoffs change likelihood; this is a piece of knowledge that is at once useful and modest.

This lack of a systematic basis for comparative analysis biases the results by directing the researcher only to look at success stories. For every social movement that grows into an overwhelming political force, there are many that never get off the ground, often with similar goals but in different times or places. Once we know that a collective endeavor is successful, it is easy to marvel at the political genius of its participants forgetting that equally talented agents failed in similar, but ultimately different, circumstances.

But if this first drawback vitiates results of ongoing research, there is a second drawback that simply makes other inquiries impossible: the current approaches are not adequate to study counterfactuals, the instances of collective action that do not even get started but that have a powerful effect on the course followed by a political process. In parallel to the previous bias, let's call this the "exceptional-times bias." A complete theory of collective action cannot be a theory tailored only to study periods of unrest. Coordination is a powerful social force even when it operates as an undercurrent. Conflicting goals among social groups are ubiquitous, but they rarely lead to open confrontation. Most of the time, all sides involved in such conflicts see the status quo as a better alternative than any other. If, as social scientists, we want to understand how this happens, we must understand what are those other alternatives, many of which involve collective action. We need to have a theoretically informed account of instances of collective action that we will never be able to observe because they simply lurk behind as threats that keep the current situation in place.

If our conceptual apparatus is entirely concentrated on mobilization strategies, we are at a loss here. Potential, counterfactual collective action is in the minds of all rulers, through all their waking hours, whether they rule the most open democracies or the harshest tyrannies. In deciding on an economic package, or a piece of legislation, or a constitutional change, all of them, or at least the really able among them, are mindful of the possible surges of collective action that may destroy their plans. In their current state, rational-choice theories cannot even start addressing this question because they rely too heavily on the role of organizations. In instances like this, however, the organization does not exist: it is simply a prospect. But even as a prospect, it is a force to be reckoned with.

The method of stability sets can study such counterfactuals. In fact, in the second part of this book I have deliberately stayed away from the study of ostensible instances of collective action, such as revolutions or mass protests. In Chapters 5 and 6 I illustrate the method by using it where its advantages are clearer: in the study of situations where collective action, even if it does not occur, contributes to shaping the polity's outcomes. For all their differences, the reader of these chapters will be able to discern a pattern. First, I will spell out a politico-economic model where some agents, clients of a political machine in one case, workers with no capital in the other, could potentially benefit from collective action (voting against the patron or creating a strong union with full bargaining powers). The likelihood of them doing so depends on the problem's structure, the type of economy they inhabit, just as the method of stability sets would have it. Collective action is neither a necessity, dictated by the shrewdness of some entrepreneur, nor an impossibility always trammeled by free-riding: it is a counterfactual. Although this counterfactual may never materialize, it exerts a potent effect because it is the benchmark against which agents evaluate their current status quo and decide on it. By calculating the likelihoods of the different counterfactual scenarios, we can understand better the sources of stability (or disruption) of the status quo.

The preceding statement may seem to exaggerate the situation because most of the times organizations exist, even if not yet mature and in full swing. That is correct, but for the same reason, our knowledge of the belief conditions of collective action is so hazy that we should not put too much stock in it. It is wiser to acknowledge that we can only surmise what those conditions are and combine this uncertainty with the knowledge obtained from the stability sets. In the applications I will supply, I arrive at the likelihood of collective action, leaving room for improvement if we incorporate our knowledge about belief conditions. The fact remains, though, that this likelihood allows us to study counterfactual instances of collective action. More knowledge about beliefs would not make counterfactuals useless but would instead allow us to understand them better.

Rational-choice theorists often consider contemporary economics the most succesful social science, an example to be imitated by the rest. Whatever truth one may find in this perception of economic science, rational-choice approaches to collective action have thus far failed to live up to that standard in one critical aspect: comparative statics. Economics as a discipline would not be where it is now without comparative statics. The exercises of formalization typical in economics and that so baffle observers foreign to the discipline are, ultimately, procedures to enable comparative statics involving long chains of causal reasoning.

An example might help. The law of supply and demand can be expressed easily without any formalization. If we want to find out the effect of a drought on the price of wheat in a country, we do not need formal models of any kind: this is a chain of reasoning that involves only one link. But if we want to find out the effect of said drought on that country's interest rate, more links are involved. We need to know whether it is a net importer or net exporter of wheat, whether it has a fixed or floating exchange rate, whether the central bank targets inflation or growth or some hybrid of both, and so on. Any estimate of the final impact will depend on our estimates of each of the stages of reasoning involved. Economic models are the tools to negotiate each of these steps, keeping all the pieces in sight at the same time. Much of economic analysis is about this type of comparative statics, about finding the effect of exogenous shocks over endogenous variables that are not immediately or transparently related to them. If it did not contribute to comparative statics, most of economic formalization would be an exercise in futility.

Ultimately, the methodological purpose of the analysis of stability sets is to put the rational-choice approach to collective action in the service of comparative statics. Coordination is the key to most political processes and understanding how structural conditions shape coordination is the key to a rigorous treatment of political economy. This type of political economy cannot dispense with a comparative statics of collective action because its polar star is the study of how exogenous changes in the economic structure affect the realm of political alternatives that the actors in a polity face.

The chapters that follow illustrate the research agenda I have in mind. Simplified as they are, these models help us transform our intuitions about the interactions between economics and politics into testable hypotheses, derived from the analysis of rational decision making. In that sense, they show that the method of stability sets does not see the macrostructural dimensions of collective action as in conflict with their microlevel logic. It combines both to arrive at a picture of social interactions that is both textured and informative.

A theory of collective action compatible with rational-choice theory, attuned to the context where agents act, general enough to encompass successes and failures, to encompass times of calm and times of agitation, able to illuminate broader questions of political economy: such is the theory we need to develop. Such is the theory the method of stability sets is meant to facilitate.

Part II

Applications

Introduction to Part II: Structural Inequalities and Democratic Governance

Analytical precision and mathematical rigor are not ends in themselves. Ultimately, the approach developed in the preceding chapters must prove its usefulness in generating insights about substantive questions. Here I will take two small stabs at one such major question: the connection between democracy and equality.

At the dawn of the contemporary democratic era, many saw democracy as a formidable force that, once unleashed, would transform all the societies that embraced it. When observing what was at the time the only sizeable democracy, de Tocqueville (2000 (1835)) concluded that the American experiment in democratic government was heading to a future that would be shared by the rest of the world, a future where all the inequalities entrenched over centuries would collapse under the pressure of masses newly armed with the right of suffrage. In one country after another, blood was spilled in the struggle to extend the franchise because both friends and foes of democracy thought that, upon taking hold, this new form of government would overhaul the preexisting allocations of power and resources.

Soon a rival, skeptic account emerged, one in which democracy, far from ushering in an era of equality, would simply give new garb to the inequalities and injustices of the past. In a famous passage, Marx and Engels (1992 (1848)) called the modern state the "executive committee of the bourgeoisie" and, although both later revised their views, they never became much more flattering of contemporary democratic strictures. Arguably, Marx's scorn should be understood within the context where it emerged: a time when universal suffrage was still heavily restricted and when the notions of mass parties and open political competition would defy the most fertile imaginations. But, although many Marxists later came to embrace electoral democracy, notably social democrats, his statements were influential enough to start a tradition of doubting the potency of democracy as a force for equality.

With the hindsight of a century and a half, it is safe to say that none of these prognoses has turned out to be literally true. Perhaps a larger share of the world's population lives in democratic regimes now than at any previous point in history but large disparities of income and opportunities subsist and often even have grown. But it is also true that several democracies, especially some of the wealthiest ones, devote a larger share of their resources and efforts to attaining equality than at any preceding era.

When facts do not lend themselves to sweeping generalizations, it is wise to turn the ambiguities into a source of questions aimed at finding the mechanisms at work. This is the path followed by a large and vibrant body of scholarship of political economy informed by rational-choice theory. The mechanism through which democracy could in principle lead to greater equality is clear: once the fundamental instruments of redistribution are in the hands of a majority, it is to be expected that said majority will use them to extract as much resources as possible from the wealthiest members of the polity. This idea, which animated much of the early debates about electoral franchise, received a new formulation in the language of contemporary economic theory in the work of Meltzer and Richard (1981). But the logic of this argument is too powerful for its own good: it fails to explain why democracies retain some inequalities. A complete account needs other mechanisms to counteract this first one.

Meltzer and Richard suggest that, since taxes have incentive effects, electoral majorities abstain from full progressive taxation lest it shrink the size of the pie available for redistribution. Roemer (1997, 1996) claims that, since electoral competition is rarely only about taxation, but instead includes other issues (policy dimensions), these issues may end up fracturing what would have been otherwise a redistributive majority.

Before the advent of democracy, a polity's anti-egalitarian bloc can resort to another mechanism: slowing down the march toward democracy or stopping it altogether, with fire if necessary. Recent studies about the emergence of democracy and its spread throughout the world draw on this intuition and probe how it works in different environments (Acemoglu and Robinson, 2006; Boix, 2003; Ellman and Wantchekon, 2000). Negotiated transitions are a closely related mechanism. In an authoritarian polity facing pressures to democratize, it is possible for elites to offer, and get accepted, a democratization package so tied in knots that not much can be expected from it (Przeworski, 1990).

Here I want to explore a related idea: democratic institutions may not lead to full equality, even once they are consolidated, because the socioeconomic structure in which they are embedded trammels their putative equalizing power. This topic has a long lineage in Marxism and theories influenced by it. Gramsci (1992) famously stated that elections are but the last stage of a long process destined to confer legitimacy to bourgeois rule. Poulantzas (1975) argued that the modern state's scope for action is only one of "relative autonomy," determined as it is by the underlying class structure. Offe (1987) considers that the welfare state as a redistributive arrangement depends on the mutual recognition of individuals of a normative principle of solidarity and that the functioning of a market economy puts pressure on individuals to abandon such a compact. Habermas (1984) considers that the economic rationalization typical of capitalism crowds out genuine democratic deliberation, leaving an imprint on the political institutions that keeps them from addressing the inequities inherent in the system.

It would be a major understatement to say that rational-choice theorists remain unimpressed by such theses since they are not couched in terms of individual decision making (although Offe and to some extent Habermas do rely somewhat on such categories). But this does not make them absurd. After all, their starting point is hardly controversial: an institution's performance, we have many reasons to believe, depends on the environment in which it operates.

I have no interest here in starting a polemic for or against overarching theories of the state, Marxist or otherwise. The models I will put forward will barely resemble the arguments I just alluded to. I will not make any effort to translate or formalize them to make them palatable to rationalists. Instead, I will use the tools developed in the preceding chapters to spell out ways in which socioeconomic realities place limits on the type of redistribution that can result from electoral politics.

In a nutshell, the reasoning I will follow is fairly simple. In every democratic polity, some ground rules are not subject to democratic decision making. Property rights and social hierarchies, two such ground rules that will play a prominent role in the next chapters, are cases in point. They have far-reaching consequences in determining what is and what is not possible in the realm of politics but they themselves are not routinely up for consideration: they are only called into question in times of a major constitutional shift or perhaps even a revolution. In normal times, political actors in a democracy are expected to accept the established ground rules, which is to say that they are expected to accept the outcome of the last constitutional shift or the last revolution.

When it comes to property rights and social hierarchies, this may prove to be a tall order. They are both exclusionary and depend on who was defeated the last time they were up for decision. It should come as no surprise if those defeated parties give at best a grudging acquiescence or even try to force a reconsideration of the issue. Seen from this perspective, there is no such thing as neutral democratic mechanisms.

To turn this notion into an analytical argument, we still need to make explicit the ways in which the ground rules of the socioeconomic structure condition the possibilities on the table during an electoral contest. The plural in "ways" is crucial: perhaps there is no single mechanism and therefore, no guarantee that it will always work in the same manner and with the same effects. Perhaps we have to work through the logic of the scheme one case at a time. Incidentally, this is a major methodological difference between the approach I want to articulate and the one most closely identified with "structuralism." Whereas we may share the view that "structures matter" (to use the trite expression), structuralists try to arrive at one unifying principle that explains how this happens. By my reckoning, the debates among structuralists about the place occupied by categories such as "capitalist mode of production" or "suprastructure vs. infrastructure," while somewhat objectionable to those foreign to the tradition, are relevant to those in it because whatever the outcome is, it will determine the final shape of the model, the way all the pieces fit together in one general account. But I do not think there is any need for the pieces to fit together. Societies are infinitely complex and it may well be that no unified principle accounts for all the connections between structures and outcomes. Instead of a unified theory, we should try to detect different mechanisms and explain how they work in different times and places, letting the final aggregate be a matter of empirics, dependent on the specific case analyzed.[1]

Just like any other rule, social ground rules are worthless unless they enjoy some measure of collective recognition.[2]

---

[1]In this regard, my methodological views agree with those of Elster (1989) to the extent that he rejects the notion of a general theory of society and calls for an account of mechanisms. But I do not go with him all the way: he extends this call to the very microfoundations of a theory while I have more confidence than him that the benefits of deductive models, based on orthodox decision theory, can make up for their undeniable drawbacks. Waldner (2006) offers a forceful critique of Elster's stance in ways akin to the ones I defend in this book.

[2]This topic is central in phenomenological sociology (Berger and Luckmann, 1967; Habermas, 1996) and in the philosophy of social facts (Searle, 1995; Gilbert, 1989; Bratman, 1993).

In that sense, they are akin to the equilibria of coordination games: provided everyone adheres by them, individuals are discouraged from unilateral departures. Herein resides the power of collective action. Whereas an equilibrium works to punish unilateral deviations, coordinated deviations may destroy it altogether. Conceivably, collective action could destabilize and reestablish the most fundamental practices and institutions in any society, its laws, its currency, its customs and even its language. Yet it rarely does so. Instead, such social facts display remarkable endurance, sometimes measured in millenia.

In my approach to collective action problems, this is the point where the technical and the substantive converge. How stable a social fact is depends on how willing society's members are to accept it. The likelier it is that individuals coordinate in a collective endeavor to reject a social fact, the more fragile it is. The game-theoretic treatment of coordination in Part I of this book taught us that the likelihood of such coordination depends on objective, structural circumstances. For the purposes of a research agenda in political economy, this suggests a line of inquiry: make explicit how a society's economic structure lends stability or disrupts its political institutions by forestalling or promoting collective action directed against them.

In Chapters 5 and 6 I will exemplify such a take on political economy by developing models where economic and social conditions influence the possibilities of political collective action, electoral or otherwise, on the part of the citizenry. In Chapter 5 I will focus on clientelism to study how political monopolies based on patronage, often entrenched in the social structure thanks to longstanding inequalities of power, confront the voters-clients with a collective action problem that limits their possibilities to coordinate in favor of policies more to their liking. In Chapter 6 I will study how the functioning of the labor markets, often regulated as a result of workers' collective action, has downstream effects on politics that change the distributive options available electorally. The result of this analysis will largely be compatible with the initial conjecture:

inequalities in the underlying socioeconomic structure blunt the equalizing power of electoral competition.

Thus stated, this may seem either a platitude or a sweeping indictment against democracy. We do not need sophisticated game-theoretic machinery to conclude that unequal societies will not stop being so only because they have elections. Many people already have arrived at this same conclusion without arduous mathematical weight lifting. By the same token, one could take this to be an incendiary conclusion, some sort of denunciation of democracy as a sham.

There is a third possible reading, the one I favor in these pages, that turns this simple notion into a source of social-scientific questions. What type of inequalities can reinforce themselves in the face of electoral competition? How? Are all economies equally prone to this? Are there any discernible socioeconomic trends that undermine this state of affairs? These and other related questions pertain to specific details about specific economies and societies. To answer them we need the right precision tools. Without scalpels we would not have anatomy treatises. The following chapters are not an anatomy of democracy, but a display of a special type of scalpel that may lead to some anatomic findings of interest in their own right.

Chapter 5

Clientelism as Political Monopoly

5.1 Introduction

Some elections, especially in the Third World, are almost literally an exercise in "Brechtian democracy" whereby the government dissolves the people and elects a new one. During the process, government officials scrutinize the track record of the populace to see how much those aspiring citizens behaved with the ruling party's interest at heart. The election rallies are an opportunity to see up close the degree of loyalty of the masses and, since democracy needs accountability, once the returns are in, underperforming citizens are shown the door, either by firing them from their public sector jobs, or denying them access to certain services. The results are impeccable. Whereas in an ordinary democracy, the government that emerges mirrors the preferences of slightly more than 50% of the population (percentages above 60% are called landslides), in these other democracies the electoral returns are far more impressive: often more than 90% of the elected people can be considered a reliable supporter of the incumbent.

While this description might conjure images of totalitarianism, similar patterns are discernible in clientelistic democracies. True, the national elections of clientelistic countries rarely fit the implacable pattern of incumbents winning with more than 95% of the vote, but local clientelistic machines manage to reelect themselves with clockwork regularity and overwhelming majorities. Clientelistic regimes do not usually resort to violence as a tool of control the same way dictatorships do but their citizens are subjected to smaller threats, less intimidating but sometimes more pervasive, threats of being fired, of having the public works program scaled back, of being bumped down a waiting list.

Thus clientelism mocks the idea that in a democracy ultimate power resides with the people. In fact, the contemporary client of a political machine is a direct descendent, often also in the strictly familial sense, of the subordinate party in patron-client relations of feudal and semifeudal societies. Whereas in the past the patron would provide security in exchange for loyalty and services, modern political clientelism seems to follow a similar pattern except that this time the loyalty takes the form of electoral support and instead of security, patrons offer resources garnered from the public sector. It would seem as if, while the forms of exchange and its asymmetries of power remain, only its material contents changes.

Believers in the power of institutional reform may find here a sobering lesson on how social mores assert themselves in the presence of putatively profound constitutional changes. Arguably, this substantive lesson carries over to methodological questions. If established practices that operate, so to speak, behind the citizens' backs can have such a powerful influence over the efforts of those same citizens to change their forms of government, one has reason to wonder about the wisdom of an approach that sees individuals as the main explanatory categories. This much has been argued by critics of rational-choice theory. For instance, for Weyland (1996), rational-choice theory is ill-equipped to study clientelism because, by design, it places the main explanatory burden on free-standing agents at the expense of a nuanced understanding of the structures that constrain their action.[1]

---

[1] "Basic institutional structures are not flexible products of choice that adapt easily to changes in actors' preferences and power capabilities. Rather, they are resilient and persistent in shaping the definition of individual interests and setting parameters of political behavior. Indi-

This chapter can be read as an attempt to refute this criticism with a concrete example. The charge that rational-choice theory ignores the role of social structures has been raised at many different levels, some of them involving highly abstract conceptualizations within social theory, and this is not the place to discuss such arguments. Instead, for the present purposes it seems more useful to discuss specifically what the role of clientelistic structures is in shaping individual agency and, given this role, what can be learned about clientelism from a game-theoretic perspective.

A satisfactory analysis of a clientelist system must examine how it affects its members' possibilities of engaging in collective action. Seen in this light, the causes and consequences of clientelism can be brought into sharper focus with the aid of the tools I have discussed in the first part of this book.

Although it is nowhere written in the theoretical canon, rationalist models of collective action often assume that collective action is the realm of politics in "extraordinary times." At least this is the impression one would get from the many models of public goods, tipping games and focal points that refer to protests, insurgencies, and revolutions. Without any individual author intending it, rational-choice theories of collective action rarely speak to problems of "politics as usual." Against this backdrop, it may seem odd to use tools from the study of collective action to understand the everyday workings of political clientelism. Yet, political clientelism is, ultimately, the outcome of a sophisticated collective action problem.

5.2   Clientelism in Society and in Politics

Political clientelism has been defined in many different ways. Even in the analytically oriented literature we find significant conceptual diversity. For Robinson and Verdier (2001), clientelism means that politicians distribute to voters goods that are reversible, rather than permanent. For Estévez and his as-

---

vidual actors operate inside these institutional constraints. Contrary to rational choice's methodological individualism, these constraints should be the starting point of political analysis" (Weyland, 1996, pg. 4).

sociates (Estévez, Magaloni and Díaz-Cayeros, 2002), it means that politicians distribute goods to individual voters, instead of distributing public or club goods. For Wantchekon (2002), it means that politicians offer voters concrete benefits in the lead-up to elections, rather than promises of programmatic benefits that will materialize after the election. For Lyne (2001) and for Brusco and her associates (Brusco, Nazareno and Stokes, 2002), it means that politicians use the criterion of expected political support rather than more abstract criteria of identity of need to decide which citizens get what.

Interestingly, all these definitions of clientelism choose as benchmark a notion about what a perfectly competitive electoral system would do. This is hardly surprising since much of the interest on clientelism in recent years has been spurred by the remarkable differences between the performance of advanced industrialized democracies and those in the developing world or of recent consolidation. Thus, scholars have used the term "clientelism" to capture some of these differences in recent studies of Argentina (Auyero, 2001; Brusco, Nazareno and Stokes, 2002; Levitsky, 2001; Szwarcberg, 2001), Brazil (Gay, 2001, 1998; Hagopian, 1996; Mainwaring, 1999), Mexico (Fox, 1994; Estévez, Magaloni and Díaz-Cayeros, 2002), Peru (Stokes, 1995), Bulgaria (Kitschelt et al., 1999), Russia (Van Loo and Taran, 2001), Benin (Wantchekon, 2002) and Vietnam (Malesky, 2001).

I share with this literature the belief that, for clarity's sake, we should compare clientelism with a "pure" type of democracy, even if no such thing exists on the face of the earth. Ostensibly, politics in clientelistic societies differs greatly from a well-functioning democracy, however defined. But I also believe that we do not take full advantage of this methodological procedure if we limit our comparison to the specific nature of exchanges and promises in the two types of polities compared. We run the risk of mistaking the symptom for the disease.

Nothing in the definition of a democracy says that politicians cannot or will not compete by offering personalistic benefits to their supporters, or by making promises contingent on each individual's vote, or by providing private goods in the

lead-up to the election. When we describe a "pure" democracy
as a system where politicians compete through programmatic
appeals, focusing on public goods at the expense of private
goods, we are, perhaps inadvertently, conflating the specific
rules for electing a government (democracy) with an elaborate set of practices in a polity, practices that remain, for the
most part, unspecified.

If there is one lesson that anthropologists and sociologists
have taught those of us who think about political clientelism,
it is that political clientelism never appears ex nihilo; it always emerges against the background of a society that is already clientelistic in other nonelectoral, and even nonpolitical,
realms.[2] The patron-client relations we observe in electoral
politics are little else than a late addition to a long list of
patron-client relations prevalent in security provision, labor
exchange, appropriation of agricultural surplus, conflict resolution and personal loyalties.[3]

This leads me to side with sociologists such as Eisenstadt
and Roniger (1980) who claim that all these exchange patterns
emerge from the same type of power relations. As in other
types of clientelism, in political clientelism one of the parties
has privileged access to a set of resources that he (more often
than not, patrons are males) can grant or deny to the client
at his discretion. This discretion is a source of power since it
allows the patron to impose several constraints on the client's
behavior. The resource *exchange* in clientelistic systems in
general, and in political clientelism in particular, owes its form
to a deeper structure of resource *control*. But, beyond this,
political clientelism can occur even if the resources exchanged
and the resources controlled are not the same.

Clientelism can be likened to a monopoly in an economic
market with the patron occupying the role of a monopolist
with the power to extract a surplus from the customer. Students of clientelism on the ground may cringe at the comparison, given all the differences there are between the exchange

---

[2]I owe this crucial point to a discussion with Federico Estévez.

[3]See, for instance, the models of clientelism discussed by Lemarchand
and Legg (1972) and Eisenstadt and Roniger (1980).

within patron-client relations and the exchange between monopolists and customers. For instance, sociologists have observed that patron-client relations display traits of personal proximity between both parties that we would rarely expect and observe in an economic market.[4] Such differences speak to a related and important, but ultimately different, issue: each relation's source of legitimacy. The ideal type of monopoly that populates economics textbooks does not depend upon any legitimacy other than the one that emanates from the monopolist's property rights, enforced in a court of law, if needed. In contrast, patrons often need to nurture their own legitimacy through an elaborate set of practices. Important though these differences are, they should not distract from the fact that both the monopolist that owns, say, a country's only railroad, and a patron that is the sole provider of security and conflict adjudication enjoy a position of power vis-à-vis the agents with whom they deal. Just as monopolists can use their power to charge prices higher than the cost of the goods they provide, patrons can use theirs to extract from their clients resources, material or otherwise.

In economics, pure monopolies are hard to come by. Much more common is the case of *contestable* monopolies, that is, monopolies that are always threatened by the potential entrance of a challenger.[5] Likewise, it is misleading to think that patrons do not need to be mindful of the possibility of being displaced by another would-be patron.[6] In practice, there are few resources and services such that the existing patron is the only one able to dispense them, be they protection from marauding gangs, access to a grain elevator, transfers of

---

[4]See, for instance, the studies of Clark (1994) on clientelism in American cities.

[5]The concept of contestable monopoly has a long history in economics, Baumol, Panzar and Willig (1982) being its classic presentation.

[6]I am not the first to use the analogy of contestable monopolies to think about politics. A long tradition within "Chicago's political economy" has done the same. A recent exponent is Casey Mulligan and i Martin (2004) and an older source is Stigler (1971). Despite this commonality, my approach in this book differs from that tradition in many other aspects, especially in our attitudes towards the Olsonian view of organized interests.

food and clothing or jobs in the public sector. Like the economic monopolist, the patron needs to forestall the entry of a competitor that could offer the same resources under less onerous conditions.

In this sense, there is a difference, if not in kind, then at least in degree, between political clientelism and the other expressions of clientelism to be found in society. Operating in a context of electoral competition, political clientelism is always subject to a explicit set of rules that institutionalize contestability. If a patron's monopoly comes from being an elected official, in principle he can be stripped of his powers by an action of his very own clients: a vote for an opponent in a contested election. Even in environments without election, one could think of parallel instances of contestability in, say, the monopoly enjoyed by a protection racket in a community without state-provided police services. But it is fair to say that the electoral mechanisms for demoting a patron are much more fluid and transparent than the mechanisms for switching from one Mafia-style organization to another.

5.3 Contestability and Entry Deterrence in Political and Economic Monopolies

For all the powers a monopolist may enjoy, there is one whose extent is very debatable: the power to keep would-be competitors at bay. In economic competition, barring illegal interferences with the operation of other businesses, it seems as if there is only one way in which the monopolist can manipulate the price and quality of his goods to avoid contestation: providing goods at a price so low and a quality so high that customers do not need to switch to another firm. But if the mere prospect of contestation forces the monopolist to behave as in a competitive environment, one is left wondering what is the real power of the owner of a contestable monopoly. In the tradition of economic and legal analysis initiated by Posner (1976) and Bork (1979), a firm's inordinate share of the market does not constitute evidence of an abuse of monopoly power; such a share may simply be the result of that firm being the best possible provider.

Aghion and Bolton (1987) have shown that this argument is less general than it may appear. Consider, for instance, a customer about to sign a contract with a monopolist. In a contestable market, the theory claims, the monopolist cannot overcharge, threatened as he is by a potential challenger, able to produce the same good at a lower cost. But, in an uncertain world, the customer knows there is a risk that the incumbent is the best possible provider of the good and will, then, be able to overcharge, at least up to the price the higher-cost challengers would offer. Facing that risk, the customer is willing to enter into an *exclusive-dealing contract* that stipulates two different prices, one if the customer remains with the incumbent, and the other a "switching fine" that the customer pays if she decides to take her business elsewhere. Contrary to the canonical doctrine on contestable markets, this contract is both acceptable to the customer *and* able to deter the entry of some low-cost challengers. By accepting to pay a "switching fine," the customer gives up part of the surplus she could obtain from dealing with a low-cost challenger but, in return, avoids being fully exploited by the monopolist if such challenger does not exist. Uncertainty about the challenger's entrance is also a source of power for clientelistic incumbents only that here, unlike what happens in the Aghion-Bolton model, such uncertainty is endogenous because a challenger succeeds only if he wins the election, something that depends on actions the "customers" themselves must take.

Suppose that a patron monopolizes the access to a resource useful to the voters, say, jobs in the public sector, slots in the local schools, good beds in the town's hospital or swift adjudication of conflicts in the local courts. In light of the debates on contestable markets, we should not hurry to conclude that this monopoly will give him a special advantage in winning elections unless we have a clear, logical argument. Such an argument is possible thanks to the models of exclusive dealing.

Although experience suggests that clientelistic patrons are often reelected, the Posner-Bork criticism cautions us about inferring from this some abuse of democratic mechanisms. A clientelistic patron may be consistently reelected simply because he is better than the alternatives at providing goods and services. If we want to know if clientelism, by itself, gives patrons an advantage, we must eliminate this possibility and assume instead that both the patron and the challenger are just as efficient in administering the public resources (although, of course, they may follow different allocation rules). That way we can be sure that whatever reelection rates result from our analysis are not because of some intrinsic, unobserved, "better" quality of the patrons but to the mechanisms through which clientelism distorts the putative equality of conditions for participants in an electoral process.

Another possible explanation for the patrons' high reelection rates could be that, whereas challengers offer programmatic appeals and public goods, the patrons' campaigning strategies focus on personalistic transfers and private goods. Although consistent with the observed patterns of clientelism, this explanation, which assumes a difference in nature between patrons and challengers, is ad hoc and unconvincing. Analytically, we should assume that, when it comes to making offers to the voters, both candidates have the same battery of strategies at their disposal.

This already introduces a distinction between resource control and resource transfer. Although the candidates are identical in their freedom to choose the type of transfers they want to offer, they differ because it is the patron, not the challenger, who is the one who controls a resource the voters need. Close observers of clientelistic polities continuously report that the patrons offer private goods to their supporters, such as small amounts of food, construction materials, etc. But other candidates could also make offers of the same type, and many often do. What makes the patron a patron is his control over some other resource that is beyond the challenger's reach.

It is not self-evident how the patron can use his monopoly to improve his prospects in a contested election. Many of the resources he controls are typically dispensed by the state so his control over them depends on his ability to retain elected office. Thus, it would seem as if the patron of a political machine has no special advantage. Voters can simply vote against him if they so wish, and, if enough of them do so, he will lose the privilege of dispensing patronage. The patron, however, has at hand a resource challengers do not have: a political version of exclusive-dealing contracts.

To visualize how such contracts work in a clientelistic monopoly, consider an extreme, unrealistic case in which the patron can observe perfectly the individual voting decision of every voter, whereas the challenger cannot do so. Then, the patron could offer voters access to the resource he monopolizes conditional upon each voter's decision in the voting booth and the patron's electoral victory. Unlike regular elections, here voters that receive a better offer from the challenger do not automatically vote for him because they have to weigh the risk that with this choice, they would lose the resource monopolized by the clientelistic machine, should the patron win.

Then, the patron's power to retaliate against voters who do not support him is the source of his advantage. How plausible is this situation? In countries yet to adopt the Australian ballot, the assumption of perfect monitoring closely approximates reality. But even in other countries, what matters for our purposes is that incumbent politicians can induce in each voter the belief that her expected payoff depends on her individual voting choice, not just on the electoral results. In programmatic politics the opposite is true: each voter's fate depends only on the aggregate results of the election, not on how she votes. In joint work with Susan Stokes (Medina and Stokes, 2001), we offer the example of a small city in Northeastern Argentina, where a local magnate controlled employment opportunities for and services to much of the population and threatened to retaliate against suspected defectors if his preferred candidate lost: voters consistently elected this candidate, even against popular opponents.

As holdovers of other patron-client systems in society, political machines do not only operate on election day. A machine at peak performance constantly has people on the ground gathering information about the voters' individual choices. At the very least, the threat of being denied access to crucial resources forces voters to act as "spontaneous" campaigners for the patron, giving the impression in public that they will vote for him. So, as voters conduct their informal polls through everyday talk, they find that the candidates in control of key resources have an electoral edge. With their individual livelihood depending on them, voters take these informal polls as seriously as they take more "scientific" ones (if not more so). Patrons thus enjoy extra "campaign resources" unavailable to their opponents.[7]

The monitoring of voters' choices is never perfect but the patron can use his informational advantage to get the support even of voters that would otherwise vote for the challenger. This information undergirds the patron's ability to retaliate against "faithless" voters, something that in turn, bolsters his electoral fortunes.

Given the role this kind of monitoring plays in a clientelistic polity, it is reasonable to expect challengers to invest substantially in acquiring them as well. After all, quite often alternation in power in clientelistic countries is, by and large, alternation between political machines. Thus, in this analysis I will assume that both the patron and the challenger can monitor, up to some degree, the voters' decisions and deliver punishment accordingly. But, by the same token, we need an analytical framework where the candidates differ in their ability to monitor. The monitoring capacities of a clientelistic patron are not a mere asset that can be acquired overnight in a spot market. They are the result of entrenched patron-client relations extending back in time and across the social life of the citizenry. It is plausible to assume that one can-

---

[7]I know firsthand that in Colombia, in the public sector of the 1970s and 1980s, employees had to be very mindful about giving the "right" impression when it came to discussing for whom they would vote. Although American audiences are not always attuned to this argument, in my experience it immediately resonates with audiences of other countries in the developing world (at least in Latin America, where I have had the chance to present it).

didate, which for the sake of argument I will assume is the incumbent, has a more efficient machine, with better abilities to intrude into people's voting decisions and, for that reason, better monitoring capacities. This will give the incumbent an advantage: his threats will be more intimidating.

5.4   Clientelism and Collective Action

When a patron threatens voters who defect from him, his threats are hollow unless he wins the election. Voters who prefer the challenger's offer could defeat him if they are a majority. But they face a typical coordination problem. No voter can unilaterally defeat the patron and if anyone tries to do so without the cooperation of others, she will lose access to the resources controlled by the machine. Would-be opponents play a "threshold game."

This coordination problem has been repeatedly recognized in the literature on clientelism with Fox (1994), Díaz-Cayeros, Magaloni and Weingast (2000) and Lyne (2000) being some recent examples. But with the conventional tools of the rational-choice theory of collective action, we reach the same dead-ends already discussed. Not having an operational comparative statics for it, not being able to make any ex ante probabilistic predictions about the success or failure of voters' coordination, we are reduced to developing ex post narratives about the downfall of particular clientelistic machines instead of developing a general theory of clientelism.

Without an operational theory of collective action, we cannot know how political clientelism reacts to changes in its economic and social environment. In contrast, the formalism I proposed in the previous chapters allows us to make such operational statements about the severity of the collective action problem, i.e., the likelihood of its resolution as a function of its environment.

I will illustrate this advantage by developing a model of clientelism and will show how this approach leads to general conclusions about the political economy of these regimes, conclusions that cannot be obtained with the standard tools of collective action theory. With this model we can understand regularities of clientelism that, although empirically robust, have eluded many attempts at theoretical explanation.

Economic development erodes the political power of patrons. In the felicitous coinage of Auyero (2001), clientelism is "poor people's politics" (although there are always Chicago and Boston (Clark, 1994)). But, by themselves, the data will not tell us if a deep causal connection runs between a country's prosperity and the demise of its clientelistic strongholds, or if the connection between poverty and clientelism requires other conditions, or if different types of economic development have different effects over clientelism, or even if there is no real connection but just a spurious correlation. Only a rigorous analytic account can answer these questions. The model that follows explores this problem from an analytical point of view and shows that, in fact, ceteris paribus economic development of some specific kind can alleviate the coordination problem faced by clients, thus reducing the patron's electoral advantage.

Clientelistic polities tend to have bloated public sectors and to afford a relatively small role to universalistic policies of income redistribution. This is no accident. The combination of bloated bureaucracies and scant safety nets (except the ones that can be targeted to proven political supporters) creates an environment where clientelistic machines increase their power over their voters. But only an operational treatment of the collective action problem inherent in clientelism can turn this argument into a precise theory, a theory with which to study, say, the impact of different types of public sector spending over the stability of clientelism.

An analysis colored by tipping models, or public goods, or focal points, can point to the existence of this collective action problem and the sufficient conditions for its solution, but cannot assess its severity or the variables that modify it. As such, it cannot clarify the effects of economic development or the size of the public sector over the stability of a monopoly.

5.5   A Politico-economic Model of Clientelism[*]

In light of the previous discussion, a parsimonious model of clientelism needs the following elements:[8]

1 A political monopoly over some specific resource, a monopoly whose continuity is contingent on electoral victory.

2 A gap between the monitoring capabilities of the candidates, the patron being the one who has an advantage in gathering information about the voters.

3 A vast latitude in the candidates' ability to make proposals, so that the effects of the clientelistic monopoly are not confused with possible effects of some arbitrary ideological difference between the candidates.

The model in this section captures these three elements and draws their implications. Property 3 implies that this model belongs to the category of "divide-the-dollar" electoral games, where two candidates compete for elected office by offering each voter a share of some resource (e.g., national income). This means that both candidates can offer, if they so wish, purely personal transfers to the voters, independent of any ideological or programmatic commitment to a universalistic rule.

While the practice of transferring private goods is pervasive in every clientelistic polity, we should not consider it *the* difference between clientelistic democracies and the rest. Rather, Properties 1 and 2 offer a better characterization of clientelistic democracies. In clientelistic electoral competition, a monopoly uses its linkages to voters, linkages that transcend the purely electoral arena, to create for itself an advantageous monitoring capacity.

---

[*]Technical section.

[8]This section formalizes the intuitive arguments made above and, as such, makes intensive use of mathematics. Readers not interested in such details can find a qualitative statement of these results in the next section.

To formalize Property 1, consider an economy in which voters (denoted with lower case subindexes i, j) have an endowment ω which they can use for production. Voters can generate income through two possible activities: a risk-free one (ϕ_0) and a risky one (ϕ_1). I describe these activities by the following production functions: $\phi_0(x) = k_0 x, \phi_1(x) = \sigma k_1 x$. The term σ is a stochastic shock taking value 1 when exogenous conditions are good, say, when there is good weather for agriculture, with probability p and 0 when these same conditions are bad, with probability $1 - p$. The actual value of the shock is not known at the time of the election. Access to the risk-free activity is controlled by the patron, who sells the voters access to it at price q.

Voters decide how to allocate their endowment between the two activities. Therefore their income is $y_i = k_1(1 - \theta_i)\omega_i \sigma + (k_0 - q)\theta_i \omega_i$ where θ_i is the share of endowment allocated to the risk-free activity. The voters are risk-averse and their preferences are represented by a utility function u such that: (a) $u' > 0$, (b) $u'' < 0$, and (c) $x u'(x)$ is increasing.[9]

Voters optimally allocate their endowments between risky and risk-free activities following this rule:

$$\theta_i^*(q) = \arg \max_{0 \leq \theta_i \leq 1} Eu(y_i).$$

Hence, both income (y_i) and the optimal allocation rule (θ_i^*) depend on the price of access to the risk-free activity, q.

This formalization accurately represents how resources monopolized by the patron are essential to the voters' livelihood. Moreover, it is consistent with the narratives of clientelism in many Third World societies. In a world subjected to the vagaries of an agrarian economy, without adequate financial markets where individuals can diversify their risks, patrons gain their clout over voters by providing a modicum of economic

---

[9]The first two of these assumptions about preferences are straightforward. They imply that agents have well-behaved preferences with risk-aversion. The last one has been introduced by Hadar and Seo (1988) in the literature on portfolio choice. Its role is to ensure that the demand for risky assets increases as their yield increases, a very intuitive property.

security. In such environment, securing a slot at the impossibly overbooked local school, jumping ahead in the queue for the aid package sent after the latest flood, or having a household member appointed as porter of the municipal building are all welcome protections against the risks of the market economy, protections that are dispensed by the patron through his "recommendations."

The economy formed by these individuals collects taxes at a flat rate τ. Two would-be patrons compete as candidates, an incumbent (I) and a challenger (C), compete in elections by proposing the N-dimensional distribution of this tax revenue. The tax policy is exogenous: both the challenger and the incumbent can decide how to allocate the tax revenue but they cannot decide the total amount of revenue available to redistribute. Through N-dimensional policies, the victorious candidate can transfer resources to the voters in any way he wants.

One of the central properties of a clientelistic regime, as discussed previously, is the fact that many goods and services are subject to a political monopoly. Access to them is controlled by the politicians in office who condition it to displays of loyalty, especially electoral support. To formalize this idea, I shall suppose that the patron's control over the risk-free activity allows him to offer voters exclusive-dealing contracts. These contracts stipulate two prices, each contingent on the voter's decision in the ballot box. If the voter supports the patron she will pay one price (q_0) but if she does not, she will be charged a higher price ($q_1^J : q_1^J > q_0$) for $J = \{I, C\}$.[10] I am assuming that each candidate J charges a different price to punish defectors. In fact, there are several ways we could model the asymmetry in monitoring abilities between the incumbent and the challenger but they all come to the same. We could assume that although they charge the same price (i.e., an infinite price, tantamount to absolute exclusion from the risk-free activity), the incumbent can detect defectors with a

---

[10]An interesting possibility is that the contracts are also contingent on *other* voters' decisions, thus engaging in tactics of collective punishment. I will not pursue that analysis here but its logic is similar to the one discussed in the main text.

higher probability. This would be equivalent to assuming that, in terms of expected utility, the price the incumbent charges for defectors is higher than the one the challenger can charge.

Formally, divide-the-dollar games of this kind present several technical difficulties. With full certainty, they are the quintessential example of a multi-dimensional policy space with no generic Nash equilibrium (Plott, 1967). It is known, however, that if the environment is modified to allow for some uncertainty, then it is possible to find a Nash equilibrium (Calvert, 1985; Coughlin, 1992). In this particular instance, I will borrow from the model developed by Myerson (1993) where, instead of being deterministic vectors of transfers, the candidates' platforms are probabilistic distributions of income. This eliminates the main culprit of the nonexistence of equilibria: the fine-tuning of electoral platforms that each candidate could perform in an environment with certainty, fine-tuning that would allow him to adjust his coalition and defeat his opponent.

I will denote as $t_i^J(\sigma)$ the transfer that voter i receives from candidate J if the state of the economy is σ. To avoid unnecessary complications, I assume that a transfer $t_i^J(\sigma)$ is a fixed share of aggregate output that does not vary from one state σ to the other. This assumption simplifies matters because with it, if, say, $t_i^I(0) > t_i^C(0)$ then $t_i^I(1) > t_i^C(1)$ and so, in a very precise sense we can say that $t_i^I > t_i^C$.[11]

The expected utility of each voter depends then on the transfer he receives from the victorious candidate and the price he has to pay for access to the risk-free technology, in turn a function of his individual voting decision. In general, such expected utility will be $Eu((1-\tau)y_i(\theta^*(q), \sigma) + t_i^J(\sigma)) \equiv v(t_i^J, q)$. To know the exact value of this general expression we need to determine who is the victorious candidate and whom did the

---

[11]In other words, we are excluding the possibility that the candidates use the transfers to offer insurance to the voters. This is not a big loss because the model is already capturing the availability of insurance through the risk-free activity. Furthermore, relaxing this assumption would not change anything of substance. The only difference would be that, in deciding which transfer is preferable for a voter, we would have to compute the expected utility of the transfer itself.

voter support in the elections. Knowing the victorious candidate we can determine the transfer that the voter will receive, and knowing the candidate he supported we can determine the price he will have to pay for the risk-free technology. For example, if the voter supports the challenger and the incumbent wins, his expected utility will be $v(t_i^I, q_1^I)$ because he receives the transfer the incumbent offered him and is forced to pay price q_1^I to use the risk-free technology as punishment for his having supported the challenger. For any utility function, the voter always prefers to pay lower prices. Since we are assuming that the incumbent can punish voters with more accuracy, or, what comes to the same, charge defectors with higher prices, we have that: $v(t_i, q_1^I) < v(t_i, q_1^C) < v(t_i, q_0)$.

With probabilistic platforms, the transfer each voter is offered by a candidate is a draw from the lottery that this same candidate chooses strategically. Thus, any strategy of candidate J is a probability distribution over transfers. To describe such strategies, I use their cumulative distribution functions $F_J^\sigma(t_i)$ which must satisfy the following properties:

- $F_J^\sigma(0) = 0$;
- $\int_0^\infty x \, dF_J^\sigma = \tau y_\sigma$.

The first property means that no candidate can offer to a voter a negative transfer. In the present context, this is in keeping with the assumption that tax collection is independent of the political process so that candidates are only competing over how to allocate the tax revenue already levied. The second property means that the schedule of transfers a candidate proposes must conform (in its expectation) to the balanced-budget constraint stipulating that total transfers equal total tax revenue.

I will not be interested in the way these platforms depend on the actual stochastic state and instead will focus on those propositions that are true regardless of it. So, for notational purposes, let's use the following convention to denote the pair of state-specific distributions: $(F_J^0, F_J^1) \equiv F_J$.

In Myerson's model, the optimization problem of the candidates consists of choosing a probability distribution that maximizes the expected size of their coalition. In that setting, the probability that a randomly sampled voter i receives an offer from the patron better than the one he receives from the challenger is $\int_0^\infty F_C(x)\, dF_I(x)$. With a large electorate, this probability converges to the expected size of the coalition of voters supporting the patron. If this expected size is larger than $1/2$ the patron will win the election.

In the present model, the existence of the monopoly and the monitoring capacities introduce several modifications. In a standard voting model, if a voter receives a better offer from candidate I than from candidate C, he is sure to vote for I. Here that is not necessarily true because the supporters of any candidate are trapped in a collective action problem: although they may prefer "their" candidate, they have to consider that, if this candidate is defeated, they will be punished with a higher price q.

Technically speaking, the subgame that follows once both candidates have proposed their platforms has multiple equilibria. With the standard methods, this would mean that, since the candidates cannot know what comes out of their platforms, they cannot evaluate the probability of victory resulting from their strategic choice and, so, we cannot solve this game at all. But this is not a problem with the method of stability sets. For any given pair of platforms, we can compute the probability with which voters will overcome their collective action problems and use this to compute the resulting probability of victory. That way we have well-defined payoffs for every platform and we can compute the game's equilibrium. The fact that the method of stability sets allows us to solve games that otherwise would not even be well-specified is an eloquent illustration of its advantages.

To compute the probability of victory for each candidate, we need to make explicit the coordination problem their supporters face. To fix ideas, let's study the coordination problem of the challenger's supporters. The resulting expressions will be analogous to the ones for the incumbent's supporters.

For any pair of strategies of the two candidates, define the size of the group of the challenger's supporters as $s_C(F_C, F_I) =$

$N^{-1}(\#\{i : t_i^C > t_i^I\})$, the voters that receive a higher offer from the challenger than from the incumbent. Each member i of this group faces four possible payoffs depending on whom he votes for and who wins: $v(t_i^C, q_0)$, $v(t_i^I, q_1^I)$, $v(t_i^C, q_1^C)$, $v(t_i^I, q_0)$. These payoffs are conceptually analogous to the ones we denoted as w_1, w_3, w_2 and w_4 in Chapter 4. In fact, the first term is the payoff a supporter of the challenger receives if he decides to cooperate in his candidate's victory and succeeds, the second term is the payoff if he cooperates but is defeated, the third represents the payoff if he does not contribute and still his candidate wins and, finally, the fourth term represents the payoff if he does not cooperate and the incumbent wins. The results on stability sets obtained in Chapter 4 rely on distributions of strategies that can be summarized by their average turnout. So, we can describe the size of the stability sets of this game as a function of the average payoffs of the challenger's constituency. More exactly, we can define average values w as:

$$w_{1C} = \int_{i:t_i^C > t_i^I} v(t_i^C, q_0)\, di;$$

$$w_{2C} = \int_{i:t_i^C > t_i^I} v(t_i^C, q_1^C)\, di;$$

$$w_{3C} = \int_{i:t_i^C > t_i^I} v(t_i^I, q_1^I)\, di;$$

$$w_{4C} = \int_{i:t_i^C > t_i^I} v(t_i^I, q_0)\, di.$$

Given these payoffs we can compute the probability with which the challenger's supporters will coordinate. If the challenger's supporters are a minority the incumbent's supporters can ensure their own victory simply by coordinating, regardless of what the challenger's voters do. Likewise, if the incumbent's supporters are in a minority, then the challenger's supporters are the ones who can secure victory independently of their opponents' choices. Finally, if both groups are of the same size, then there will be a tie if both coordinate or if none does, a tie that will be broken by the toss of a fair coin. Denote by $\Omega(t^I, t^C)$ the probability of victory of the incumbent given both candidates' platforms and, as in the preceding chapters, by $\Pi_J(1)$ the probability that group J will coordinate. So, following this reasoning, we can express this probability depending on the size of the two constituencies.

If the group of the incumbent's supporters is larger than that of the challenger's supporters, that is, $s_C(F_C, F_I) < 1/2$:

$$\Omega(t^I, t^C) = \Pi_I(1)$$
$$= \frac{w_{1I} - w_{2I}}{(w_{1I} - w_{2I}) + (w_{4I} - w_{3I})}.$$

If, instead, there are more supporters of the challenger $(s_C(F_C, F_I) > 1/2)$:

$$\Omega(t^I, t^C) = \Pi_C(1)$$
$$= \frac{w_{1C} - w_{2C}}{(w_{1C} - w_{2C}) + (w_{4C} - w_{3C})}.$$

If both groups are of the same size $(s_C(F_C, F_I) = 1/2)$:

$$\Omega(t^I, t^C) = \begin{cases} 1 & \text{with probability} & \Pi_I(1)(1 - \Pi_C(1)), \\ 1/2 & \text{with probability} & \Pi_I(1)\Pi_C(1) \\ & & + (1 - \Pi_I(1))(1 - \Pi_C(1)), \\ 0 & \text{with probability} & (1 - \Pi_I(1))\Pi_C(1). \end{cases}$$

This is, then, a compound lottery so that we can obtain the total probability of victory by computing its expected value:

$$E(\Omega(t^I, t^C)) = 1/2(1 + \Pi_I(1) - \Pi_C(1)).$$

This last expression is of special interest because, as Myerson has pointed out in his analysis of electoral games with probabilistic platforms, they are, ultimately, zero-sum games so that their Nash equilibrium is the minmax strategy profile. More exactly, for any $s_C = 1/2$ represents the only case where both candidates are choosing minmax platforms.

If we denote by F_C^*, F_P^* the pair of equilibrium platforms of the electoral game with political monopoly, the following theorem describes how the probability of victory of the patron changes as the structural parameters governing the technology and the redistributive politics change.

Theorem 4 *In an electoral equilibrium F_C^*, F_P^*, the probability of victory of the patron Π satisfies the following properties:*

- $\frac{\partial \Pi}{\partial k_1} < 0$;

- $\frac{\partial \Pi}{\partial \tau} < 0$.

Proof: The first statement is true because the probability of victory of the patron is an increasing function of the individual terms $(w_{4i} - w_{3i})/(w_{1i} - w_{3i})$ and they are all decreasing in k_1. To prove this, we notice that u is concave, $w_{1i} > w_{4i} > w_{3i}$, and all these values are increasing in k_1 so that:

$$\frac{1}{w_{1i} - w_{3i}} \left| \frac{d}{dk_1}(w_{1i} - w_{3i}) \right| < \frac{1}{w_{4i} - w_{3i}} \left| \frac{d}{dk_1}(w_{4i} - w_{3i}) \right|.$$

The second statement results from a similar argument. In fact, increases in τ increase the expected value of the candidates' budget constraint. But it is not optimal to spend this increase on voters who, even with the improved offer, will still receive a higher offer from the opponent. Thus, the difference $\bar{w}_1 - \bar{w}_4$ increases which, in turn, reduces Π.

Remark: Intuitively, increases in k_1 reduce the dependency of voters on the monopoly, thus alleviating their collective action problem and increases in τ reduce the relative importance of the sanctions imposed by the patron. To take the argument to the extreme, if $\tau = 0$, then there is no money to be distributed, $w_{1i} = w_{4i}$ for every voter and, hence, $\Pi = 1$.

5.6 Concluding Remarks

Occurring in many different latitudes, among different political traditions, institutional frameworks and social structures, political clientelism is such a widespread phenomenon, especially in the Third World, that it is startling to verify the extent to which its instances resemble each other. Clientelistic polities tend to be poor and highly unequal, afflicted by bloated public sectors and with precarious safety nets. Such regularities can hardly be coincidental and, hence, in explaining them we should not resort to variables that are specific to certain times and places. Instead, we must look into the nature of clientelistic relations, as a general phenomenon, in order to understand them.

The model of this chapter identifies one important property of clientelism that helps explain why clientelism coexists with such economic performance. Political clientelism owes its success to the collective action problem it forces upon voters who depend on the patron's political monopoly. Such collective action problem often leads them to reject at the ballot box alternative candidates they would prefer, lest they lose access to the monopolized resource, thus depressing electoral competition with insalubrious consequences.

In developing countries where a large segment of the electorate is poor, democratic theory would suggest that income inequalities would decline over time as pure office-seeking candidates promote distribution. But the developing democracies frequently identified as clientelistic display persistent inequality. The present model makes sense of this puzzle by showing that clientelistic patrons who are fundamentally office seekers also favor nondistributive policies. This is not in spite of their electoral motive, but precisely because of it. The political monopoly they enjoy is more stable in environments with little redistribution because such environments give more salience to the monopoly while leaving the challengers without tools to mount a successful opposition.

This model implies that monopoly plus monitoring produces states that are antiredistributive but not necessarily small. Patrons may use large states to increase the dependency of the electorate on their monopoly. Taxes used not for redistribution but for employing people in a bloated bureaucracy increase his probability of victory.

Economic development, conceptualized as an increase in the productivity of private, risky activities over monopolized, risk-free ones (such as public employment), undermines the electoral strength of the patron. As the private economy becomes more productive, agents depend less on the patron's monopoly and, at the same time, universalistic redistribution becomes more salient. It is a small step to speculate that the patron, knowing this is true, is less than energetic in his pursuit of economic development (a point that Chubb (1981, 1982) drives home in her analysis of southern Italian politics in the post-World War II decades).

Clientelistic monopolies are buttressed by the collective action problem clients face when challenging them. Any mechanism that reduces the severity of such collective action problem undermines the grip of the monopoly. Economic growth and universalistic redistribution are two such mechanisms: they both offer voters alternatives to the resource monopolized by the patron. While the first mechanism does so by increasing the productivity of the nonmonopolized assets, the second one makes more resources available to the monopoly's political challengers. This analysis of the microfoundations of clientelism and its connections with wider economic processes would not be possible without a systematic treatment of the collective action problem, a treatment that tells us how serious the problem is and how its magnitude changes with changes in its environment. An exclusive focus on sufficient conditions for collective action, with no comparative statics, can only tell us how voters may try to overcome free-riding but cannot place their efforts against the backdrop of the political economy they inhabit.

Chapter 6

The Political Economy of Wage Bargaining and Electoral Redistribution

6.1 Introduction

The dichotomy between state and market has been a powerful conceptual template for understanding how the power that individuals derive from their property rights and the power they obtain from their political rights interact in contemporary societies. The study of how capitalist economies based on private property operate against the backdrop of one-man-one-vote decision making has brought about a period of remarkable intellectual fertility for political economy. The vast literature on electorally driven redistribution is just one such example. Recently, a large and valuable crop of scholarship informed by rational-choice theory has weighed in on this topic, adding much to our systematic understanding of the problem (Meltzer and Richard, 1981; Boix, 2003; Roemer, 2001a).

But elections embody only a fraction of the political rights citizens enjoy in modern democracies; voting is not the only source of power besides property. The polis and the market interact, and often clash, in ways that overflow the channels of majority rule. Democracy is more than voting, so much so that we often hesitate to label countries as democratic if all they do is hold elections. Democracy also confers upon individuals the right to engage in collective action through the freedoms of thought, speech and association.

Through the systematic analysis of citizens' preferences and electoral institutions we have attained some degree of understanding of the implications of voting rights for the political economy of contemporary, market-based societies. Likewise, I believe that an operational theory of collective action can help us understand the politico-economic ramifications of these other democratic rights.

In this chapter I will offer a thumbnail sketch of how this could be accomplished by providing a simplified model of a market economy where agents can not only vote but also combine in collective action. Not much can be expected by the way of precision and detailed texture from such a model, but I believe it can serve as a useful benchmark for future research in much the same way as the earlier formulations of economic redistribution through electoral mechanisms made possible more detailed work over time.

6.2   A Limitation of Electoral Models

By now it is a well-established proposition that if the majority in a country is "poor," that is, if median income is below average, something that occurs in virtually all the sizeable world economies, we should expect universal suffrage to lead to redistribution. Powerful as this insight is, it is deficient in a way that, although originating in a purely technical matter, has tremendous conceptual implications.

One of the best-known results in the mathematical theory of voting is that, under some general conditions, voting on the distribution of some amount of money constitutes a game with no equilibrium (e.g., Coughlin (1992)). To circumvent this difficulty, the standard models of progressive taxation impose constraints over the game until it becomes amenable to the median-voter theorem. The single most important constraint of this kind is the restriction to a one-dimensional policy space: a flat tax rate.

What begins as a seemingly innocent technical assumption creates a substantive problem. True, under standard conditions, the median voter is likely to form a coalition with those poorer than him to expropriate (at least part of) the wealth of the rich. But, could not the rich counteract this by offering the median voter the possibility of joining an alternative coalition to expropriate the *poor*? On the face of it, this seems unlikely. By definition, the poor have little wealth to expropriate; such coalition would not be very attractive.

This will not do. Conceivably, the rich could make the deal more attractive by sharing some of their wealth, but less than what would otherwise be expropriated. Satisfying the distributional demands of the median voter is likely to be cheaper than satisfying the demands of the poorest ones.

Mathematically, this opens a can of worms. If we allow all types of distributive coalitions, we are back to the original problem of the nonexistence of an electoral equilibrium. Recently, by introducing the concept of Pary Unanimity Nash Equilibrium (PUNE) John Roemer has addressed this problem, showing that these type of models do have equilibria, albeit of a different kind (Roemer, 2001*b*). One major reason for restricting ourselves to the one-dimensional case is thus removed.

For simplicity, in what follows I will relax the assumption of one-dimensional economic policy but will not adopt a policy space encompassing all the possible distributive policies. My focus is not exclusively on electoral distribution but also on how it interacts with organized collective action.

Let me state bluntly my central thesis, even if later I will have to add the corresponding qualifiers to make it more scientific: the basic mechanism through which the poor can stop this coalition of the rich with the median voter is collective action. Moreover, such a coalition has, in fact, emerged when collective action has not been able to stop it.

This statement may sound outlandish. Taken at face value, it would imply that in some countries we should observe poll taxes or even regressive taxes, two fiscal arrangements that are hard to come by. But this fixation with taxes as the distributive mechanism par excellence, although a convenient analytical tool, can fail descriptively in any but the simplest exchange economies, populated by independent producers. In a modern economy we need to look at the distributional aspect of the factors' markets, the quintessential site of collective action in contemporary politics.

6.3 Distributive Coalitions in an Economy with Factors' Markets

To fix ideas, let's imagine an economy with only two factors of production: capital and labor. We can let capital stand for all the forms of accumulable wealth, including land or even skills. For simplicity, assume that the stock of capital is fixed but that its distribution is unequal so that the median holding of capital is smaller than the average. Much of the basic intuition can be understood by thinking of an economy with three sets of agents: *proletarians*, that is, agents with no capital; the *middle classes*, or agents with median capital holdings; and *capitalists*, agents with above-average capital.

If every agent in this economy were an independent producer, combining his labor with whatever capital he happens to hold, taxing income would be the only possible vehicle of redistribution. But in a modern economy, capital and labor are traded in markets. This implies that an agent's income is determined not only by the market value of his output, but also by the market value of his factor endowment; factor markets, especially the labor market, have a large component of implicit redistribution.

To stick as closely as possible to the standard models of political redistribution, let's restrict our attention to flat tax rates. As a mechanism to transfer income from the rich to the poor and the middle classes, taxes have several advantages. Even with a flat tax, the rich will end up financing a larger share of the public transfers, and the richer they are, the more they will do so. But, as economists have long recognized, taxes, except poll taxes, have distortionary effects that reduce economic output. Taxes that affect the choice of labor over leisure will reduce labor supply and, through it, aggregate income. Let's call this the "incentive effect" of taxation. Beyond a certain point, the incentive effect is so large that further increases in taxes may reduce the total amount of income transferred to those on the bottom half of the income distribution.

There is, however, a problem that complicates the political economy of taxation: even within the pool of net recipients of transfers from the rich, the incentive effect is felt differently by different agents. For a proletarian, the incentive effect has two components: the reduction in net transfers once the tax rate hits a certain threshold and the reduction in employment. Increased tax rates reduce tax revenue only at very high levels whereas the effects on employment can be felt before that extreme arises: the second component kicks in faster. But taxation also offers a way to mitigate the impact of this employment effect. Through public spending, the proletarian can obtain some degree of income support, some degree of nonmarket income, so to speak, to compensate, at least in part, for the loss of market income.

For middle-class citizens, the situation is different because the incentive effect has a third component: reduced labor supply reduces the marginal productivity of capital, thus reducing the return they obtain from their capital holdings. Income transfers that are large enough to compensate workers for the loss of wages are not large enough to compensate the middle classes for the additional loss of capital returns; as a tool for redistribution, taxation is less attractive for the middle classes than for the proletarians.

This creates a fracture in the would-be redistributive coalition. Once we consider factor markets, it becomes misleading to speak of the "poor" as a unified group; agents that we could classify as poor for having income below average are at odds with each other because of their different factor endowments.

In this model, the optimal policy for the middle classes would be a combination of instruments to transfer income from the rich while at the same time keeping the supply of labor as abundant as possible, in other words, keeping the workers' leisure as expensive as possible in order to keep high employment levels with their positive effect on the marginal productivity of capital. In such a world, the middle classes would be extracting income from both the capitalists and the proletarians.

What kind of public policies would we expect from such arrangement? There would be some transfers, perhaps substantial from the upper half to the lower half of the distribution, but coupled with high degrees of "labor commodification" (Esping-Andersen, 1985). Low levels of income support for non-wage-earners would make it harder for workers with no capital to opt for leisure. We would expect low- or non-paid leaves (vacation, sickness, maternity) and little job security because keeping redundant labor during economic downturns negatively affects the returns to capital. The economy would display low levels of unemployment and would operate at or close to its "potential output."

In this case, from the proletariat's point of view, electoral democracy would not deliver all the redistribution it wants. If we look only at the effect of taxes, that is, the difference between "before-government" and "after-government" inequality, it would seem as if this economy has a progressive mechanism of redistribution in place. But this comparison masks a "before-government" inequality that the proletariat would want to address: the returns on accumulable wealth enjoyed by the owners of capital are paid for with high implicit transfers away from the proletariat's leisure.

Having extracted all the redistribution that was possible through electoral mechanisms, a proletarian in this model can only redistribute further income toward himself by accumulating political power in other arenas. In other words, he can engage in collective action.

Thus far we have analyzed an economy where markets operate without any regulation. Although government intervention through taxes affects the choices between labor and leisure, it leaves all the outcomes of these choices to be sorted out by the market. Now let's consider what would happen in an economy in which the proletariat, by engaging in collective action, forces the polity to accept labor-market regulations. For simplicity, let's focus on the issue of a minimum wage. Just as the usual assumption of a flat tax is flexible enough to capture much of what distributive policies do, the issue of a minimum wage can also serve us as a template to think of many of the available tools to regulate labor markets.

As the conventional analysis shows, the minimum wage generates unemployment. In that sense, it has an incentive effect similar to the one that taxes have. Just as before, this incentive effect reduces the marginal productivity of capital and hence is felt disproportionately by the middle classes who, to compound things, do not participate much, if at all, in the benefits.

This has a crucial political consequence: organized collective action aimed at bringing about a regulated labor market shifts the electoral center of gravity by inducing the middle classes to support levels of tax redistribution that it would have otherwise opposed. The reason is that labor-market regulation changes the costs and benefits of the mechanisms of redistribution available to the middle class.

To see how this happens, let's go back to the unregulated economy we were studying before and imagine that the middle classes have obtained their optimal redistributive package: a combination of some taxes that capture income from the rich and labor commodification, which keeps the returns of capital high. If suddenly this economy were to introduce a minimum wage, the resulting decrease in labor supply would reduce capital returns. There is now a gap in the package that needs to be made up. But one of the sources for it is now closed by definition: labor supply has already fallen and, short of going back to the status quo ante, there is no way of raising it again. This means that the transfer shortfall can only be compensated for with higher taxes. Higher taxes have incentive effects and so it would seem as if this attempt to make up for

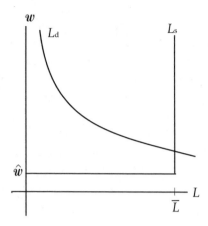

Figure 6.1: A Purely Competitive Labor Market

the gap would backfire. But this ignores that the incentive effects of taxation occur *at the margin*, when taxation in fact reduces labor supply. With the new reality, with the minimum wage, the previous level of taxation is no longer reducing labor supply at the margin; the minimum wage has already done that. Within some interval, additional tax increases will have no incentive effect. A few diagrams may clarify this.

Figure 6.1 represents a simplified version of the supply-and-demand curves that describe the labor market. Wage rate $\hat{w}$ is what is commonly known as the reservation wage, the wage rate below which workers are not willing to sell their labor because their outside option is better. For wages lower than $\hat{w}$ labor supply is zero. Since wage $\hat{w}$ is exactly the wage that makes them indifferent between selling and not selling their labor, at that level, labor supply is perfectly elastic. Finally, at wages above the critical level $\hat{w}$, every worker in the economy is willing to supply labor services, so that the supply is perfectly inelastic.

The critical level $\hat{w}$ depends on the workers' outside option, which, in turn, depends on political decisions over income support. Policies that increase the amount of income that workers can obtain without concurring to the labor market will increase $\hat{w}$. In the economy we have been analyzing, this means that higher tax rates, used to finance universalistic income transfers, raise the safety net, improve the workers' outside option and hence reduce labor supply.

With the particular shape of the labor-supply curve depicted here, the incentive effects of taxes kick in only if they raise $\hat{w}$ above w_{fe}, the highest reservation wage compatible with full employment. At reservation wages higher than w_{fe}, the equilibrium employment level, determined by the intersection between labor supply and demand, drops below $\bar{L}$. For the sake of argument, imagine that the middle classes' capital endowment is such that the optimal tax rate for them is the one that generates a reservation wage of $\hat{w} = w_{fe}$.

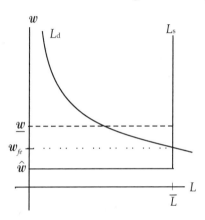

Figure 6.2: A Labor Market with Minimum Wage ($\underline{w}$)

Now introduce a minimum wage regulation, presumably as a result of the pressure exerted by trade unions. The new labor market, with a minimum wage, is depicted in Figure 6.2. There is now unemployment in the economy.[1] To be sure,

---

[1]Technically speaking, there is a difference between the unemployment generated by minimum wages and the one generated by increased safety nets. The latter one is often called "voluntary" whereas the former is considered "involuntary." According to this terminology, voluntary unemployment occurs at equilibrium wages because workers who are out of a job could find work if only they wanted to supply labor at a cheaper rate. I do not think this distinction is illuminating, especially in this model where many of the important effects have to do with output, which is affected by unemployment, whatever its nature. I register it, however, for the sake of completion and to allow the reader to situate this model in the context of the larger literature on labor markets.

unions may constitute something of a "labor aristocracy," as
their critics would put it, to the extent that they obtain secure
and high-paying jobs for themselves at the expense of creating unemployment for other workers in the economy. On these
grounds, it would seem as if unions are working against the
interest of other propertyless agents in the economy. Whether
this is true depends on many specific details. Conceivably,
trade unions could devise job-sharing and wage-sharing mechanisms (often dubbed "socialism in one class" (Scharpf, 1991))
to extend the gains obtained from these high-paying jobs to
those who are left out. There might be good political reasons
to do so.

But if we look beyond the shop floor, the minimum wage
has another far-reaching distributional effect, one that works
through the political system: it changes the trade-offs faced
by the middle classes in their electoral choices in the direction
of more redistribution. Before the minimum wage was introduced, taxes resulting in a reservation wage above w_{fe} would
generate unemployment. With the minimum wage, this is no
longer the case so long as the reservation wage remains below $\underline{w}$. Since the middle class has below-average capital and
income, it is now in its best interest to support higher taxes.
That way it can benefit from the transfers from the rich without incurring any additional costs because of incentive effects:
the incentive effects operate only at the margin and the current
tax rate associated with $\hat{w} = w_{fe}$ has become infra-marginal
by virtue of the minimum wage.

In other words, through collective action, the workers in
this economy attain a labor-market regulation that also shifts
the political balance in their favor. In an unregulated labor
market, the middle classes are not a reliable partner of the putative coalition of the "poor" because they benefit also from
an alliance with the rich against the proletariat. Labor-market
regulation changes this political balance: once "cheap labor,"
with its resulting high capital returns, is no longer an option,
the middle classes become a firmer ally of the proletariat in
the support of taxation. Collective action is, thus, what undergirds this type of interclass collaboration.

The public policies resulting from this type of alliance are different from the ones we would expect in the previous case. In this economy labor-market regulations will coexist with a high social safety net. The difference between "before-government" inequality and "after-government" inequality will be larger, suggesting more redistribution through taxes, but also there will be lower levels of labor commodification. From a macroeconomic point of view, this economy will seem to operate below par, with aggregate output below potential output.

Of course, this is class compromise in the same sense as shanghaied travel is tourism. The middle classes are constrained to reach this arrangement because of the collective action capabilities of the proletariat. Two factors determine how strained this "alliance" will be: the capital endowment of the middle classes and the organization of the proletariat. Large income disparities between the proletariat and the middle classes, coupled with high levels of labor union strength make for heightened tensions between the two groups. The middle classes will resent the proletariat's use of its rights to collective action, and is likely to fight the regulation of labor markets every step of the way. This makes for some ambiguity in the middle classes' political stance. Given their interest in labor market flexibility, they will be opposed to organized labor but, if and once some degree of regulation becomes a fait accompli, it is in their interest to turn around and support labor in its call for higher redistributive taxes.

I submit that this line of reasoning offers us a good starting point for analyzing some aspects of distributive policy making in contemporary economies. But some loose ends remain and to clarify them we need to express formally the main connections of the model. That way we will be able to turn the model's basic intuition into a source of operational hypotheses. The next section, then, presents the model in its mathematical form. This exercise will allow us to obtain results of comparative statics that a purely intuitive discussion would not be able to reach. Toward the end of this chapter, I will present such results in words.

6.4 The Political Economy of Labor-market Regulation and Income Support[*]

In this section I will formulate a model that captures the intuition of the previous section, showing its microfoundations. This will give us the analytical expressions from which we can derive the model's comparative statics.

6.4.1 The Economy

Consider an economy with a continuum of agents. Their preferences are represented by a concave utility function $u(x)$. This economy uses two factors, capital and labor, henceforth labeled K and L respectively and produces one good Y with the Cobb-Douglas production function $Y = K^\alpha L^{1-\alpha}$. To avoid complications coming from the analysis of consumption, let's simply assume that good Y is sold on the world market where final demand, Y_d, is a decreasing function of the price p and parameter Γ, with constant and unitary price elasticity $Y_d = \Gamma/p$.

To analyze the incentive effects of public policy we need to know the behavior of the markets for production factors. Since the effects we are interested in are those pertaining to the regulation of the labor market, we cannot rely only on the standard computations of a full-employment equilibrium. But these computations, nevertheless, constitute a good analytical benchmark that simplifies several expressions.

By the standard method of solving a cost-minimization program and applying Shephard's lemma (Appendix 6.A.1), we conclude that the following equations represent capital demand (K_d) and labor demand (L_d) as functions of their prices (that is, interest rate r and wage rate w):

$$K_d = \frac{Y\alpha}{r},$$

$$L_d = \frac{Y(1-\alpha)}{w}.$$

---

[*]Technical section.

It will be convenient to have a notation for the "potential per capita income," that is, the per capita income that the economy could obtain if it used all its production factors. Let's call it $\bar{y} = Y/L$. Likewise, the capital-labor ratio (K/L) of the economy will also play an important role in our analysis so I will denote it by k. If we consider labor supply and capital supply as fixed at L and K respectively, these demand functions would lead to the following equilibrium factor-prices:

$$
\begin{aligned}
w &= \bar{y}(1 - \alpha), \\
r &= \frac{\bar{y}\alpha}{k}.
\end{aligned}
$$

Convenient as these expressions are, they are not useful for studying an economy that operates below its potential output, which is what happens if public policies affect the factors' supply, especially, as in our case, labor. So, the next step is to lift the assumption of a fixed amount of production factors. For simplicity, I will retain the assumption that capital supply is perfectly inelastic so that $K_s = K$. Capital constitutes the wealth of the economic agents and they differ on this dimension so that, from now on, k_i will label the capital endowment of individual i. In contrast, I will impose a more detailed structure on labor supply.

Individuals in this economy can obtain a nontaxable income z if they engage in home production rather than working in the market. The polity levies taxes at a flat rate τ and uses the tax revenue to finance transfers to individuals in the form of a universal program of income support. Later I will make more assumptions about this program but, for the time being, it suffices to assume that each individual receives a transfer t_i which may vary from one agent to the next. So, agents decide to work in the labor market, forgoing home production, if:

$$
\begin{aligned}
(1 - \tau)(w + rk_i) + t_i &\geq z + (1 - \tau)rk_i + t_i, \\
w &\geq \frac{z}{1 - \tau};
\end{aligned}
$$

where we can define:

$$\hat{w} \equiv \frac{z}{1-\tau}.$$

This results in the labor-supply function:

$$L_s(w) = \begin{cases} 0 & \text{if} \quad w < \hat{w}, \\ [0, L] & \text{if} \quad w = \hat{w}, \\ L & \text{if} \quad w > \hat{w}, \end{cases}$$

so that the labor market is described by the supply-and-demand curves depicted in Figure 6.1.

Therefore, in this economy higher taxes reduce employment through their effect on labor supply. Denote the employment rate of the economy as $E(\tau) = L_d(\tau)/L$. If we normalize the value of z to 1, since it will not play any further role in the analysis, we conclude that:

$$E(\tau) = \min[\bar{y}(1-\alpha)(1-\tau), 1].$$

Given these expressions, we conclude that the highest tax rate compatible with full employment is $\tau_{fe} = (\bar{y}(1-\alpha) - 1)/\bar{y}(1-\alpha)$.

Reductions in employment will obviously reduce output and, perhaps less obviously, also reduce the interest rate. In fact, less labor available means lower marginal productivity of capital and, therefore, a lower equilibrium interest rate. To calculate this, let's express the interest rate as a function of τ and let $y(\tau)$ be the per capita income, also a function of τ, which may differ from $\bar{y}$:

$$\begin{aligned} y(\tau) &= \frac{K^\alpha L_d^{1-\alpha}}{L} \\ &= \bar{y}E(\tau)^{1-\alpha}; \\ r(\tau) &= \frac{\partial K^\alpha L_d^{(1-\alpha)}}{\partial K} \\ &= \frac{\alpha\bar{y}}{k}E(\tau)^{1-\alpha}. \end{aligned}$$

6.4.2 Electoral Preferences

Given this economic background, we can now determine the preferences of voters over distributive policies and, through these preferences, the outcome of the political process. Thus far I have not made explicit the role of taxes in this economy. As far as the previous computations are concerned, it does not matter if tax revenue is used productively or simply dumped in the sea. But to understand the trade-offs voters face in making their political choices, we need to be more explicit. To that end, I will assume that the transfers an individual receives are, all else being equal, an increasing function of the tax rate. For simplicity, and in keeping with much of the literature, we can suppose that tax revenue is distributed evenly among all the citizens. Together with this assumption, the balanced-budget constraint implies that each citizen receives a transfer equal to $\tau y(\tau)$.

In choosing their ideal tax rates, voters have to be mindful of the fact that, while higher taxes increase the size of their transfer, they also have an incentive effect that reduces aggregate output and the marginal productivity of capital and increases unemployment. So, for any given voter i, the optimal tax rate is the one that solves the following maximization problem:

$$\tau^*(k_i) = \arg\max_{\tau} u((1 - \tau)(w + r(\tau)k_i) + \tau y(\tau))E(\tau)$$
$$+ u((1 - \tau)r(\tau)k_i + \tau y(\tau))(1 - E(\tau)).$$

There are several analyses of comparative statics that one could conduct with this model but in this chapter I will focus on two of these. I want to study the political effects of asset inequality and technological change. The following result will serve as the basis for such analysis:

Lemma 2 *For any voter i, the optimal tax rate $\tau^*(k_i)$ in an economy without a minimum wage has the following properties:*

- $\frac{\partial \tau^*(k_i)}{\partial k_i} < 0;$

- $\frac{\partial \tau^*(k_i)}{\partial k} > 0$;
- $\frac{\partial^2 \tau^*(k_i)}{\partial k \partial k_i} > 0$.

Proof: See Appendix 6.A.2. This lemma describes the voters' preferences in an unregulated labor market. But from the preceding discussion we have concluded that labor-market regulations have effects beyond the shop floor because they also change the role of tax policies and, hence, the way voters evaluate said policies. The following corollary formalizes this notion.

Corollary 1 *Denote by* $\tau^*_{\text{reg}}(k_i, \underline{w})$ *the optimal tax rate for an agent with capital endowment* k_i *in an economy with a regulated labor market where the minimum wage is* $\underline{w}$. *Then, there exists a critical capital endowment* k_g *such that* $\tau^*_{\text{reg}}(k_i, \underline{w})$ *is described by the function:*

$$\tau^*_{\text{reg}}(k_i, \underline{w}) = \begin{cases} \tau^*(k_i) & \text{if} \quad k_i < k_g, \\ \tau^*(k_g) & \text{if} \quad k_g < k_i < \bar{k}, \\ 0 & \text{if} \quad \bar{k} < k_i. \end{cases}$$

Furthermore, the value k_g *is a decreasing function of* $\underline{w}$.

Proof: With a regulated labor market, the demand for labor is not always responsive to changes in the tax rate: lowering the tax rate cannot increase labor demand beyond $L_d(\underline{w})$, the demand for labor at the minimum wage $\underline{w}$. In particular, for taxes below $(\underline{w} - (1 - \alpha)z)/\underline{w}$, labor demand is $L_d(\underline{w})$. If we denote by $\tilde{L}_d$ this truncated labor demand, we obtain:

$$\tilde{L}_d(\tau) = \begin{cases} L_d(\underline{w}) & \text{if} \quad \tau < \frac{\underline{w} - (1-\alpha)z}{\underline{w}}, \\ L_d(\tau) & \text{if} \quad \tau > \frac{\underline{w} - (1-\alpha)z}{\underline{w}}. \end{cases}$$

So, in an economy with a regulated labor market, citizens choose their optimal tax rate according to the following maximization problem:

$$\max_{\tau} u(z + (1 - \tau)rk_i + \tau y(\tau)) \frac{\tilde{L}_d(\tau)}{L} + u((1 - \tau)rk_i + \tau y(\tau)) \frac{L - \tilde{L}_d(\tau)}{L}.$$

This maximization problem is identical to the one studied in Lemma 2 for tax rates $\tau > (\underline{w} - (1 - \alpha)z)/\underline{w}$. Therefore, agents that prefer a tax rate in this interval in an unregulated economy will still do so in this new case. Lemma 2 establishes that those agents have a capital endowment lower than k_g. By the same token, the optimal tax for agents with a capital endowment larger than k_g is not larger than $(\underline{w} - (1 - \alpha)z)/\underline{w}$. Those voters will face the following decision problem:

$$\max u(z + (1 - \tau)rk_i + \tau y(\underline{w}))\frac{\tilde{L}_d(\underline{w})}{L} + u((1 - \tau)rk_i + \tau y(\underline{w}))\frac{L - \tilde{L}_d(\underline{w})}{L}$$

subject to the constraint $\tau < (\underline{w} - (1 - \alpha)z)/\underline{w}$. From the proof of the previous lemma, we know that if $k_i < k$, income is increasing in τ. Since in this maximization problem, as long as τ remains inside the constraint set, the employment level does not vary, the agent's income and expected utility both increase with τ. Thus, the optimal tax rate is $\tau^* = (\underline{w} - (1 - \alpha)z)/\underline{w}$.

Since $(\underline{w} - (1 - \alpha)z)/\underline{w}$ is an increasing function of $\underline{w}$, and the optimal tax rate is a decreasing function of k_i, then the capital endowment for which $\tau = (\underline{w} - (1 - \alpha)z)/\underline{w}$ is optimal, k_g in the notation of the corollary, is a decreasing function of $\underline{w}$.

6.4.3 Organized Collective Action

The preceding analysis does not differ much from the standard approaches to distributive taxation in the tradition of (Meltzer and Richard, 1981). But the goal of this model is to make explicit the role of collective action in the political economy of redistribution.

To that end, I shall focus on the collective action problem that the proletariat faces in this economy. The preceding results formalize the intuition already explained: labor-market regulations have effects that go beyond the shop floor. In fact, the existence of a minimum wage forces the middle classes, that is, the median voter, to support taxes higher than those they would support in a purely unregulated labor market. Formally, this can be seen in the schedule of optimal taxes and its truncation at k_g.

But such minimum wage will not result from electoral politics: a coalition of the middle class and the capitalists can defeat it electorally. Instead, in this model the proletariat's only possibility of regulating the labor market is by exerting organized pressure, in other words, through collective action. At this level of abstraction there is little point in spelling out the details of this process, but it could happen in many ways: workers can stage a general strike so successful that the country is brought to its knees and the only way out is to agree to their salary demands, or they can form an effectively enforced cartel that prevents firms from hiring workers at wages lower than what it declares acceptable. Whatever the process that leads there, we can assume that, if successful, mobilized workers would impose a wage rate w_M, the optimal wage they would choose if they could act united as a monopoly. From the previous results, we know that the proletariat's preferred taxes are the highest among the electorate so that, given the direct relationship between taxes and minimum wages, this means that left unchecked, the proletariat would impose a minimum wage that is higher than that preferred by any other agent in the polity.

This suggests the analytical procedure that I will follow in this section. The model's economic structure determines the incentive effects of taxation, key factor of the electoral preferences that shape the political process. Together, these incentive effects and these electoral preferences will determine the potential benefits that the proletariat obtains from regulating the labor market, in this case, by forcing the introduction of a minimum wage.

In Part I we learned that the prospects of collective action depend crucially on the payoff schedule. If, in case of success, cooperators get rewarded above and beyond what defectors do, the collective action problem has multiple equilibria and it is inaccurate to say that every agent will attempt to free-ride on the others, even if collective action results in a public good from which no one can be excluded.

Labor mobilization can produce a public good in the form of higher wages. This is why unions have been a classical topic of collective action theory since Olson (1965, Ch. 6). But, if successful, they are also in a position to reward their members for their contribution in addition to the public good. In keeping with the discussion of 2.6.3, these rewards are *not* the same as the Olsonian selective incentives: they are contingent on success and, therefore, they do not make cooperation strategically dominant.

Union membership may result in benefits of different kinds but, to keep the model parsimonious, I will focus on one benefit that already shows up in the formalization above: job protection. Consistent with the norm in many unionized industries, in this model union members are at a lower risk of being fired than the rest. For simplicity, I will assume that it is impossible to fire a unionized worker.[2]

In Part I I modeled collective action problems described by four different payoffs. The discussion thus far allows us to determine two of them. If the proletariat succeeds in forcing the introduction of monopoly wages, it will benefit from two sources: the minimum wage itself (w_M) and the increased tax rate that will result from the electoral process, as demonstrated above. Since the monopoly wage is optimal for the proletariat, by the logic of Corollary 1, so will be the tax rate.

In terms of our notation, the tax rate of this economy will be $\tau^*(0)$, that is, the tax rate deemed optimal by an agent with capital endowment $k_i = 0$. The payoff of successful collective action for participants (w_1) is the utility they obtain from earning the monopoly wage w_M. In turn, nonparticipants do not enjoy the same degree of job protection so their expected utility calculations must consider the likelihood of being unemployed.

Putting these elements together we can obtain the payoffs of the proletariat's collective action problem, in keeping with the notation introduced in the previous chapters:

---

[2]Strictly speaking, the reward of job protection would be trivial if union membership were equal to the size of the employed labor force. This is too much of a rare occurrence to be a major concern. Even if it happens, all we need in this model is that workers perceive ex ante that belonging to a union will reduce their risk of being jobless.

$$w_1 = u(w_M + \tau^*(0)y(w_M)), \tag{6.1}$$

$$w_2 = u(w_M + \tau^*(0)y(w_M))\frac{L_d(w_M)}{L}$$
$$+ u(\tau^*(0)y(w_M))\frac{(L - L_d(w_M))}{L}. \tag{6.2}$$

For notational convenience, I will refer to $(L - L_d(w))/L$ as $U(w)$ and to $L_d(w)/L$ as $1 - U(w)$. This is mnemonically appropriate because the first expression denotes the unemployment rate of the economy (U) at wage w and the second one the employment rate.

Like the general collective action models discussed above, here cooperators enjoy higher payoffs when collective action succeeds, but also are punished when it fails. In the notation of Part I, $w_3 < w_4$. This describes adequately the collective action problem at hand. If the workers' union fails to materialize, those who attempted it are likely to face steep costs. I will take that cost to be exogenous to the model, an outcome of established legislative and judicial practices in the polity. The model already gives us the elements to determine the payoff w_4, that is, the payoff workers receive if they simply abstain from a failed attempt at collective action. If the proletariat's collective action fails, the economy will be operating with the fully competitive wage so that nothing will stop the median voter from imposing his favorite tax rate. If we denote the median voter's capital endowment by k_m, the payoffs in case of failure become:

$$w_3 = c, \tag{6.3}$$

$$w_4 = u(w + \tau^*(k_m)y(\tau^*(k_m)))(1 - U(\tau^*(k_m)))$$
$$+ u(\tau^*(k_m)y(\tau^*(k_m)))U(\tau^*(k_m)). \tag{6.4}$$

In these definitions, w is the going wage of the economy in an unregulated labor market. For generality, I allow here for $w > w_c$ so that there may be unemployment in the economy. The level of redistribution (τ), and the option outside the market (z), determine w and, in turn, result from the political process.

The coordination workers try to accomplish in this model has a probability of success directly proportional to the number of them that do cooperate. For simplicity, I will assume that the "production function" of this collective action problem is linear: $F(\gamma) = \gamma$.

This threshold game has multiple equilibria: players may cooperate or may decide to free-ride. Facing this prospect, employers can voluntarily accept the imposition of a minimum wage legislation that pacifies labor relations by deterring workers from trying to impose monopoly wages. To that end, employers accept a minimum wage that makes workers indifferent between obtaining this legislation and embarking upon the arduous path of organized collective action. The minimum wage is, thus, determined by the threat of collective action. This approach fleshes out the standard tool of analysis of minimum wages in the economic literature: Nash bargaining between employers and employees, exemplified by Booth (1995). Formally, the expected utility workers obtain from the minimum wage is the same as the expected utility they obtain from the threshold game. To make this latter term precise, we need to know the relative probability of success and failure in this threshold game. So, the minimum wage $\underline{w}$ is the solution to the equation:

$$u(\underline{w} + \tau_m y(\tau_m))(1 - U(\tau_m))$$
$$+ u(\tau_m y(\tau_m))U(\tau_m) = \Pi(0)w_4 + (1 - \Pi(0))w_1, \qquad (6.5)$$

where τ_m is the tax supported by the median voter if the minimum wage is introduced.

At this juncture the method of stability sets plays a critical role. We cannot know the clout wielded by labor in determining the minimum wage if we do not know how serious its collective action problem is and how likely it is to be solved, that is, if we do not know the probabilities $\Pi(0)$ and $\Pi(1)$. These parameters can be calculated by studying the stability sets of this problem and I doubt that they could be ascertained with any of the standard methods. The value $\Pi(0)$ is the probability of the noncooperative equilibrium we calculated in Chapter 4. This probability depends, as we already discussed, on the distribution of initial belief conditions. Here, for simplicity, I will adopt the Laplacian approach. I am not interested right now in comparative statics results involving changes in such conditions; assuming they are uniformly distributed will remove one extra complication. So, we can conclude that:

$$\Pi(0) \;=\; W, \tag{6.6}$$

$$W \;=\; \frac{w_4 - w_3}{(w_4 - w_3) + (w_1 - w_2)}. \tag{6.7}$$

These expressions allow us to prove the main comparative statics results of this collective action problem, which are summarized in the following lemma. In a nutshell, this result states that, all else being equal, increases in economic inequality and in the productivity of capital increase the benefits of the proletariat's collective action and, so, increase the likelihood of its success and, with it, the resulting minimum wage.

Lemma 3 *The probability of success of collective action* $\Pi(1)$ *and the minimum wage* $\underline{w}$ *are such that:*

- $\frac{\partial \Pi(1)}{\partial k_m} > 0$;
- $\frac{\partial \Pi(1)}{\partial k} < 0$;
- $\frac{\partial \underline{w}}{\partial k_m} > 0$;
- $\frac{\partial \underline{w}}{\partial k} < 0$.

Proof: Since w_1 and w_2 are payoff functions evaluated at $k_i = 0$, and with a tax rate independent of k_m or k, the only effect of changes in k and k_m on these expressions is felt through w_4. The results in the previous section show that w_4 is decreasing in k_m and increasing in k. Since $\Pi(1)$ and $\underline{w}$ are increasing in w_4, this establishes the results.

6.5   Interpreting the Results

The previous section formally presents the results of comparative statics of this politico-economic model. Given that they are derived from the study of the model's mathematical properties, it is necessary to discuss them conceptually as well.

The first result to notice refers to electoral preferences. In that regard, this model does not differ in essence from the canonical studies of redistributive policies: the richer voters prefer lower taxes. Consistent with the logic of that previous literature, we can conclude that increased inequality in the form of a larger gap between average income and median income will lead to heightened demands for redistribution.

This result holds in general for any economy that redistributes income through a flat tax. Beyond that, however, we can arrive at other results once we consider the role of production and the markets for production factors. In particular, an important conclusion of the preceding section is that the disparity in preferences over taxation across voters will increase with increases in the productivity of capital. This can be appreciated in the role of k, the economy's capital-labor ratio, in the calculations above. In computing comparative statics over k I looked only at, so to speak, "income-compensated" increases in the capital stock, that is, increases in the capital stock resulting from changes in the technology needed to produce one unit of output. This isolates the effect of increases in k on income distribution from the effect of, say, a larger capital stock over output. For any given level of output, a lower capital-labor ratio corresponds to a higher productivity of capital.

Thus, the lemmata above show that as the marginal productivity of capital increases, so does the gap between the preferred tax rates among the populace. This is hardly surprising. Increases in the tax rate decrease the supply of labor and thus reduce the marginal productivity of capital, something that does not affect the proletariat as it does the middle classes. The relative size of this effect is larger the higher the productivity of capital. Thus, were the middle classes' capital stock to become more productive, the added effect of taxation over income will become larger: the disparity between the tax rates deemed optimal by each class will grow.

Furthermore, we also know from the preceding analysis that labor-market regulations have an effect on the voters' electoral preferences. In particular, when a minimum wage is in place, this creates a level of unemployment higher than what some voters, with capital endowment above a critical level, would have preferred. But, confronted with the new levels of unemployment, they find it optimal to support higher degrees of taxation: at their otherwise optimal tax rate, marginal increases in taxation do not lead to higher unemployment. Those voters are now, so to speak, pressed into service of a redistributive coalition they would not have joined in an unregulated labor market.

These interactions between the economic and the electoral processes form the backdrop against which collective action occurs. Together with the guarantees, or lack thereof, for union activity, they constitute the costs and benefits that the proletariat will face in its attempts to transform the structure of the labor market through collective action.

This is where the current model departs both from the standard models of economic redistribution and from the conventional approaches to collective action in rational-choice theory. Unlike models of electoral redistribution that focus solely on the preferences that the citizenry expresses through the ballot box, this model makes explicit how those preferences are in part the result of deeper conflicts that play themselves out in the workplace. Unlike the extant rationalist theories, the approach I present connects the process of collective action to its underlying economic structure.

The preceding results on electoral preferences allow us to formulate some explicit conclusions about the role of organized union activity in this economy. The lemmata of the previous section prove that, all else being equal, the larger the economic gap between the proletariat and the middle classes, or the higher the productivity of capital, the higher the minimum wage. Here the "all else being equal" clause is fundamental; it results in an important qualification of the result. But, before qualifying it, we need to understand its meaning.

In a way, this result is intuitive. Consider two economies A and B that differ only in their degrees of economic inequality or in their capital productivity: *A* is more unequal and more productive than *B*. Given what we know about electoral preferences, if their labor markets are entirely unregulated, *A* will have lower tax rates, that is, less redistribution, than *B*. By the same token, were the proletariat to succeed in imposing monopoly wages, say through a general strike or an enforced labor cartel, it would obtain a larger increase in taxation and redistribution in economy *A* than what it could in *B*. In other words, economy *A* displays a higher degree of politico-economic tension between the proletariat and the middle classes. An analysis equipped with a canonical Olsonian model of collective action would not grant any importance to this fact. To it, in both economies the proletariat would be irremediably hampered by the public goods problem so that we should not expect any differences between them in this regard. But, as I have repeatedly stated, such Olsonian analysis is too restrictive and fails to do justice to the existence of multiple equilibria in coordination problems. Instead, with the method of stability sets we can use this knowledge of the economic structure of *A* and *B* to understand their political outcomes.

Since the potential benefits of collective action are larger in *A* than in *B*, the method of stability sets allows us to conclude, in a way fully consistent with the principles of rational-choice theory, that, all else being equal, *A*'s proletariat is more likely to succeed in its attempt at imposing monopoly wages than its counterpart in *B*. Therefore, if the owners of capital want to avoid such monopoly wages, they must agree to a higher minimum wage in *A* than in *B*, a minimum wage that dissuades the proletariat from engaging in full-scale, risky, but potentially powerful coordination.

Not all else is equal, though. Thus far I have assumed that *A* and *B* display equal degrees of tolerance with respect to unionizing, in other words, that both polities impose the same costs on the proletariat's collective action. But these costs are not a given and there is no reason to believe that they remain the same across time and place. Instead, it stands to reason that, faced with an economic structure so prone to proletarian belligerence, the middle classes and the capitalists will try to clamp down on it by increasing the costs of collective action. We would expect A to have harsher anti-strike legislation and perhaps even more instances of labor repression than B. In the formal language of the model, the middle classes and the capitalists of A will try to lower the payoff w_3 as much as possible to offset the incentives to collective action that the proletariat faces given the underlying tensions in the economic structure.

6.6 Class Struggle and the Political Economy of Redistribution: Sweden and Germany in the Interwar Years

The model presented thus far is not ready for the type of heavy-duty empirical testing that we often expect from mathematical models in the social sciences. Its assumptions about the economic structure are exceedingly simple: it focuses only on the labor market at the expense of other factors of production, assuming a fixed supply of capital and erasing the distinction between physical capital, human capital and land. Perhaps more limiting, it also presents an oversimplified view of the political process. In particular, it treats as exogenous the determination of w_3, the costs of unionization. As mentioned above, these costs are the outcome of strategic choices by the classes with power to modify them and, as such, also depend on the underlying economic structure. Absent such an analysis, the model presented thus far should be considered an exercise in "partial equilibrium," to use the term reserved in economics for models that leave out of the analysis some crucial adjustment mechanisms.

But while partial equilibrium models do not make for outstanding scores in statistical testing, neither are they useless: they can suggest lines of inquiry and clarify some mechanisms, suggestions and clarifications that may ultimately inform a more complete theory. I believe that the model developed in this chapter can pass this milder test, as I will illustrate with some considerations about the collapse of some liberal economic orders in interwar Europe, notably, in Germany and Sweden.

The rise of fascism in Europe and its ultimate collapse in the bloodiest war in recorded history is one of the great epochal crises of all times and, among that small league, is the one chronologically closest to our own time, the one whose consequences can be felt most vividly. As such, it towers as a challenge for scholars in comparative politics. Given the enormity of the events, any attempt at explaining them is likely to fall short but, at the same time, no paradigm of comparative politics can ignore them without risking irrelevance. Not surprisingly, this period has generated an enormous literature, some of which can be counted, as was to be expected from such an outpouring of intellectual power, among the very best work this subdiscipline has produced.

Here, for the sake of precision and clarity, I will focus at some length on two particular works on the subject that, apart from being splendid scientific pieces in their own right, have theoretical sensibilities similar to the ones that animate this book: the now classic book by the late Greg Luebbert, *Liberalism, Fascism or Social Democracy*, and the politico-economic model based on it that John Roemer develops in his *Political Competition*.

At this point it should already be clear that I intend to launch a research program that combines the tools of rational-choice theory with the insights of structural analysis in the social sciences. But many rational-choice theorists believe that their approach refutes the previous structuralist paradigms and, likewise, many believers in the power of structural explanations regard as anathema the premises of rational-choice theory. Against this backdrop, it is a rare occasion when a work applies the tools of rational-choice theory to examine a structural argument proposed by a political sociologist, an occasion rendered even more exceptional by the fact that the subject matter of this dialogue is a most intriguing question in comparative politics. Unlikely though this was, it is exactly what happened.

Although Luebbert's book barely needs presentation or any added praise, let's summarize its basic argument and Roemer's take on it. For Luebbert, the history of Europe during the half century that preceded World War II is, by and large, the history of different responses to the political mobilization of the newly enfranchised masses. Whereas the major European countries had a similar initial response, over time their paths differed dramatically and even lethally. As the nineteenth century drew to a close, most of these political regimes can be described as Lib-Lab alliances, that is, as regimes where the nascent labor movement was still looking for its political home inside the historic liberal parties that emerged after the revolutionary waves originating in 1789. Clearly it was an uneasy alliance, especially given that during the nineteenth century there had been occasions of overt and violent conflict between liberal governments and the workers' movements. But, in principle, there were plenty of opportunities for mutual benefit: the liberal party gained access to a fast-growing constituency and labor gained from the political expertise of the liberal party in an era when its own electoral skills were not yet honed.

Luebbert's book is largely an attempt at reconstructing the dissimilar fates of similar Lib-Lab alliances across Europe. On the face of it, the results could not be more disparate. By 1938, the first year in which one of the regimes in Luebbert's sample (Czechoslovakia) was cut short, not by its internal dynamics but by the meddling of foreign powers, only Britain, France, Switzerland and Czechoslovakia could still be described as liberal regimes. The remaining regimes had been transformed beyond recognition either by becoming fascist (Italy, Germany, Spain) or social democratic (such as the Scandinavian countries).

Luebbert's central claim is that in those countries where the Lib-Lab alliance collapsed, the key to the final outcome was in the hands of the rural middle class: in countries where the peasantry supported the urban middle classes, the outcome was fascism and in those where it threw its support behind labor, the outcome was social democracy. This begs two questions: 1. What accounts for the weaknesses of those Lib-Lab coalitions that collapsed? 2. What accounts for the behavior of the peasantry in the cases where Lib-Lab was replaced?

Luebbert responds to both questions by resorting to the notion of pre-existing political cleavages. With respect to the success or failure of liberalism, Luebbert summarizes his position by claiming that:

> Where liberals failed to establish their prewar hegemony, they failed because they could not straddle pre-industrial cleavages within the middle classes. Having failed to establish their hegemony, liberal parties found the mobilization of a socialist working class enormously threatening — so threatening, in fact, that they consistently refused to ally themselves with socialist movements. Normally left without allies, and always without useful allies, socialist parties and trade unions concentrated on the comprehensive and coherent organization of the working classes. (Luebbert, 1991, pg. 9)

In another passage he clarifies further:

> [L]iberal movements in [...] societies [where liberalism failed] were crippled by divisions within the middle classes that originated in the pre-industrial epoch. Conflicts of national territory, religion, the center versus the periphery, the city versus the country, and the national communities remained decisive at the time of mass mobilization. (Luebbert, 1991, pg. 63)

His basic thesis on the divergent fates of the failed liberal regimes is that:

> Whenever socialists sought to organize the agrarian proletariat in politics and in the labor market, the family peasantry was pushed into the arms of

> fascists. Whether or not socialists sought to orga-
> nize agrarian workers was in turn determined by
> whether those workers were politically available or
> had been previously organized by another move-
> ment. [...] When the family peasantry sided with
> urban workers, the outcome was a social demo-
> cratic regime. When it sided with the urban mid-
> dle classes, the outcome was fascism. (Luebbert,
> 1991, pg. 11)

Drawing on his own work on electoral equilibria in multi-
dimensional policy spaces, Roemer has developed a politico-
economic model to test Luebbert's hypothesis about the emergence of fascism versus the emergence of social democracy.
There is no point in reproducing here Roemer's analysis. Suffice it to say that in it he formulates an elegant model of
electoral redistribution where the Left and Right parties compete for votes by offering different vectors of income allocations among the classes involved. This implies computing
the Party Unanimity Nash Equilibria (PUNE) of a four-class
model (workers, middle classes, landed peasantry and agricultural proletariat) and comparing the behavior of those equilibria with that of the PUNE one would obtain in a three-
class model (fixing the income allocation between the landed
peasantry and the agricultural proletariat). Upon computing
these two models with demographic parameters from Sweden
and Germany in the 1930s Roemer is able to analyze counterfactual models of each country (that is, a "Sweden" with class
struggle in the countryside and a "Germany" without it) to
see whether Luebbert's proposed mechanism does in fact explain the difference in outcomes. In specifying the equations
that generate an electoral equilibrium, Roemer has at his disposal two extra degrees of freedom coming from unobservable
parameters, viz. the relative weight that both Left and Right
give to the interests of their rural constituencies. He makes
use of these degrees of freedom to simulate various alternatives
in what amounts to a test of the robustness of the mechanism
proposed by Luebbert.

Roemer's results lend credence, albeit not unqualified credence, to Luebbert's theory. In fact, for a large family of parameters, class struggle in the countryside is detrimental for the Left. For some parameter values, though, Luebbert's hypothesis is not borne out by the equilibrium results.

It may seem at first glance that Roemer's model simply translates Luebbert's verbal argument into mathematical symbols. But Roemer is too sharp a methodologist not to realize this. Thus, he supplements his work with an admirable "Methodological Coda," two pages that constitute as measured and cogent a statement as one can find about the relative merits of analytical and historical methods and the dialogue between them. There, Roemer writes:

What does the formal analysis with PUNE add to Luebbert's abstraction? I think, principally, it shows that it was not a coincidence that the Left supported the agricultural workers, thus alienating the peasantry, when agricultural class struggle was active. This was, if you will, a consequence of the factional intraparty struggle and, in particular, the role of militants in the Left. The opportunists in the left would, presumably, have been happy not to have supported land reform, but the militants would not settle for that. The equilibrium analysis shows that, given parties with factions guided by rather simple and clear motivations, the left will win with smaller probability in a country where agricultural class struggle is active than where it is passive, ceteris paribus. In this sense, the analysis instructs us not to view left support for land reform as a tactical error: it was part and parcel of the historical development of social democratic parties, which emerged in every case with militant factions — factions in the absence of which these parties might well have lost their socialist character. (Roemer, 2001*a*, pg. 243)

Thus, there are nuanced differences between Luebbert's account and Roemer's. Roemer assigns more explanatory weight to conflicts over land tenure, whereas Luebbert emphasizes the pre-industrial political cleavages as the main impediment to the penetration of the socialists in the countryside. By the same token, I am not sure that Luebbert's position can be characterized as one that attributes to a tactical error the Left's defeat in fascist countries, but that may be besides the point. What matters is that, for Roemer, important though socioeconomic structures may be, the organizational imperatives faced by any political party worthy of its name also play a role in shaping the outcomes of the political process.

These distinctions notwithstanding, the result of combining these two approaches is a theory of the origins of fascism that traces the effects of the underlying socioeconomic structure on the political process of a Europe that had just recently completed the transition to mass politics. But, while assigning conceptual preeminence to structural factors, this theory does not deny the role of individual, rational agency and instead draws heavily on it to analyze the mechanisms of electoral competition. In that sense, it is a good example of the type of political economy that I think is possible once we combine rational-choice theory with structural analysis. The model I have developed in this chapter is too crude to become a serious competitor of this theory but can illuminate aspects that it overlooks.

The analyses of Luebbert and Roemer raise some questions that cannot be answered given their analytical framework but that, instead, can be addressed by a more developed version of the model I have just discussed. A key element in Luebbert's theory is the persistence of pre-industrial political cleavages, especially in the countryside. It is not clear why such political conflicts would trump the newer ones. More precisely, it remains to be explained why age-old tensions over religion or conflicts of center versus periphery held a grip over the citizenry that hindered effective coalition building around class issues that were already becoming pressing. In fact, it may seem as if Luebbert's hypothesis explains too much. He offers a compelling portrait of the difficulties liberals in Germany and Sweden faced in trying to unify middle class segments of the population that had been politically seasoned in previous, pre-industrial, conflicts. But if such pre-industrial conflicts were so deeply entrenched, it is not clear why other parties, viz. the fascists, succeeded in overcoming them. After all, fascism succeeded in doing exactly what Luebbert argues the liberals could not: bringing together the middle classes despite their pre-existing divisions. In the processes that culminated either in fascism or social democracy pre-industrial political cleavages are far from a static presence: while they proved fatal for the liberal forces, the new movements, especially the fascists, were able to cut through them in the span of a few years. The political geography of such pre-industrial cleavages also remains somehow opaque: it is one of Luebbert's central claims that in those societies that would ultimately become fascist, the socialists could not successfully establish a foothold in the countryside, divided as it was because of pre-existing cleavages. But this attributes to the countryside a specificity that needs to be explained. After all, these same socialist parties had overcome formidable obstacles in the cities, going from virtual nonexistence to sizeable political actors, sometimes during the course of just a few years and confronting urban middle classes every bit as hostile and fixated in pre-industrial conflicts as its rural counterparts.

Roemer's approach makes explicit the organizational dilemmas faced by the European Left. But, although it is hard to disagree with his view that a nascent socialist party without a sizeable militant faction is something of an oxymoron, and that, hence, socialist parties in the interwar period were prone to get saddled with electorally suboptimal platforms, this explanation of the fate suffered by some socialist parties needs to be supplemented. Arguably, the Nazi party was not going out of its way to maximize its vote share but was instead waiting for the electorate to come over to its side, as it in fact did after the Depression. This suggests a limitation to Roemer's analysis, one that he himself has explicitly acknowledged: even if the German Left was beholden to militants that

got in the way of its vote maximization efforts, it is remarkable
that the ultimate victory went to that group of pragmatic and
level-headed reformers known as the Nazi party.[3] The role of
militant factions that would hamper the parties in their efforts at maximizing votes is rather nuanced: while arguably
fatal for the German Left, it did not stop the Nazi party from
attaining victory.

It is possible to complement the approach of Luebbert and
Roemer by expanding on their blind spots. For good reasons,
both authors place special emphasis on the electoral angle of
the process under study. But the struggles that led to the
emergence of fascism and social democracy in the countries
discussed were not only fought through the ballot box. In a
democracy, no matter how imperfect, elections are the mechanism through which political parties come into office but they
are not the only source of political power, sometimes not even
the most important one. Deeply entrenched socioeconomic
realities often confer the real power to actors others than the
party in government. The model analyzed in the preceding
sections allows us to bring out this point in ways that may illuminate some aspects of the collapse of liberalism in Germany
and Sweden.

During the early decades of the twentieth century, these
countries went through intense political turmoil over the regulation, or lack thereof, of the labor market. The allocation
of economic rights in the workplace has, ultimately, electoral
repercussions because, indirectly, it also allocates across economic agents the costs of the incentive effects resulting from
any redistributive policy, thus affecting these agents' electoral preferences. It is not gratuitous, then, that in a crucial
formative stage of their politico-economic process, the German and Swedish democracies went through decisive battles,

---

[3]Roemer recognizes as much in his final assessment of the model: "I
must remark that the Right has been modeled, here, as a conservative
party which represents the propertied classes. There is nothing in the
model that captures the fascist nature of the victorious parties in Germany, Italy, and Spain. This analysis, therefore, has nothing to say about
why fascism, rather than traditional conservatism, became the scourge of
Europe in the interwar period." (Roemer, 2001a, pg. 241)

extra-electoral but nonetheless political, over how to define the rights and duties of employers and employees.

Germany is a case in point. The transition of the Nazi party from a group of heavy-drinking, unemployed World War I veterans to a serious contender in national politics is only partially the result of electoral, vote-maximizing decisions. As late as 1928, only five years before the takeover, the Nazi party had a disastrous showing in the elections. But since its creation it had already established its presence in the German political scene as the anti-Spartacist shock troops.

Both Luebbert and Roemer are right in pointing out the instructive contrast between the outcomes in Sweden and Germany. But focusing on the electoral results understates the magnitude of the contrast. When Hitler was sworn in as Chancellor, the Swedish Social Democrats had already been in power for a few months. By the year 1936, while the Swedish trade unions and employer organizations began the negotiations that would culminate in Saltsjöbaden, the Nazi party had already killed, imprisoned or exiled most of the Left opposition and the first concentration camps for political prisoners were already active. The Nazi victory in Germany was more than just a swing in the proverbial political pendulum; it was the ascent to power of one of the most ruthless and uncompromising political groupings ever known. When it comes to visions of class conflict or compromise, whatever the attitudes of the Swedish Social Democrats toward the employers, they were no match for the brutal anti-labor stance of the German Nazis.

If outcomes are important, trajectories also matter. Luebbert's attention to detail in his analyses of the different European political processes should give pause to anyone who tries to supplement his views, but it is worth noticing that, aside from the electoral shifts that ultimately destroyed the Weimar Republic, the interwar years were for Germany the period of a heated struggle in the workplace. Even at times when the Nazi party was still a nonentity, the German Left's labor movement was under attack by the "yellow unions," unions of clear right-wing credentials, such as those associated with the Stahlhelm, which had the explicit goal of undermining the Left's potential for collective action at the factory level (Fischer, 1989).

It would be a mistake to project back into the Swedish politico-economic process of the 1920s the social democratic hues that marked it in the postwar period. If anything, the Swedish labor movement in that era had to stomach more than one bitter defeat at the hands of the remarkably cohesive employers' organization, the SAF (Swenson, 2002). But there are differences in nature and in degree between the German situation and the Swedish one. The Swedish labor movement, already bludgeoned into accepting basic principles of management autonomy after its first setbacks, was perceived as a legitimate interlocutor of the employers and an acceptable partner in steering the labor markets through troublesome economic waters. The fortunes of the German labor movement follow something of an inverse trajectory: a key and formidable actor even in failure as in the aborted uprising of 1918, it finds itself fighting a rearguard action in the defense of Weimar against the Right's reaction, first successfully, as when it contributed to the collapse of Kapp's putsch, then unsuccessfully in the agony of Weimar, until the ignominious end with the dissolution of unions and the formation of the Nazi Labor Front, during the early stages of the Third Reich.

Overall, the conflict over labor-market regulation polarized the German society of the 1920s and 1930s in ways unparalleled in the Sweden of the time. This suggests an explanation for the difficulties we encountered in the study of Luebbert's and Roemer's studies. Conceivably, the urban middle classes in Germany were not entirely frozen in pre-industrial cleavages but, instead, once overt class struggle broke out in the workplace, reaching unprecedented heights in the early years of the Weimar Republic, they started converging around parties that could credibly claim to pacify the conflict by force, shedding the disagreements over older issues that had plagued the liberals' attempts to win them over. Once this process was under way, that is, once the Spartacist Left became something of an existential threat for the middle classes, a threat exacerbated by the Depression, right-wing militancy stopped being a liability. Instead, the more extremist its antisocialist stance, the more ruthless its rhetoric against the Left, the more a party (viz. the Nazi party) could claim to be in possession of a solution fully acceptable for the middle classes, both urban and rural.

But this begs the question of why there were such high levels of polarization in Germany compared to Sweden. The model developed in this chapter can offer some insights in this regard. We have seen that in a market economy, structural conditions pertaining to its production technology and asset distribution determine the severity of the workers' collective action problem as they try to force the regulation of labor. Since such regulation imposes a cost on the middle classes, in an economy where the workers can easily overcome the barriers to collective action, the middle classes will want to counteract this effect by supporting high costs for unionization. In the language of the model, the higher the magnitude of collective action's potential benefits relative to its costs, that is, the higher w_1 and w_2 relative to w_3 and w_4, the more the middle classes will try to increase the costs over which they have control in the political process by reducing w_3. Harsh anti-union legislation or, if that fails, overt, even physical, confrontation with labor are some of the tools we can expect to be used in this process.

The comparative statics results demonstrated above allow us to focus on two properties of an economic structure that raise the benefits of proletarian collective action and that, hence, make for especially tense labor relations: high productivity of capital and high disparity of endowments between the proletariat and the middle classes. High productivity of capital means that the workers can derive higher benefits from regulating the labor market. In a way, the minimum wages are a transfer from capital rents to labor and so, the higher the productivity of capital, the more of these rents can be transferred. High differences between the factor endowment of the middle classes and that of the proletariat mean that there is a larger gap between the taxes favored by each in an unregulated labor market. Thus, there is a larger incentive for the proletariat to force the implementation of minimum wages to counter the anti-tax bias of the middle classes, forcing them to go along with larger redistribution.

From this point of view, Sweden and Germany in the years before World War II corresponded to what the model would lead us to expect. The parameters of endowment distribution that Roemer used to calibrate his model provide some hints. Using the data from Przeworski, Underhill and Wallerstein (1978), he concludes that around 1930: "the propertied classes constitute 51% of the adult population in Germany and 45% in Sweden. Germany is more urbanized than Sweden: 77% of the population live in cities, versus 66% in Sweden. In sum, Sweden is less urbanized but more proletarianized than Germany" (Roemer, 2001a, pg. 218). For the rural sector, other data confirm Roemer's assessment. Moller (1990) concludes that from an early stage the Swedish land was concentrated in large agro-industrial holdings, with little room for a middle-class landed peasanty. Instead, Niehaus (1933) shows that in Germany, aside from the notorious Junker, by the 1920s a sizeable portion of land was in middle-sized holdings. Judging from these pieces of evidence we can conclude that the German proletariat found itself in a predicament foreign to its Swedish counterpart: in pushing for larger redistribution it was pitted against propertied middle classes that would benefit from a deregulated labor market and would, therefore, be willing to ally with large capitalist interests over that issue. It is a widely recognized fact that the key constituency of the Nazi party in its final push for power was made up of shop-keepers, farmers and middle-class professionals, all of whom had been rendered economically insecure by the Depression (Childers, 1976).

Factor productivity in both countries also resonates with the theoretical expectations from the model. Figure 6.3 shows data on the productivity of capital, labor and land in Sweden and Germany between 1875 and 1914. The single most salient feature of this graph is the gap in capital productivity (F_K) between Germany and Sweden. Whereas labor was slightly more productive in Germany than in Sweden (as shown by their respective F_L values), only to a tiny extent, and there is hardly any discernible difference in the productivity of land (F_T) between both countries, it is unmistakable that Germany's capital stock was much more productive than that of Sweden.

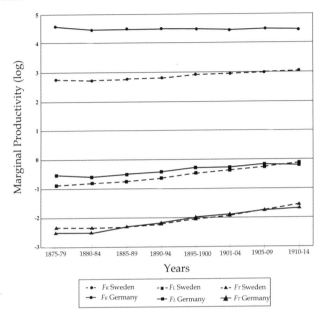

Figure 6.3: Factor Productivities in Germany and Sweden (1875-1914). Source: Author's Computations from O'Rourke, Taylor and Williamson (1996).

In light of these data, the political economy of both countries makes sense. Sweden's middle-class section of the population was small, with modest levels of productivity, and, therefore, would not have been much of a formidable opponent for labor in its struggle with capital. To be sure, capitalists themselves proved to be determined, ruthless and cohesive in their confrontation with labor, perhaps as much as their German equivalents. But the political lines of battle were, arguably, more straightforward, something that, ultimately, helped labor shape the terms of the conflict. Instead, the German labor movement had to be constantly mindful of the behavior of the sizeable and highly productive middle classes, who could be counted on to turn against it on key issues such as the regulation of the labor market.

It is worth recalling that the model of collective action developed here has an additional degree of freedom: the level of mutual expectations among the participants. I have made no effort to quantify this or even to conduct a comparative static analysis of it. But, clearly, higher levels of labor's mobilization will lead to higher likelihood of success in its collective action endeavors. In this regard, we should not forget that, already at the end of nineteenth century, the German labor movement was among the world's most active and organized, its political branch, the SPD, being the envy of left-wing sympathizers the world over. Likewise, after World War I the German Communist party became the largest Communist party outside of the newly-founded Soviet Union. This was not accomplished through electoral calculations. In fact, the KPD grew while rejecting any half-measures, or any collaboration with bourgeois parties. Its impetus came more from a tradition of labor militancy than from its scant skill in the halls of power. With a working class with levels of militancy hardly rivaled anywhere, and a sizeable middle-class segment in control of a highly productive endowment, Weimar Germany seems, from the point of view of this chapter's model, a political perfect storm.

Interestingly, this model allows us to go beyond World War II in ways that the models of Luebbert and Roemer do not. The developments post-1945 offer an interesting challenge to any theory of fascism. From the ashes of the Third Reich emerged a welfare state with few equals in its comprehensiveness and its guarantees for labor. Ironically, much of this occurred under governments of the Right. After the war, the SPD, even in opposition, was able to push for measures that were unthinkable during its short spell in government during the Weimar period. This chapter's model suggests an explanation. With the destruction of the Nazi regime, gone were the days when the German labor movement could be confronted with the heavy-handed tactics of the 1920s. For a host of reasons, negotiating with labor on an equal footing became the only politically feasible option. In the language of the model, the mechanism of increasing w_3, even with extra-legal mechanisms, in hopes of defanging labor was no longer possible. In this new type of environment, with a regulated labor market, the middle classes became a reliable partner of labor in its demands for increased redistribution. Only then, with the issue of the incentive effects of taxation adjudicated in favor of the working class, can the voters with below-median income be properly called a coalition.

6.7 Concluding Remarks

Prominent economist Jean Drèze once said that models in economics serve the same purpose and run the same risks as models in fashion: though a good way to put ideas on display, the author should not get carried away with them, nor should the customer forget that reality is messier. This is all the more true when the subject matter is as elusive as class struggle and income redistribution in a market economy. We might be well advised, then, to step back and take a critical look at the model presented here, to see what its limitations are and what we can, nevertheless, learn from it.

The model in this chapter cannot legitimately be considered a theory of why Germany became fascist and Sweden social democratic in the early 1930s. To begin with, no serious historical account of this process can omit the humiliating conditions of Versailles and the dislocations they produced in Germany. There are so many specificities in each of these countries that perhaps no single theory will explain their trajectories. By the same token, just like Roemer in his empirical analysis, I have focused only on Germany and Sweden. But Italy also became fascist, in fact, much earlier than Germany, and so did Spain, although not without a civil war of gigantic proportions. If we wanted to attribute real explanatory power to this model, we would have to establish whether these two countries faced the same tensions in their labor relations as Germany did and, in case they did, whether such tensions responded to the underlying economic structure in the ways the model claims.

Since the model just developed does not come close to a testable theory of the political economy of class struggle, it is appropriate that we ask what is, then, its payoff. I wish to claim that there are several useful conclusions we can draw from it, both substantive and methodological.

The classical paper of Meltzer and Richard (1981) inaugurated a tradition in formal political economy of studying how inequalities in the asset distribution of an economy map into distributive conflicts that, presumably, can be arbitrated through electoral mechanisms. In a one-dimensional policy space, the tax rate chosen by the median voter reflects the degree of redistribution possible for any given level of inequality. But this simplified template cannot deal with two facts of modern capitalist democracies: (a) the fact that much of the redistribution in contemporary societies is, so to speak, "off the books" since it occurs implicitly through the policies that regulate the markets for factors of production, especially labor and (b) the fact that many of those policies are not themselves the outcome of an electoral process, but instead reflect the capability of different agents in the economy of engaging in collective action outside of the ballot box.

The model developed in this chapter introduces these two additional complications to the original framework, arriving at three general results. The first is simply an extension of the classical Meltzer-Richard result to the new case: increases in the gap between the "poor" (that is, voters with income below the median) and the "rich" increase the demand for redistribution. The second result, instead, pertains only to this expanded model: all else being equal, especially the legal and extra-legal costs of labor's collective action and its degree of mobilization, the electoral majority will be in favor of higher levels of redistribution the more the labor market is regulated. Finally, higher levels of capital productivity will increase the degree of polarization of the preferences of voters for redistribution.

Having established these results, I used Germany and Sweden in the interwar period as an illustration of how they work and how they can be put to use in the study of concrete

problems. The results are satisfactory in that both politico-
economic environments followed trajectories similar to those
described by the model. Although it would be a mistake to
consider this a conclusive proof, it nevertheless constitutes
a favorable exhibit. When compared to Sweden, the German economy of the time displays features that, according
to the model presented above, should make it prone to be
destabilized by the efforts at collective action of different economic and political agents. In this, the model tracks historical events: according to most accounts of the demise of
the Weimar Republic, those were years marked by heightened
tensions that pitted the left-wing workers' movement against
fascist groups in battles that were anything but electoral. Collective action, rather than vote maximization was the tool of
choice of the relevant forces; if the Weimar Republic was cre-
mated in the ballot box, it is because it had already been bled
to death in the streets.

In the introduction to Part II I claimed that a rigorous
study of collective action, informed by the tools developed
above, could help us understand how the socioeconomic structure of a democracy places constraints over the degree of equality it could possibly attain. The model in this chapter displays
one such mechanism. Although the incentive effects of taxation can, as Meltzer-Richard claim, represent a brake on the
amount of redistribution a society may want to pursue, the
magnitude of that effect depends on the way such incentive
effects are spread out across the economic agents. This, in
turn, depends on deeper institutional constraints, such as the
structure of the labor market, constraints that are defined, to a
large extent, through extra-electoral mechanisms that involve
the agents' ability to coordinate through collective action.

From a purely methodological point of view, this model
exemplifies the approach to the study of collective action I
have defended in the first part of this book. Undeniably, the
ultimate fate of the collective action efforts of German and
Swedish workers depended on many organizational and individual choices that determined whether they could coordinate
their expectations. These individual choices can be and often

have been described with the tools of the game-theoretic analysis of collective action, tools such as focal points and tipping games. In fact, it is not entirely inaccurate that the study of those choices has become the trademark of rational-choice approaches to the matter. Instead, such mechanisms do not play a substantial role in the preceding analysis.

There are several reasons for such departure from standard practice. There is no doubt that belief coordination is fundamental for collective action; I do not reject the contributions that rational-choice theory has already made in this area. But I believe that an exclusive focus on expectations, without looking at the impact of the structure in which collective action occurs, might create an unhealthy lack of balance in our analysis.

The dangers of this one-sidedness become apparent if we try to understand the politico-economic mechanisms discussed above with the existing tools. Much of the theorizing on this matter has attempted to answer the question, "Why does collective action occur?" But, for the purpose of the problem at hand, such question would not take us far enough. When it comes to the study of organized collective action, for the purposes of this model the question should not be, "Why workers strike?" but, "Given that workers may solve their collective action problem and strike, what are the broader consequences for electoral redistribution of the resulting conflict over labor market regulations?" In other words, in this model collective action is not the goal of the analysis but, instead, is just another link, among others, connecting the economic structure (e.g., asset distribution, technology and productivity) with political outcomes (e.g., distributive taxation and minimum wages).

I believe this is the way it should be. Few phenomena in the social sciences are as important as collective action. But when we turn it into the ultimate goal of our studies we fail to do justice to its centrality. Collective action has effects. It is the task of a systematic theory to understand those effects. In that sense, knowing that collective action is possible should be the beginning of our inquiry, not its end.

6.A   Proofs of Main Results

6.A.1   Factor Demand

To compute the factor demand functions, we first solve the cost-minimization problem of a typical firm:

$$\min_{K,L} w\,L + r\,K \text{ s.t. } K^{\alpha}L^{1-\alpha} = \bar{Y}$$

or, written as a Lagrangean:

$$\min_{K,L,\lambda} w\,L + r\,K + \lambda(\bar{Y} - K^{\alpha}L^{1-\alpha}),$$

which gives the following first-order conditions:

$$
\begin{aligned}
w - \lambda(1-\alpha)\left(\frac{K}{L}\right)^{\alpha} &= 0; \\
r - \lambda\alpha\left(\frac{L}{K}\right)^{1-\alpha} &= 0; \\
K^{\alpha}L^{1-\alpha} &= \bar{Y}.
\end{aligned}
$$

Solving these equations for the optimal values of K, L and plugging them in the original objective function, we obtain the cost function:

$$C(w,r,\bar{Y}) = \bar{Y}r^{1-\alpha}w^{\alpha}\xi(\alpha),$$

where $\xi(\alpha)$ is simply a constant that depends on the parameter α. Shephard's lemma states that the demand for each factor is equal to the derivative of the cost function with respect to that factor's price:

$$
\begin{aligned}
L_d &= \frac{\partial C(w,r,\bar{Y})}{\partial w}; \\
K_d &= \frac{\partial C(w,r,\bar{Y})}{\partial r}.
\end{aligned}
$$

In this case, this lemma results in:

$$L_d = \alpha \left(\frac{r}{w}\right)^{1-\alpha} \xi(\alpha)\bar{Y};$$

$$K_d = (1-\alpha) \left(\frac{w}{r}\right)^{\alpha} \xi(\alpha)\bar{Y}.$$

To solve for $\bar{Y}$, we use the condition of equilibrium in the market for the final good: $\bar{Y} = Y_d$, together with the condition that, in a competitive market, the price of the final good is equal to its marginal cost, which in this case is: $p = \partial C(w, r, \bar{Y})/\partial \bar{Y}$. Since the cost function is linear in $\bar{Y}$, then the equilibrium in the final good's market is:

$$\bar{Y} = \frac{\Gamma}{r^{1-\alpha}w^{\alpha}\xi(\alpha)}.$$

Substituting this value into the derivatives of the cost function, gives the factor demand functions of the main text.

6.A.2   Proof of Lemma 2

These comparative statics result from the fact that the voter's maximization problem under uncertainty inherits the basic properties of an analogous maximization problem without uncertainty. So, in this proof I will proceed in two major steps. First, I will prove that these results are true of a *non-wage income*-maximization problem, that is, the problem agents would face if, implausibly, they had linear utility functions and no job. Knowing how to prove these properties for this simple case, we will then be in a position to extend them to the more realistic case of risk-aversion.

Step 1: Income Maximization.   Given the previous definitions, we can rewrite the voter's income as a function of his capital endowment, the economy's capital-labor ratio and the tax policy:

$$\begin{aligned} y_i(\tau, k_i, k) &= ((1-\tau)(r(\tau)k_i) + \tau y(\tau)) \\ &= \bar{y}E(\tau)^{1-\alpha}\left(\alpha\frac{k_i}{k} + \tau\left(1 - \alpha\frac{k_i}{k}\right)\right). \end{aligned}$$

This function is concave in τ so that the tax rate that maximizes income is the one that solves $\partial y_i / \partial \tau = 0$. In particular:

$$\tau^* = \frac{1}{(2 - \alpha)(1 - \alpha \frac{k_i}{k})} - \frac{\alpha \frac{k_i}{k}}{1 - \alpha \frac{k_i}{k}}.$$

This expression satisfies the comparative statics results contained in the lemma.

Step 2: Expected Utility Maximization. The condition $\partial y_i / \partial \tau = 0$ is also the optimality condition when $z = 0$. We now need to study how the optimum behaves as z increases. The first-order condition for expected-utility maximization is:

$$\begin{aligned}
\frac{\partial y_i}{\partial \tau} &= \bar{y}(1 - \alpha) \frac{u(y_i(\tau, k_i, k) + z) - u(y_i(\tau, k_i, k))}{u'(y_i(\tau, k_i, k) + z)E(\tau) + u'(y_i(\tau, k_i, k))(1 - E(\tau))} \\
&= R(z, \tau, k_i, k).
\end{aligned}$$

When $z = 0$, $R = 0$ but for any value $z > 0$, R is decreasing in k and increasing in k_i. Instead, $\partial y_i / \partial \tau$ is increasing in k and decreasing in k_i. As a result, the τ that solves the first-order condition is also increasing in k and decreasing in k_i. To prove the third statement consider $k_i < k_j$ and $k < k'$. From the behavior of the income-maximizing problem we know that if $z = 0$, $\tau^*(k_i, k) - \tau^*(k_j, k) > \tau^*(k_i, k') - \tau^*(k_j, k')$. If $z > 0$, then for every τ, $R(k_i, k) - R(k_j, k) < R(k_i, k') - R(k_j, k')$. Together with the fact that $\partial y_i / \partial \tau$ is decreasing, this implies that the solutions to the first-order conditions for expected-utility maximization also satisfy the same inequality as the income-maximizing case.

Chapter 7

Final Remarks

No society can exist without collective action. Throughout all seasons, whether of innovation or restoration, of comity or enmity, of turbulence or tranquility, individuals lead their lives as members of a polity by assembling in groups. Collective action is not an instance of politics, let alone an exceptional one; it is what makes politics possible.

Politics always involves power and, more even than sheer brute force, collective action makes individuals powerful. Co-operating, individuals can accomplish mighty goals that would otherwise be unthinkable. No theory of how societies change is complete without a systematic effort at understanding this most potent agent of transformation. In this book I have taken the first steps of what I consider a research agenda necessary to supplement the current efforts in this matter.

To understand the power of collective action it is not sufficient to behold it in the rare instances where it is operating in all its fury. Earthquakes are eloquent lessons in plate tectonics but they will not teach us all there is to be learned about the subject; we also need to look at smaller tremors and even at periods and places of calm. Something similar happens with the study of collective action. As much as we can learn from observing the dramatic instances that focus the mind of existing scholarship, such as the mass mobilizations of the American Civil Rights Movement or of the Eastern European revolutions of 1989, by themselves they will not add

up to a systematic theory if we do not also understand why
they are so rare, why they occur only at certain times and in
certain places, under some specific circumstances, and why it
is quiescence that is the normal tone of historical processes.
This focus on the exceptional diminishes the importance of the
phenomenon under study. Continental plates are constantly
drifting and in the process they not only unleash earthquakes,
but also give rise to mountains, perhaps a less spectacular outcome but one with more far-reaching consequences. Collective
action is also a constant force operating in society. Every day
millions of individuals try to engage in it with all kinds of
purposes. Only a handful succeed but in their failures the rest
exert an undeniable influence over the shape of our societies.

In these pages I have argued for the need of a compre-
hensive research program that studies how collective action is
connected to its environment, why some social structures are
more prone to some types of collective explosions than others
and what the political, social and economic consequences are
of these multiple attempts, both successful and unsuccessful.
In short, I believe that the theory of collective action will not
mature beyond its current stage until it develops a rigorous
comparative statics approach to its subject matter.

Comparative statics does to data what reverse engineering
does to machines: it decomposes them into their basic parts,
one at a time, to see which one does what, and what would
happen were they shaped or combined differently. Without
this conceptual exercise, theoretical understanding is impossible. In the study of collective action, such comparative statics
starts by asking: what external changes make a particular
instance of collective action more or less likely? If we can answer that, we are on the way toward an operational theory of
collective action.

Common sense offers an answer: all else being equal, collective action is more likely if its benefits increase, and less
likely if its costs increase. But rational-choice theories have
never embraced this answer and, instead, have attempted to
undermine it with elaborate models.

The first chapter of this book presented the main flaws

of such attempts. Public goods models adopt a fragile framework that, in the end, misrepresents the collective action problem. These models focus on a simplistic and highly implausible structure of costs and benefits. Once we abandon that structure in favor of a more realistic one, the model's main conclusion, that, absent selective incentives, agents will always free-ride, evaporates. Models of focal points and tipping games offer a richer and more robust framework for a systematic theory. But they do not make the most out of their own insights for lack of a rigorous technique to deal with the multiplicity of equilibria they generate.

To address this theoretical bottleneck, in this book I have proposed and developed a game-theoretic tool that shows some promise: the method of stability sets. The method is neither entirely new nor entirely unparalleled. Its basic ideas are borrowed from work in the mid-1980s by John Harsanyi and Reinhardt Selten and, in its attempt to go beyond the pure computation of equilibria, trying also to describe the conditions that make them robust or fragile, it resembles current efforts in the topics of evolutionary game theory and quantal-response equilibria. This is a good thing. I would be disturbed if the method of stability sets were entirely at odds with the rest of game theory. Instead, the fact that it resembles other approaches suggests that they are all part of a more general enterprise and that it is possible for them to supplement each other's weaknesses.

Since the work of Harsanyi and Selten on stability sets and the tracing procedure did not attain the fame of most of their other contributions, it is easy to emphasize the weaknesses while overlooking the strengths. The tracing procedure met a cool reception from critics who considered it an ad hoc construction with no evident value. But it is neither absurd nor worthless. It is a plausible way of representing the role of the agents' beliefs about each other in a game with multiple equilibria. It recognizes, the same way more recent work does, that the outcome in such games depends on the conditions under which the players attain common knowledge of rationality. The tracing procedure adopts a explicit mathematical structure to phase in such common knowledge. Other structures are possible but, in all likelihood, adopting them does not change the main properties of the results obtained. Above all, the procedure is a convenient way to compute stability sets which form the foundation on which the concept of evolutionary basins of attraction is built. It is not possible to develop an argument about evolutionary convergence to an equilibrium without having spelled out what forces operate outside of an equilibrium. Stability sets offer a clear way to calculate the impact of those forces. Scholars who embrace evolutionary game theory while rejecting the notion of stability sets run the risk of being inconsistent.

In this book I have adopted a very crude formalism to deal with the fact that, in a game with multiple equilibria, the final outcome depends on the beliefs players hold about each other and that, hence, our estimates about the relative likelihood of the equilibria will depend on this information. I have adopted a Laplacian assumption, supposing that all initial belief conditions are equally likely. This is not a limitation of the analysis. Quite the opposite, it is a degree of freedom of the method of stability sets that could be used to improve its further applications. The general principle, that changes in the size of an equilibrium's stability set change its likelihood, does not depend on the Laplacian assumption. Relaxing it will not change the essence of the results and will instead allow us to incorporate other types of knowledge about the game in order to refine our predictions.

I regard this as a major strength of the method. The approach developed in this book recognizes that in any complex social interaction strategic considerations, important though they may be, are not the only ones that matter. Instead, agents also rely on other sources of knowledge (or even sheer prejudice) in making their decisions. Here I have not taken advantage of the flexibility that this generates, but this is a promising avenue for future research. The process of developing a non-Laplacian model of initial belief conditions incorporates knowledge about the shared views players have about their own proneness to coordinate. These views do not necessarily come from strategic calculations. To be sure, they might be the outcome of previous games but this is not the only possible source. There is no need to legislate their origin at this level of abstraction when we know that the details will ultimately depend on the specific situation under study.

Some social sciences have a comparative advantage in the study of material circumstances (e.g., economics), others in the study of attitudinal changes (e.g., social psychology). A theory of collective action must recognize that no single approach will capture all the problem's wealth. In the elementary examples I presented, I used this book's techniques to analyze the impact of material changes on collective action problems by borrowing heavily from economic theory. But a scholar with different inclinations could have done otherwise, focusing instead on, say, the impact of organizational changes over a group's common beliefs and, hence, on the likelihood of success of its collective endeavors, given some material parameters.

In this book I have studiously sidelined organizations and leadership. Concrete instances of collective action usually require both, a point acknowledged in much of the literature. But it would be wrong to turn this valid insight into a scientific fixation. Not every angle of a collective action problem pertains exclusively to its participants, be they the leaders and members of an organization, first movers, free-riders or whatever else. All these participants confront objective circumstances beyond their control, which also deserve careful study. Excellent scholarship in the rational-choice paradigm shows how different groups overcome the difficulties of collective action. I have nothing to contribute to it but instead wanted to shed light on the other, neglected side of the topic: the role of exogenous, objective conditions, knowing full well that, by itself, it can never exhaust the analysis of collective action.

I do not claim that the mathematical results I offer here are the only possible ones, or even the best possible ones. I consider all these approaches, the one in this book as well as the alternatives in the literature, part of a larger agenda in game theory, an agenda that has been emerging in the last decades and that, in a salutary development, shifts attention from the equilibria themselves to their robustness and stability. I decided to use the method of stability sets because I found it to be the best suited for my specific purposes: to obtain simple illustrative politico-economic models that involved collective action problems with large numbers of players. These are not the only kind of models in which we should be interested. On occasion, we might need models with much more detailed dynamics, or models with specific parameters for the individuals' decision-making rules. In such contexts the method of stability sets may be inferior to its evolutionary or quantal-response counterparts. But, then again, sometimes we do not need such detailed information. Sometimes, rather than a careful analysis of one particular situation, we need a model that allows us to arrive at general conclusions of comparative analysis, covering many different cases, even if it comes at the price of several details.

In this book I illustrate what we can learn from such a broad-brush approach. Clientelism is a bafflingly protean phenomenon whereby voters are rendered powerless in front of their patrons through myriad mechanisms. In some places voters fear losing their job, in others their children's slot at the local school, in yet others the promised batch of construction materials. As they try to shake off this submission, they avail themselves of many mechanisms. Sometimes it is by creating a civic organization that channels their discontent, sometimes it is the local church that acts as a first mover, sometimes a new party arrives on the scene with a candidate representing a different style of politics. No list of mechanisms can even aspire to be complete. But we need to know what all these polities have in common and how, despite their differences, they react to similar exogenous shocks.

Observers of developing countries have documented consistently how economic development undermines clientelism. The intuition behind this is clear enough and already belongs to the standard description of how clientelistic machines evolve and decay. All else being equal, economic development creates opportunities for citizens to diversify their fortunes away from the grip of patrons. The less the voters depend on political machines for their livelihood, the less they have to fear from reprisals and, then, the easier it is for them to support other candidates in elections. But, to a large extent, this regularity has remained beyond the reach of formal approaches to the problem. The reason is that the reprisals upon which the effectiveness of clientelism depends is often merely a threat and is contingent on the players following an off-equilibrium path. Standard techniques to deal with collective action problems cannot analyze such situations with the precision necessary. Instead, the method of stability sets computes the relative likelihood of such reprisals as a function of the model's structural parameters.

It is incumbent upon us believers in game-theoretic approaches to show what can be gained from expressing in a formal language insights about social processes that can be formulated in everyday terms. Space limitations have kept me from illustrating these gains to the extent I would have wanted. But the model discussed already shows that other politico-economic processes, in this instance, universalistic redistribution, can serve the same role as economic development. Given the prominence of handouts in any narrative of clientelism, one is led to believe that only the growth of the private economy can erode clientelism. The previous analysis shows that, at least in principle, redistributive policies can play the same role if they are removed from the patron's discretion. But just as important as proving results is the fact that those same results are expressed in a language that is at once flexible and rigorous and, hence, apt for further research. Building on this foundation, we can go beyond generalizations about growth and tax policy and study more specific questions such as, say, the impact of different sources of growth, the relative performance of different programs of redistribution and so on.

Much of the political turmoil in modern societies can be understood as the outcome of the tension between the principles of democracy and the principles of the market, between political rights to expression and association and economic rights to property and its fruits. In some societies the two principles appear to complement each other, resulting in prosperity, peace and stability. But others are not as fortunate and, instead, see their institutions collapse, overwhelmed by social conflict. A new generation of studies on this matter has offered an analytical template with which to study what determines one outcome or the other by combining the mathematical theories of elections (especially, variations around the median-voter theorem) with economic models of growth and distribution. In this book I have tried to add something to this literature by considering the role of collective action. Democracies are not only about voting but also about giving citizens the right to come together and defend their interests as a collective. If we want to understand how those political rights interact with economic rights we need an analytical framework that does for collective action what the spatial theorems of voting do for elections: offer a guide to study how different structural conditions of the process lead to different outcomes. I have not developed such a framework but I have sketched how the method of stability sets can help in developing it.

Seen in this light, the process of coalition building around distributive conflict in a democracy looks more nuanced than what our standard results on voting would suggest. The coalition of the "poor" that would presumably expropriate the "rich" in a democracy is not an inevitable outcome. Instead, the way the markets for production factors operate in a modern economy consitutes a source of implicit distributive conflict, outside of the realm of overt taxation, that depending on its outcome may dissolve or buttress that same coalition.

Since collective action is the main vehicle for conflict in the labor markets, we cannot understand how the underlying economic structure affects the prospects of coalition building in a market economy unless we know how such structure shapes the possibilities of collective action. Thanks to the method of stability sets it is possible to arrive at analytical statements that connect, for instance, the distribution of assets and their productivity with the degree of class struggle in the workplace and its effects over the political system. The cases of Sweden and Germany in the interwar period show these mechanisms at work by tracing the effects of their different economic structures onto the type of conflict that ultimately marked the end of their respective liberal regimes, with dramatically different outcomes.

Just as in the model on clientelism, whatever the merits of its answers, this model's real value is the rigor and flexibility it brings to them. It seems plausible to conclude, as the model does, that, all else being equal, the higher the productivity of capital, the deeper the tensions separating the proletariat from the middle classes. But the model's true test has to wait until it is used to address more complex questions such as, say, the role of human capital, economic cycles and investment. Daunting as these questions can be, at least the fact that they involve collective action problems does not preclude us from addressing them.

Aside from being illustrations of a common technique, the preceding pages on clientelism and labor-market regulation suggest one common underlying concern about democratic regimes. Whether an electoral democracy is a vehicle to bring hope and prosperity to its citizens and to create harmony among them depends on how it comes to terms with deeper power structures that are validated by the citizenry's acceptance or overturned by its collective action. Perhaps, then, the process of building stable and successful liberal democracies requires more than acceptable mechanisms for the replacement of those in positions of visible political power. Perhaps, to be stable, electoral democracy needs to be more than a procedure blind to its own workings and outcomes and, instead, needs to command the lucid consent of a polity that sees it as a vehicle for its own betterment. Perhaps, in sum, in a full theory of democracy, the positive and the normative are not as neatly separated as we often think.

Like most other books, this one is not the final word on its subject matter. But unlike many of them, it does not intend to bring its readers to a tight conclusion, but instead to leave them stranded in a vast, uncharted territory. Many questions remain ahead, methodological, technical and substantive. In light of its topic, it is somewhat fitting that, to come to fruition, this book still needs the collective effort of legions of social scientists.

Bibliography

Abreu, Dilip. 1988. "On the Theory of Infinitely Repeated Games with Discounting." *Econometrica* 56(2):383–396.

Acemoglu, Daron and James A. Robinson. 2006. *Economic Origins of Dictatorship and Democracy.* New York: Cambridge University Press.

Aghion, Philippe and Patrick Bolton. 1987. "Contracts as a Barrier to Entry." *American Economic Review* 77(3):388–401.

Aumann, Robert. 1974. "Subjectivity and Correlation in Randomized Strategies." *Journal of Mathematical Economics* 1:67–96.

Auyero, Javier. 2001. *Poor People's Politics: Peronist Survival Networks and the Legacy of Evita.* Durham: Duke University Press.

Baumol, William J., John C. Panzar and Robert D. Willig. 1982. *Contestable Markets and the Theory of Industry Structure.* New York: Harcourt Brace Jovanovich.

Bendor, Jonathan and Dilip Mookherjee. 1987. "Institutional Structure and the Logic of Ongoing Collective Action." *American Political Science Review* 81(1):129–154.

Berger, Peter and Thomas Luckmann. 1967. *The Social Construction of Reality: A Treatise in the Sociology of Knowledge.* Garden City, NY: Doubleday.

Binmore, Ken and Larry Samuelson. 1999. "Evolutionary Drift and Equilibrium Selection." *Review of Economic Studies* 66(2):363–393.

Boix, Carles. 2003. *Democracy and Redistribution.* Cambridge: Cambridge University Press.

Booth, Alison L. 1995. *The Economics of the Trade Union.* Cambridge: Cambridge University Press.

Bork, Robert H. 1979. *The Antitrust Paradox.* New York: Basic Books.

Bratman, Michael E. 1993. "Shared Intentions." *Ethics* 104(1):97–113.

Bratman, Michael E. 2000. "Reflection, Planning, and Temporally Extended Agency." *Philosophical Review* 109(1):35–61.

Brennan, Geoffrey and James Buchanan. 1984. "Voter Choice: Evaluating Political Alternatives." *American Behavioral Scientist* 28(2):185–201.

Brusco, Valeria, Marcelo Nazareno and Susan C. Stokes. 2002. Clientelism and Democracy: Evidence from Argentina. In *Conference on Political Parties and Legislative Organization in Parliamentary and Presidential Regimes.* Yale University.

Calvert, Randall. 1985. "Robustness of the Multidimensional Voting Model: Candidates' Motivations, Uncertainty and Convergence." *American Journal of Political Science* 29(1):69–95.

Casey Mulligan, Ricard Gil and Xavier Sala i Martin. 2004. "Do Democracies Have Different Public Policies than Nondemocracies?" *Journal of Economic Perspectives* 18(1):51–74.

Childers, Thomas. 1976. "The Social Bases of the National Socialist Vote." *Journal of Contemporary History* 11(4, Special Issue: Theories of Fascism):17–42.

Chong, Dennis. 1991. *Collective Action and the Civil Rights Movement.* Chicago: The University of Chicago Press.

Chubb, Judith. 1981. "The Social Bases of an Urban Political Machine: The Case of Palermo." *Political Science Quarterly* 96(1):107–125.

Chubb, Judith. 1982. *Patronage, Power, and Poverty in Southern Italy.* Cambridge: Cambridge University Press.

Clark, Terry Nichols. 1994. Clientelism, U.S.A.: The Dynamics of Change. In *Democracy, Clientelism and Civil Society*, ed. Luis Roniger and Ayşe Günes-Ayate. Lynne Renner Publishers, pp. 121–144.

Collier, Paul. 2000. "Rebellion as a Quasi-Criminal Activity." *Journal of Conflict Resolution* 44(6):838–852.

Coughlin, Peter. 1992. *Probabilistic Voting Theory.* Cambridge: Cambridge University Press.

David, Paul A. 1985. "Clio and the Economics of QWERTY." *American Economic Review* 75(2):332–337. Papers and Proceedings of the Ninety-Seventh Annual Meeting of the American Economic Association.

Dawid, A. Philip. 1979. "Conditional Independence in Statistical Theory." *Journal of the Royal Statistical Society, Ser. B* 41(3):1–31.

de Tocqueville, Alexis. 2000 (1835). *Democracy in America.* New York: Harper Classics. Translated by George Lawrence.

Díaz-Cayeros, Alberto, Beatriz Magaloni and Barry Weingast. 2000. "Democratization and the Economy in Mexico: Equilibrium (PRI) Hegemony and Its Demise." Hoover Institution.

Eisenstadt, S. N. and Louis Roniger. 1980. "Fresh Applications of Familiar Models of Patron–Client Relations as a Model of Structuring Social Exchange." *Comparative Studies in Society and History* 22(1):42–77.

Ellman, Matthew and Leonard Wantchekon. 2000. "Electoral Competition under the Threat of Political Unrest." *Quarterly Journal of Economics* 115(2):499–531.

Elster, Jon. 1989. *Nuts and Bolts*. Cambridge: Cambridge University Press.

Esping-Andersen, Gøsta. 1985. *Politics against Markets: The Social-Democratic Road to Power*. Princeton, NJ: Princeton University Press.

Estévez, Federico, Beatriz Magaloni and Alberto Díaz-Cayeros. 2002. A Portfolio Diversification Model of Policy Choice. In *Conference on Clientelism in Latin America: Theoretical and Comparative Perspectives*. Stanford University.

Fearon, James and David Laitin. 2003. "Ethnicity, Insurgency and Civil War." *American Political Science Review* 97(1):91–106.

Finkel, Steven E., Edward N. Muller and Karl-Dieter Opp. 1989. "Personal Influence, Collective Rationality, and Mass Political Action." *American Political Science Review* 83(3):885–903.

Fiorina, Morris. 1996. Rational Choice, Empirical Contributions and the Scientific Enterprise. In *The Rational Choice Controversy*, ed. Jeffrey Friedman. New Haven: Yale University Press, pp. 85–94.

Fischer, Conan. 1989. "Turning the Tide? The KPD and Right Radicalism in German Industrial Relations, 1925-8." *Journal of Contemporary History* 24(4):575–597.

Fox, Jonathan. 1994. "The Difficult Transition from Clientelism to Citizenship: Lessons from Mexico." *World Politics* 46(2):151–184.

Gay, Robert. 1998. The Broker and the Thief: A Parable (Reflections on Popular Politics in Brazil). In *XXI International Congress of the Latin American Studies Association*. Chicago.

Gay, Robert. 2001. Between Clientelism and Citizenship: Exchanges, Gifts & Rights in Contemporary Brazil. In *Conference on Citizen-Politician Linkages in Democratic Politics*. Duke University.

Gilbert, Margaret. 1989. *On Social Facts*. London: Routledge.

Gramsci, Antonio. 1992. *Prison Notebooks*. New York: Columbia University Press.

Green, Donald and Ian Shapiro. 1994. *Pathologies of Rational Choice Theory*. New Haven, CT: Yale University Press.

Habermas, Jürgen. 1984. *The Theory of Communicative Action*. Boston: Beacon Press. Translated by Thomas McCarthy.

Habermas, Jürgen. 1996. *Between Facts and Norms*. Cambridge, MA: MIT Press. Translated by William Rehg.

Hadar, Josef and Tae Kun Seo. 1988. "Asset Proportions in Optimal Portfolios." *Review of Economic Studies* 55(3):459–468.

Hagopian, Frances. 1996. *Traditional Politics and Regime Change in Brazil*. Cambridge and New York: Cambridge University Press.

Hardin, Russell. 1995. *One for All: The Logic of Group Conflict*. Princeton, NJ: Princeton University Press.

Harsanyi, John. 1973. "Games with Randomly Disturbed Payoffs: A New Rationale for Mixed-Strategy Equilibrium Points." *International Journal of Game Theory* 2:1–23.

Harsanyi, John and Reinhardt Selten. 1988. *A General Theory of Equilibrium Selection*. Cambridge, MA: MIT Press.

Heath, Joseph. 2003. *Communicative Action and Rational Choice*. Cambridge, MA: MIT Press.

Johnson, James. 1993. "Is Talk Really Cheap? Prompting Conversation between Critical Theory and Rational Choice." *American Political Science Review* 87(1):74–86.

Karklins, Rasma and Roger Petersen. 1993. "Decision Calculus of Protesters and Regimes: Eastern Europe 1989." *Journal of Politics* 55(3):588–614.

King, Gary, Robert O. Keohane and Sidney Verba. 1994. *Designing Social Inquiry.* Princeton, NJ: Princeton University Press.

Kitschelt, Herbert, Zdenka Mansfeldova, Radoslaw Markowski and Gàbor Tòka. 1999. *Post-Communist Party Systems: Competition, Representation, and Inter-Party Cooperation.* Cambridge: Cambridge University Press.

Koopmans, Tjalling C. 1947. "Measurement without Theory." *Review of Economic Statistics* 29(3):161–172.

Kreps, David. 1990. *A Course in Microeconomic Theory.* London: Prentice Hall.

Kuran, Timur. 1991. "Now Out of Never: The Element of Surprise in the Eastern European Revolution of 1989." *World Politics* 44(1):7–48.

Laitin, David. 1998. *Identity in Formation: The Russian-Speaking Populations in the Near Abroad.* Ithaca: Cornell University Press.

Lemarchand, Rene and Keith Legg. 1972. "Political Clientelism and Development: A Preliminary Analysis." *Comparative Politics* 4(2):149–178.

Levitsky, Steven Robert. 2001. From Labor Politics to Machine Politics: The De-Unionization of Argentine Peronism and the Transformation of Working Class Linkages in Latin America. In *Conference on Citizen-Politician Linkages in Democratic Politics.* Duke University.

Lichbach, Mark I. 1989. "An Evaluation of 'Does Economic Inequality Breed Political Conflict' Studies." *World Politics* 41(4):431–470.

Lohmann, Susanne. 1993. "A Signaling Model of Informative and Manipulative Political Action." *American Political Science Review* 87(2):319–333.

Lohmann, Susanne. 1994. "The Dynamics of Informational Cascades: The Monday Demonstrations in Leipzig, East Germany, 1989-91." *World Politics* 47(1):42–101.

Luebbert, Greg. 1991. *Liberalism, Fascism or Social Democracy: Social Classes and the Political Origins of Regimes in Interwar Europe.* New York: Oxford University Press.

Lyne, Mona. 2000. Generalizing the Electoral Connection: The Voter's Dilemma, Party Presented Reform and Democratic Consolidation in Brazil. In *Conference of the American Political Science Association.* American Political Science Association.

Lyne, Mona. 2001. Of Citizens and Patrons: A Unified Electoral Theory of Programmatic and Clientelist Democracy. In *Conference on Citizen-Politician Linkages in Democratic Politics.* Duke University.

Mainwaring, Scott. 1999. *Rethinking Party Systems in the Third Wave of Democratization: The Case of Brazil.* Stanford: Stanford University Press.

Malesky, Edmund. 2001. Enduring Clientelism in Vietnam. In *Conference on Citizen-Politician Linkages in Democratic Politics.* Duke University.

Marx, Karl and Friedrich Engels. 1992 (1848). *The Communist Manifesto.* New York: Bantam.

Mas-Colell, Andreu, Michael D. Whinston and Jerry R. Green. 1995. *Microeconomic Theory.* Oxford: Oxford University Press.

McAdam, Doug, Sidney Tarrow and Charles Tilly. 2001. *Dynamics of Contention.* Cambridge: Cambridge University Press.

Medina, Luis Fernando. 2004. Rational Choice Theory as Formalized Common Sense. Technical report, Universidad Carlos III de Madrid.

Medina, Luis Fernando and Susan C. Stokes. 2007. Monopoly and Monitoring: An Approach to Political Clientelism. In *Patrons or Policies: Patterns of Democratic Accountability and Political Competition*, ed. Herbert Kitschelt and Steven Wilkinson. Cambridge University Press.

Medina, Luis Fernando and Susan Stokes. 2001. Clientelism as Political Monopoly. Technical Report Working Paper # 25, University of Chicago, Center on Democracy.

Meltzer, Allan H. and Scott F. Richard. 1981. "A Rational Theory of the Size of Government." *Journal of Political Economy* 89(5):914–927.

Milgrom, Paul and John Roberts. 1994. "Monotone Methods for Comparative Statics." Working Paper, Stanford University.

Moe, Terry M. 1981. "Toward a Broader View of Interest Groups." *Journal of Politics* 43(2):531–543.

Moller, Jens. 1990. "Towards Agrarian Capitalism: The Case of Southern Sweden during the 19th Century." *Geografiska Annaler. Series B. Human Geography* 72(2/3):59–72.

Muller, Edward N. and Karl-Dieter Opp. 1986. "Rational Choice and Rebellious Collective Action." *American Political Science Review* 80(2):471–488.

Murphy, Kevin M., Andrei Shleifer and Robert W. Vishny. 1989. "Industrialization and the Big Push." *Journal of Political Economy* 97(5):1003–1026.

Myerson, Roger. 1991. *Game Theory: Analysis of Conflict.* Cambridge, MA: Harvard University Press.

Myerson, Roger B. 1993. "Incentives to Cultivate Favored Minorities under Alternative Electoral Systems." *American Political Science Review* 87(4):856–869.

Niehaus, Heinrich. 1933. "Agricultural Conditions and Regions in Germany." *Geographical Review* 23(1):59–72.

Offe, Claus. 1987. "Democracy against the Welfare State? Structural Foundations of Neoconservative Political Opportunities." *Political Theory* 15(4):501–537.

Oliver, Pamela. 1981. "Bringing the Crowd Back In: The Nonorganizational Elements of Social Movements." *Journal of Politics* 43(2):531–543.

Olson, Mancur. 1965. *The Logic of Collective Action.* Cambridge, MA: Harvard University Press.

O'Rourke, Kevin, Alan M. Taylor and Jeffrey G. Williamson. 1996. "Factor Price Convergence in the Late Nineteenth Century." *International Economic Review* 37(3):499–530.

Palfrey, Thomas R. and Howard Rosenthal. 1983. "A Strategic Calculus of Voting." *Public Choice* 41:7–53.

Palfrey, Thomas R. and Howard Rosenthal. 1985. "Voter Participation and Strategic Uncertainty." *American Political Science Review* 79(1):62–78.

Plott, Charles. 1967. "A Notion of Equilibrium and Its Possibility under Majority Rule." *American Economic Review* 57(4):787–806.

Posner, Richard A. 1976. *Antitrust Law: An Economic Perspective.* Chicago: The University of Chicago Press.

Poulantzas, Nicos. 1975. *Political Power and Social Classes.* London: NLB.

Przeworski, Adam. 1990. *The State and the Economy under Capitalism.* Chur, Switzerland: Harwood Academic Publishers.

Przeworski, Adam, Ernest Underhill and Michael Wallerstein. 1978. "The Evolution of Class Structure in Denmark, 1901-1960; France, 1901-1968; Germany 1882-1933 and 1950-1961; and Sweden, 1900-1960: Basic Data Tables." University of Chicago, Photocopy.

Putnam, Robert, Robert Leonardi and Rafaella Nanetti. 1993. *Making Democracy Work: Civic Traditions in Modern Italy.* Princeton, NJ: Princeton University Press.

Richards, Diana. 2001. "Coordination and Shared Mental Models." *American Journal of Political Science* 45(2):259–276.

Riker, William H. and Peter C. Ordeshook. 1968. "A Theory of the Calculus of Voting." *American Political Science Review* 62(1):25–42.

Robinson, James and Thierry Verdier. 2001. "The Political Economy of Clientelism." Working Paper, UC Berkeley.

Roemer, John. 1996. "The Democratic Class Struggle: A Survey of Recent Results." University of California at Davis, Working Paper.

Roemer, John. 1997. "Politico-Economic Equilibrium when Parties Represent Constituents: The Unidimensional Case." *Social Choice and Welfare* 14:479–502.

Roemer, John. 2001*a*. *Political Competition.* Cambridge, MA: Harvard University Press.

Roemer, John. 2001*b*. *Political Competition: Theory and Applications.* Cambridge, MA: Harvard University Press.

Sandler, Todd. 1992. *Collective Action: Theory and Applications.* Ann Arbor: The University of Michigan Press.

Sandler, Todd and Keith Sargent. 1995. "Management of Transnational Commons: Coordination, Publicness and the Treaty Formation." *Land Economics* 71(2):145–162.

Scharpf, Fritz. 1991. *Crisis and Choice in European Social Democracy.* Ithaca: Cornell University Press.

Schelling, Thomas. 1960. *The Strategy of Conflict.* Cambridge, MA: Harvard University Press.

Schelling, Thomas. 1978. *Micromotives and Macrobehavior.* New York: Norton.

Schuessler, Alexander. 2000. *The Logic of Expressive Choice.* Princeton, NJ: Princeton University Press.

Searle, John. 1995. *The Construction of Social Reality.* New York: Free Press.

Shepsle, Kenneth and Michael Laver. 1996. *Making and Breaking Governments: Cabinets and Legislatures in Parliamentary Democracies.* New York: Cambridge University Press.

Stigler, George J. 1971. "The Theory of Economic Regulation." *Bell Journal of Economics and Management Science* 2(1):3–21.

Stokes, Susan C. 1995. *Cultures in Conflict: Social Movements and the State in Peru.* Berkeley: University of California Press.

Sugden, Robert. 1995. "A Theory of Focal Points." *Economic Journal* 105(430):533–550.

Swenson, Peter A. 2002. *Capitalists against Markets.* Oxford: Oxford University Press.

Szwarcberg, Mariela L. 2001. "Feeding Loyalties: An Analysis of Clientelism, the Case of the Manzaneras." Universidad Torcuato di Tella.

Taylor, Michael. 1987. *The Possibility of Cooperation.* Cambridge: Cambridge University Press.

Tsebelis, George. 1990. *Nested Games: Rational Choice in Comparative Politics.* Berkeley: University of California Press.

Tullock, Gordon. 1971. "The Paradox of Revolution." *Public Choice* 11:89–99.

Tuomela, Raimo. 1991. "We Will Do It: An Analysis of Group-Intentions." *Philosophy and Phenomenological Research* 51(2):249–277.

Van Loo, Jonathan and Sergiy Taran. 2001. Parties, Clientelism and Electoral Systems in the Russian Duma: Alternative Politician-Citizen Linkages. In *Conference on Citizen-Politician Linkages in Democratic Politics*. Duke University.

Waldner, David. 2006. "Anti-Antideterminism or What Happens when Schrödinger's Cat and Lorenz's Butterfly Meet Laplace's Demon in the Study of Political and Economic Development." Working Paper, University of Virginia.

Wantchekon, Leonard. 2002. Markets for Votes: Evidence from a Field Experiment in Benin. In *Conference on Clientelism in Latin America: Theoretical and Comparative Perspectives*. Stanford University.

Weyland, Kurt. 1996. "Obstacles to Social Reform in Brazil's New Democracy." *Comparative Politics* 29(1):1–22.

Wood, Elisabeth. 2002. *The Logic of Insurgent Collective Action: Defiance and Agency in Rural El Salvador*. Cambridge: Cambridge University Press.

Yamagishi, Toshio, Satoshi Kanazawa, Rie Mishima and Shigeru Terai. 2005. "Separating Trust from Cooperation in a Dynamic Relationship: Prisoner's Dilemma with Variable Dependence." *Rationality and Society* 17(3):275–308.

Yin, Chieng-Chun. 1998. "Equilibria of Collective Action in Different Distributions of Protest Thresholds." *Public Choice* (97):535–567.

Young, Peyton. 1998. *Individual Strategy and Social Structure*. Princeton: Princeton University Press.

Index

271

DATE DUE
